IMAGES
of America

THE TEXAS ASSOCIATION OF CHICANOS IN HIGHER EDUCATION

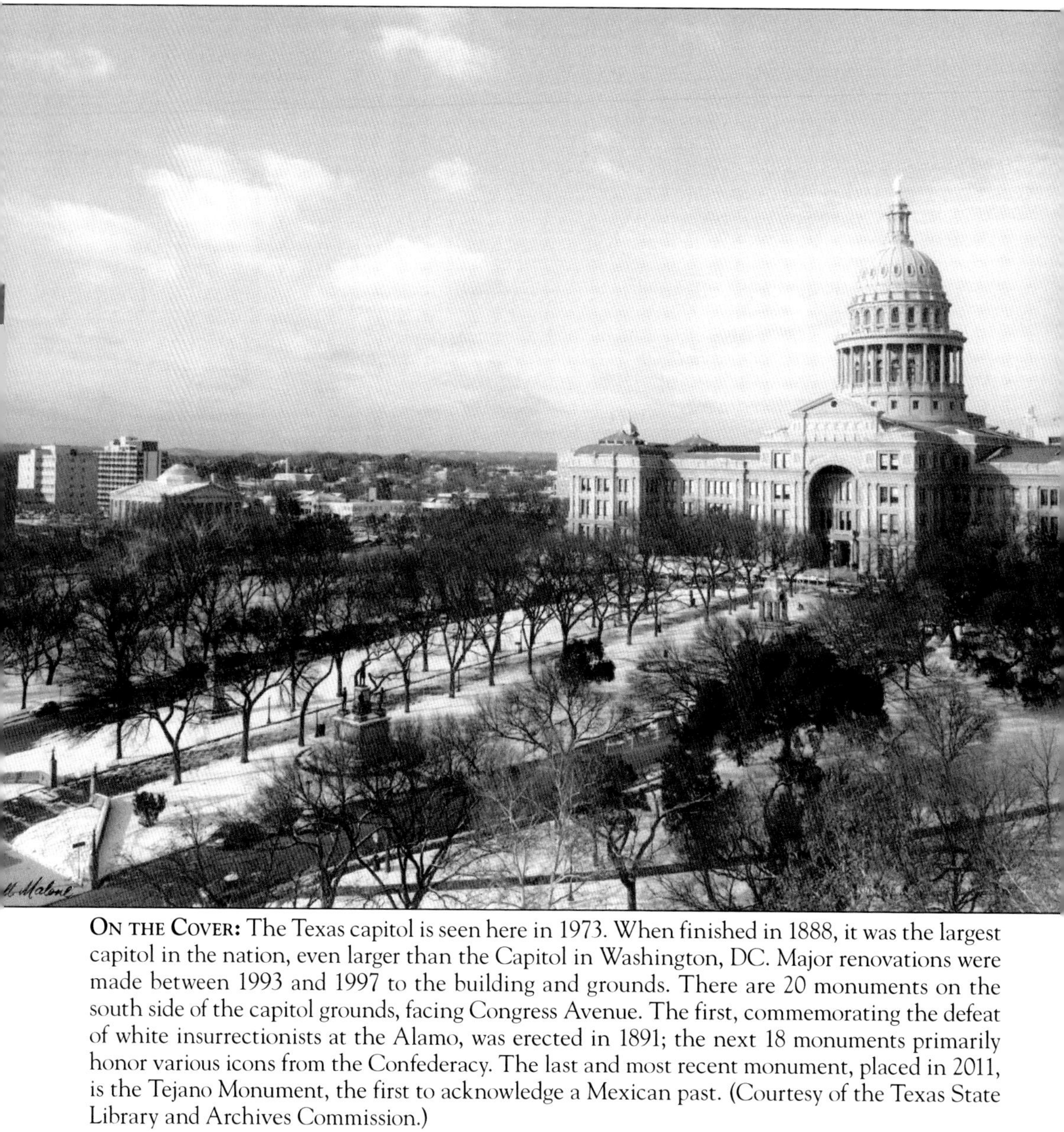

ON THE COVER: The Texas capitol is seen here in 1973. When finished in 1888, it was the largest capitol in the nation, even larger than the Capitol in Washington, DC. Major renovations were made between 1993 and 1997 to the building and grounds. There are 20 monuments on the south side of the capitol grounds, facing Congress Avenue. The first, commemorating the defeat of white insurrectionists at the Alamo, was erected in 1891; the next 18 monuments primarily honor various icons from the Confederacy. The last and most recent monument, placed in 2011, is the Tejano Monument, the first to acknowledge a Mexican past. (Courtesy of the Texas State Library and Archives Commission.)

IMAGES
of America

The Texas Association of Chicanos in Higher Education

José Angel Gutiérrez
and Natalia Verjat Gutiérrez

ARCADIA
PUBLISHING

ISBN 1-4671-3082-0

Published by Arcadia Publishing
Charleston, South Carolina

Printed in the United States of America

Library of Congress Control Number: 2013952314
For all general information, please contact Arcadia Publishing:
Telephone 843-853-2070
Fax 843-853-0044
E-mail sales@arcadiapublishing.com
For customer service and orders:
Toll-Free 1-888-313-2665

Visit us on the Internet at www.arcadiapublishing.com

To Dr. George I. Sánchez, pioneer voice; Dr. Simón González, funder; Sal Castro, teacher and mentor; and Dr. Leonard Valverde, who began organizing TACHE in 1974

Contents

FOREWORD

TACHE was formed in 1975. At that time, there was a major counterculture movement across the country; US war policy was being challenged; the Chicano movement and the civil rights movement were in full force; and traditional institutions and organizations were being criticized and confronted on relevancy. Youth, farm workers, and women from racial and ethnic minorities took to the streets in protest.

Major institutions had not provided equal treatment to minorities. Governmental policy was disparate and institutionalized. Public officials created and maintained segregation within schools, social clubs, and neighborhoods and denied public services to minorities in Houston, Chicago, Denver, Los Angeles, San José, and New York, as well as along the US-Mexico border cities in Texas, Arizona, and California.

As junior faculty at the University of Texas, we were engulfed in these times and events. We used the power of definition plus our collective thinking and consensus to our advantage. We were Chicanos, not Mexican Americans or Hispanics. The TACHE logo symbolized our Mayan, Aztec, and Mexican heritage. We placed higher education issues within the education context and the wider band of societal fabric. E. Ramiréz and I wrote in our first journal, *El Cuaderno*, "The need to bring about better conditions in higher education in Texas for students, staff, faculty and administrators still exist." We have made clear statements to those in power of who we are, what we stand for, and what we want over the past four decades. TACHE was formed to be a *strong* voice, not just a loud voice.

We have the intellectual capital to state our problems, the reasons for our imposed troubles, and, most importantly, the solutions to create a better set of conditions and environment. TACHE members feel empowered. TACHE continues to speak its knowledge to powerbrokers. I believe TACHE's original purpose and voice will stay true: strong, unified, significant, and definitive.

—Dr. Leonard A. Valverde, emeritus professor
Arizona State University, Tempe, Arizona

ACKNOWLEDGMENTS

We acknowledge the forgotten thousands of Chicano students and their parents who walked out of classrooms in hundreds of public schools across the nation in protest of the deplorable conditions of segregation, racism, and discrimination. In Texas alone, there were at least 39 such walkouts, some as early as the 1940s in San Antonio. They were followed by walkouts in San Juan in 1956 and more in San Antonio in March 1968, together with walkouts in Los Angeles; Kansas City, Kansas; Kalamazoo, Michigan; Tucson and Phoenix, Arizona; and Denver. The high school walkouts in Los Angeles have been memorialized in the HBO movie *Walkout*, and the noted Crystal City walkout of 1969 was remembered in the play *Crystal City 1969*.

These brave children and parents paid a heavy price, as many boys, including those from Uvalde, Texas, were failed and expelled for protesting. Some of them ended up in the killing fields of Vietnam. In 2013, Uvalde remains under federal court order to desegregate. Meanwhile, in Tucson, Arizona, in January 2012, the Tucson Unified School District was forced to disband its Mexican-American Studies program or lose its state funding. By the time of this printing, thousands of dollars in legal fees had been expended to overturn this discriminatory decision.

Past and current members of TACHE provided information and photographs for this book, particularly Ana Broadwater, Dr. Magdalena de la Teja, María Guerrero, Dr. Rudy Rodríguez, María Aguirre-Acuña, Javier Olguín, Sara Samano, and Dr. Dennis Bixler-Márquez. Coauthor José Angel Gutiérrez's graduate students in the political science department at the University of Texas at Arlington also conducted interviews with past TACHE presidents.

We also thank and acknowledge the families of the many past and future members, chapter leaders, regional representatives, statewide officers, and presidents of TACHE, who provided unpaid public service, often at great cost to the quality of their family life and at their own personal expense. In particular, we say *gracias* to former TACHE president Linda Contreras Bullock and the state board of 2012 for initiating this project, and to Laura Bruns of Arcadia Publishing for steering it to fruition.

INTRODUCTION

In the 1920s, early pioneers in the struggle for equal educational opportunity in Texas included Manuel C. González, with La Liga Protectora Mexicana, "The Mexican Protection League;" María and Pedro Hernández of Lytle, with Orden Hijos de América, the "Order of the Sons of America," and later with Orden Caballeros de América, the "Order of the Knights of America;" and, lastly, Eluterio Escobar of San Antonio, with La Liga Pro-Defensa Escolar, "The Pro-Defense League for Schools." Hernández and Escobar led street protests in San Antonio's west side barrio demanding better facilities and teachers for their children.

The League of United Latin American Citizens (LULAC) was founded in 1929. LULAC has historically been the plaintiff in educational litigation on behalf of Mexican-ancestry students and parents in this country.

After World War II, in 1948, another group emerged that joined LULAC as a proponent for better human conditions for returning veterans of Mexican ancestry: the American G.I. Forum (AGIF). At the time, African American students were rigidly segregated into inferior school facilities and programs based on race, and Hispanic students were as segregated because of language. The *Hernández v. Texas* case, heard by the US Supreme Court prior to *Brown v. Board of Education of Topeka, Kansas*, dealt with the racial issue of Mexican-ancestry persons in America. The court held that Mexican-origin persons, while classified as white for racial purposes, were set apart as not being white enough to be treated like whites. This case gave persons of Mexican origin their civil rights protections under the 14th Amendment.

Since 1946, in various federal and state court cases, Mexican parents, primarily in California and Texas, have fought for equal educational opportunity for their children, including demands for desegregation, bilingual education, testing, and equitable school financing. They met with success in the first two areas of discrimination and are still fighting for the latter two. LULAC and AGIF raised funds and served as plaintiffs for litigation to advance educational opportunity and veterans' rights until the advent of the Mexican American Legal Defense and Education Fund (MALDEF).

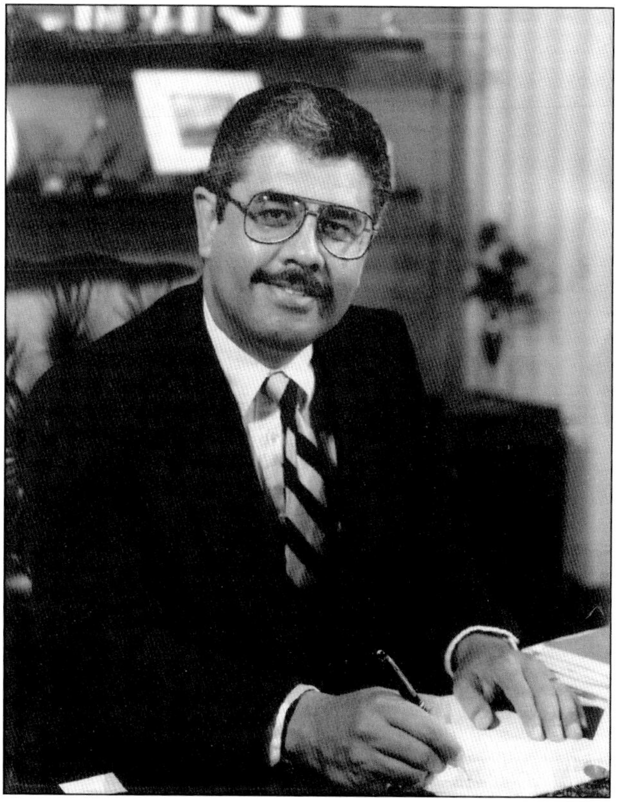

Dr. Leonard Valverde is seen at left in his office and below posing for a photograph with his wife, Josefina, (far right); Dr. Hans Mark, the chancellor of the University of Texas; and Dr. Mark's wife, Anna. (Left, courtesy of Josefina Valverde; below, courtesy of Dr. Leonard Valverde.)

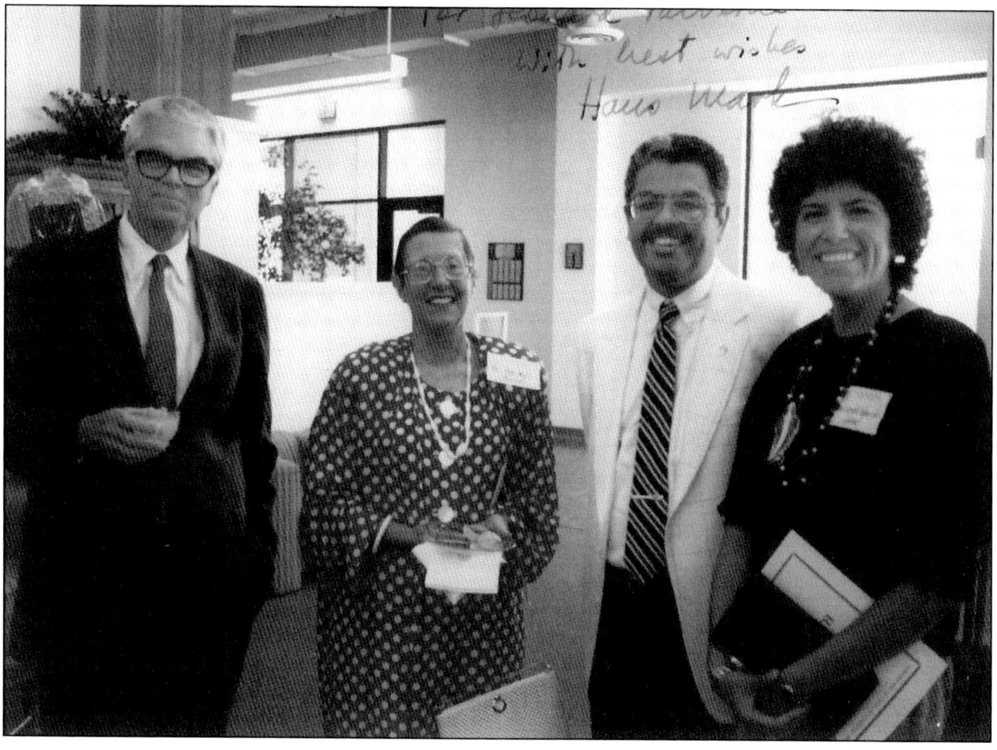

One

THE CHICANO MOVEMENT

The Chicano movement grew rapidly in the 1960s, led by youth, farm workers, and women. Chicano students took the lead in fomenting social change by boycotting classes en masse. By not attending classes, they deprived the school districts of state funding based on per-pupil daily attendance, an economic weapon. In Texas, the spearheading group for these student protests was the Mexican American Youth Organization (MAYO).

Among the Chicano student demands to return to the classroom and stop the boycott was a call for Chicano studies and Chicano teachers. This demand, in turn, caused a ripple effect in higher education, as Chicano high school graduates had to be enrolled in colleges and made into teachers. Chicano professors had to be hired to help train such teachers. The statistics of Chicano students in college were dismal, as were the faculty ranks of Chicanos. This need to fill the void of historical neglect prompted institutions of higher education to seek out and hire Chicano professors.

Once hired, these new faculty, together with early pioneers who were often the only token Chicanos in a department or a college, sought each other out across the state and the nation. The National Task Force de la Raza was formed by Chicano academics across the nation, and, in 1974, the Chicano Faculty Association at the University of Texas at Austin began the organizing steps to form TACHE.

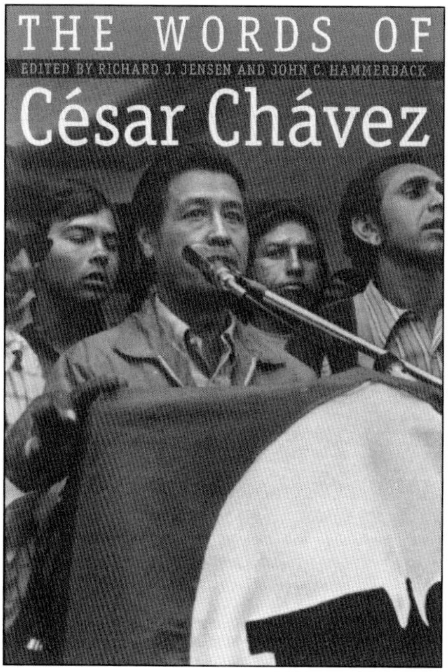

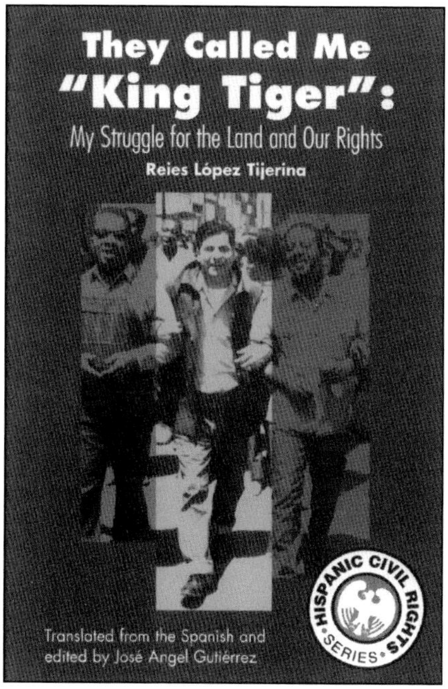

In the 1960s, the Chicano civil rights struggle took on another name: the Chicano movement. In essence, this civil rights movement emerged because there was a need for leadership renewal to augment—and supplant in some cases—the older, traditional organizations that excluded from membership agricultural workers, women, youth, and non-US citizens. Its principal leaders were described as "the Four Horsemen" in Matt Meier and Feliciano Rivera's book *The Chicanos*. These were César E. Chávez (California), Reies López Tijerina (New Mexico), Rodolfo "Corky" Gonzáles (Colorado), and José Angel Gutiérrez (Texas). (Top left, courtesy of Richard Jensen; all others, courtesy of Marina Tristán, Arte Público Press.)

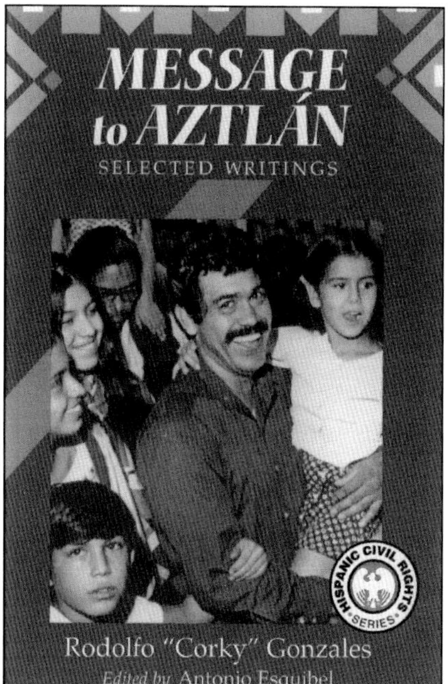

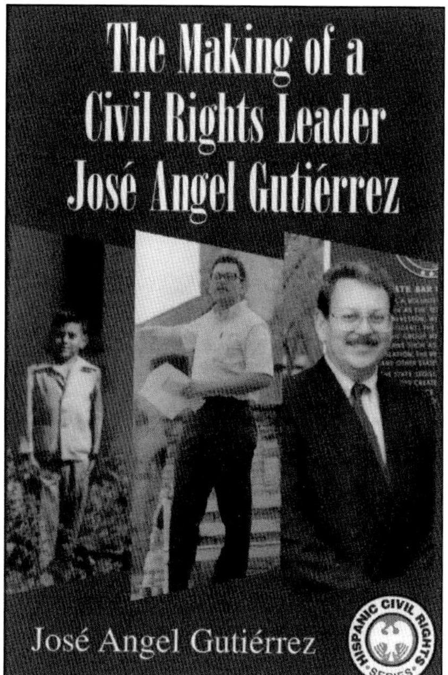

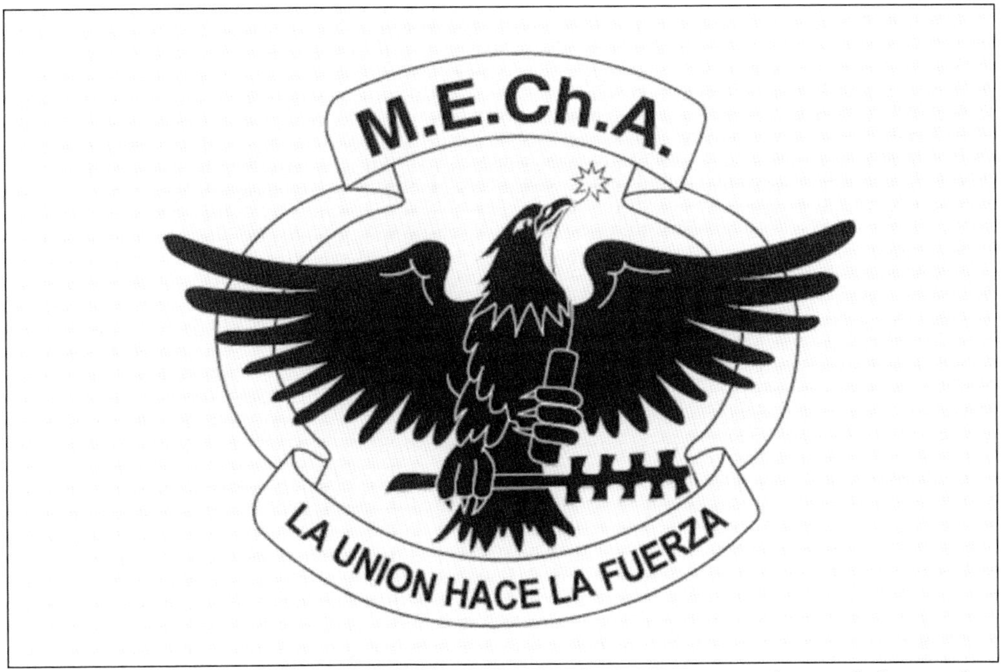

Chicano youth, male and female, formed their own organizations to press for social change; they did not want to wait until age 21 to become members of traditional organizations or be eligible to vote. The motto (above) of the Movimiento Estudiantil Chicano de Aztlán (MEChA), "La Union Hace La Fuerza," was borrowed from the 1894 Alianza Hispano-Americana. The slogan seen below on the MAYO button, "La Raza Unida," became the name of the Chicano political party in the 1970s. (Above, courtesy of John Martínez, Aztlan Media Kollective; below, courtesy of Natalia Verjat Gutiérrez.)

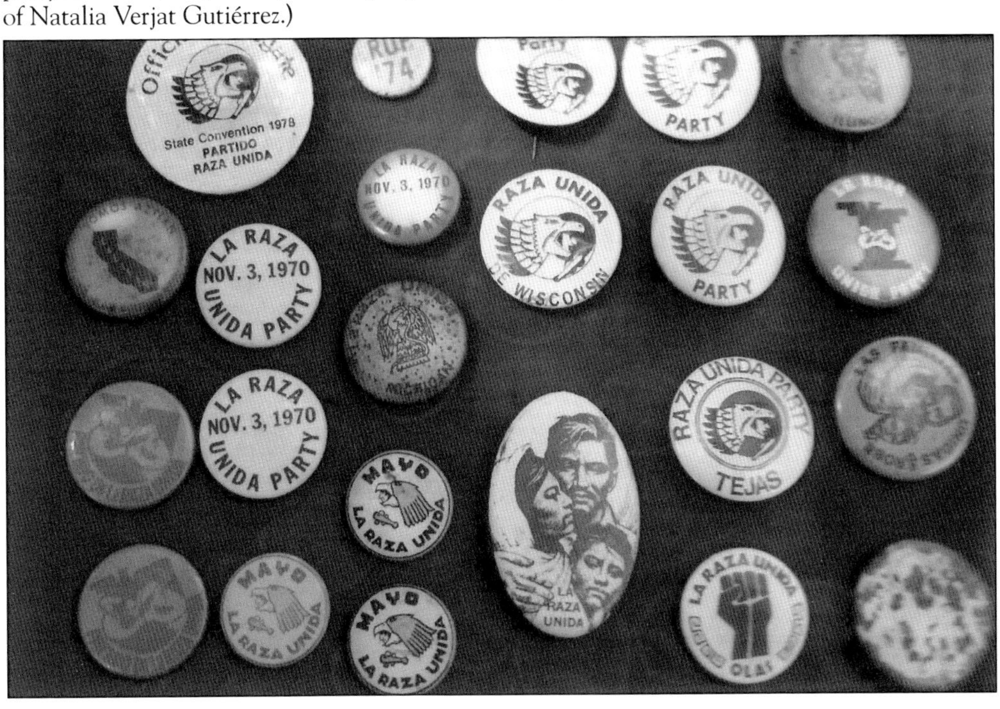

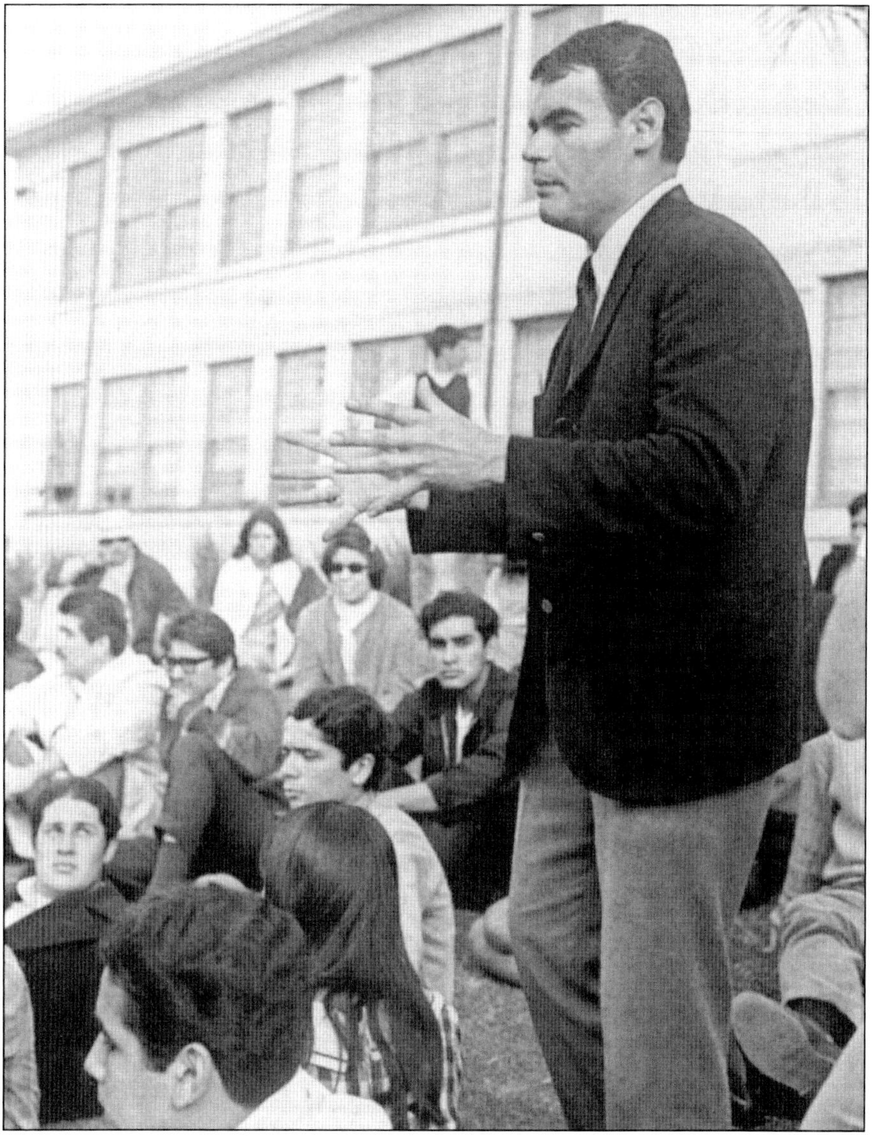

In 1968, there was unrest and dissatisfaction among Chicano high school students in East Los Angeles, the largest segregated barrio in California. A protest of the school board, teachers, administrators, counselors, and curriculum led to a series of walkouts, starting with Wilson High School on March 1, 1968, followed by Garfield High School on March 5, Roosevelt High School on March 6, and Belmont and Lincoln High Schools on March 8. Thousands took to the streets, hundreds were arrested, and many were beaten; ultimately, they had a meeting with the school board. Their mentor and teacher, Salvador "Sal" Castro, and other Brown Beret leaders were arrested. Upon his release, Castro continued his mentoring of students in an annual weekend retreat at Camp Hess Kramer, near the ocean at the edge of the Malibu Mountains. The culture camp stressed Chicano culture and heritage, as well as preparation for college admission. Castro began the Chicano Youth Leadership Conference (CYLC), after several name changes, in 1963, and it continues to this day despite his death. In *Blowout! Sal Castro and the Chicano Struggle for Educational Justice*, which he coauthored with Dr. Mario T. García, he writes that the CYLC was "for the development of youth leadership." (Courtesy of Mónica Castro.)

Dr. Rodolfo "Rudy" Acuña (left), a pioneer of the Chicano studies program at California State University, Northridge, and the author of the first Chicano history book, *Occupied America*, presents an award to Sal Castro for his role in the Los Angeles walkouts of 1968. (Courtesy of Rodolfo Acuña.)

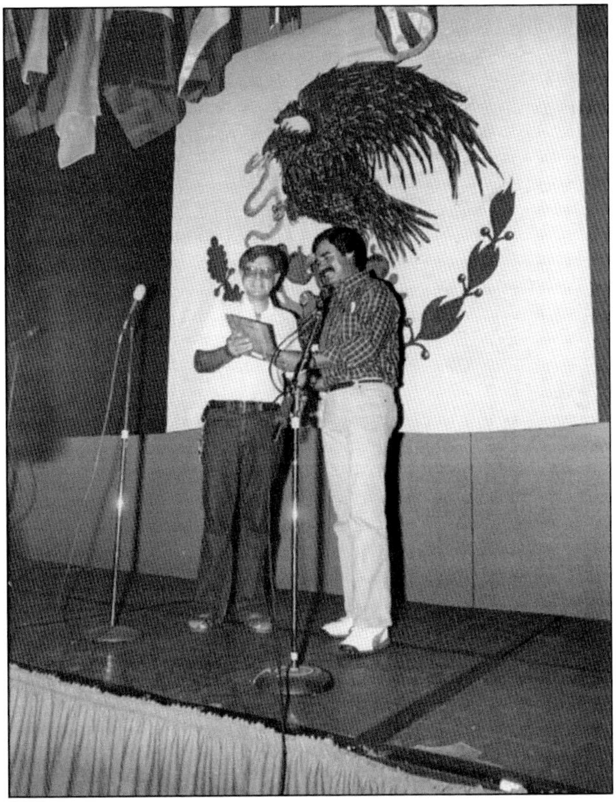

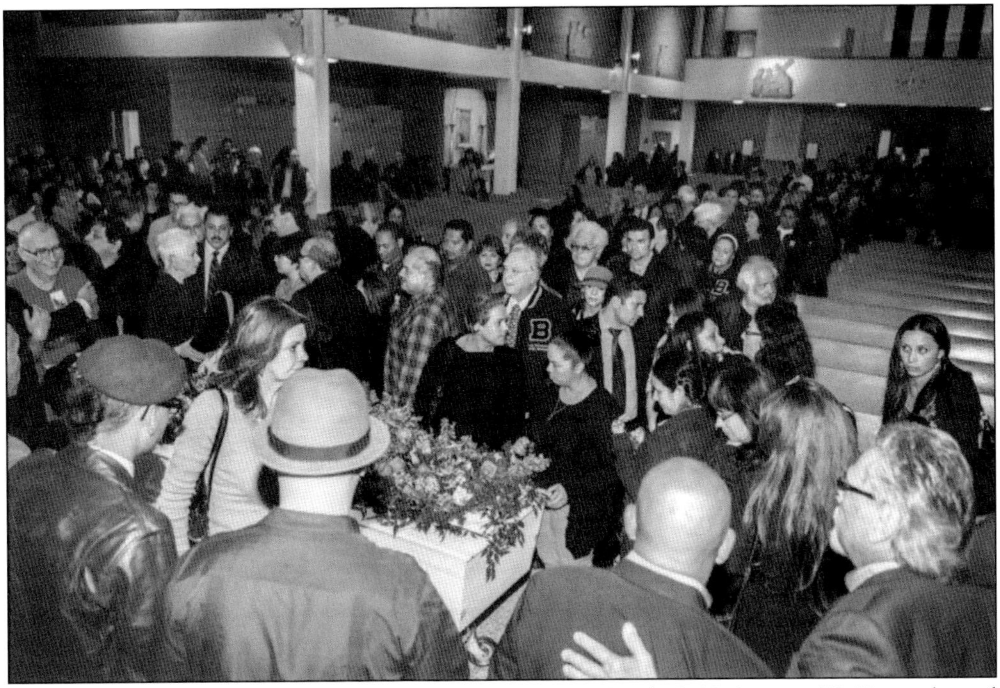

Sal Castro died after a seven-month battle with cancer on April 15, 2013, at age 79. He was buried on April 25, 2013. (Courtesy of David Sandoval.)

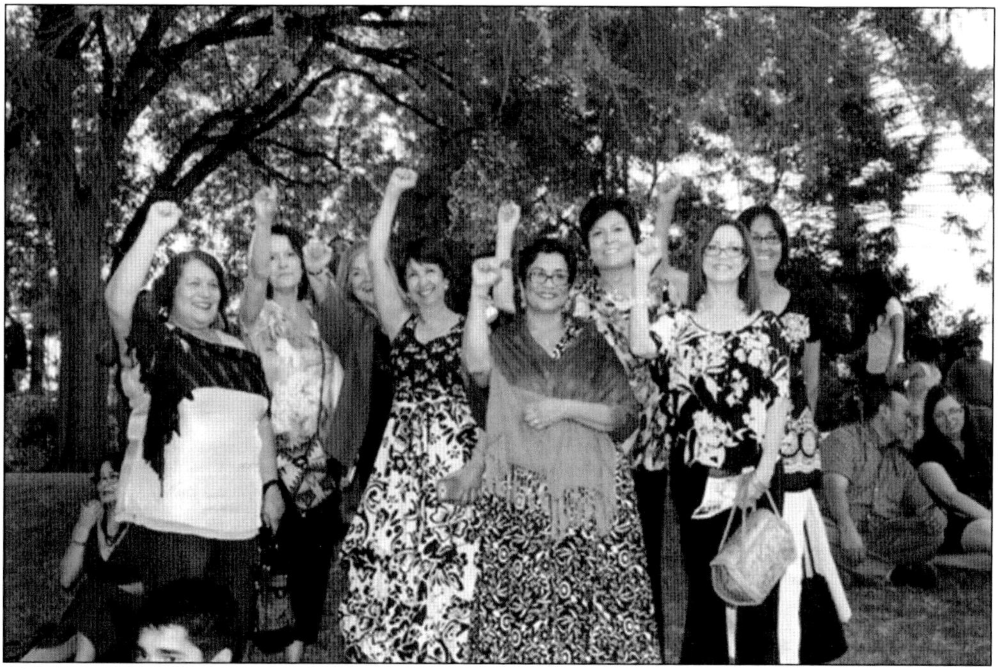

This crowd pays their last respects to Sal Castro at his funeral service. Many of them had been his students or participants at Camp Hess Kramer. (Courtesy of Rodolfo Acuña.)

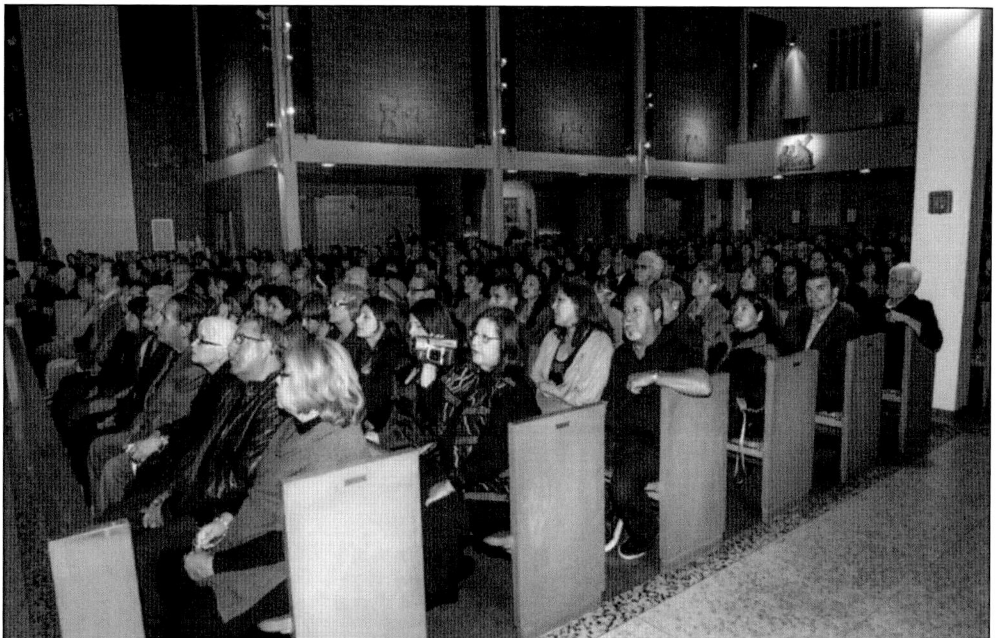

Some MEChA students were aging seniors by the time of the Castro service. These students had formed MEChA to press for Chicano studies in college and high school curriculums, as well as other reforms. (Courtesy of Rodolfo Acuña.)

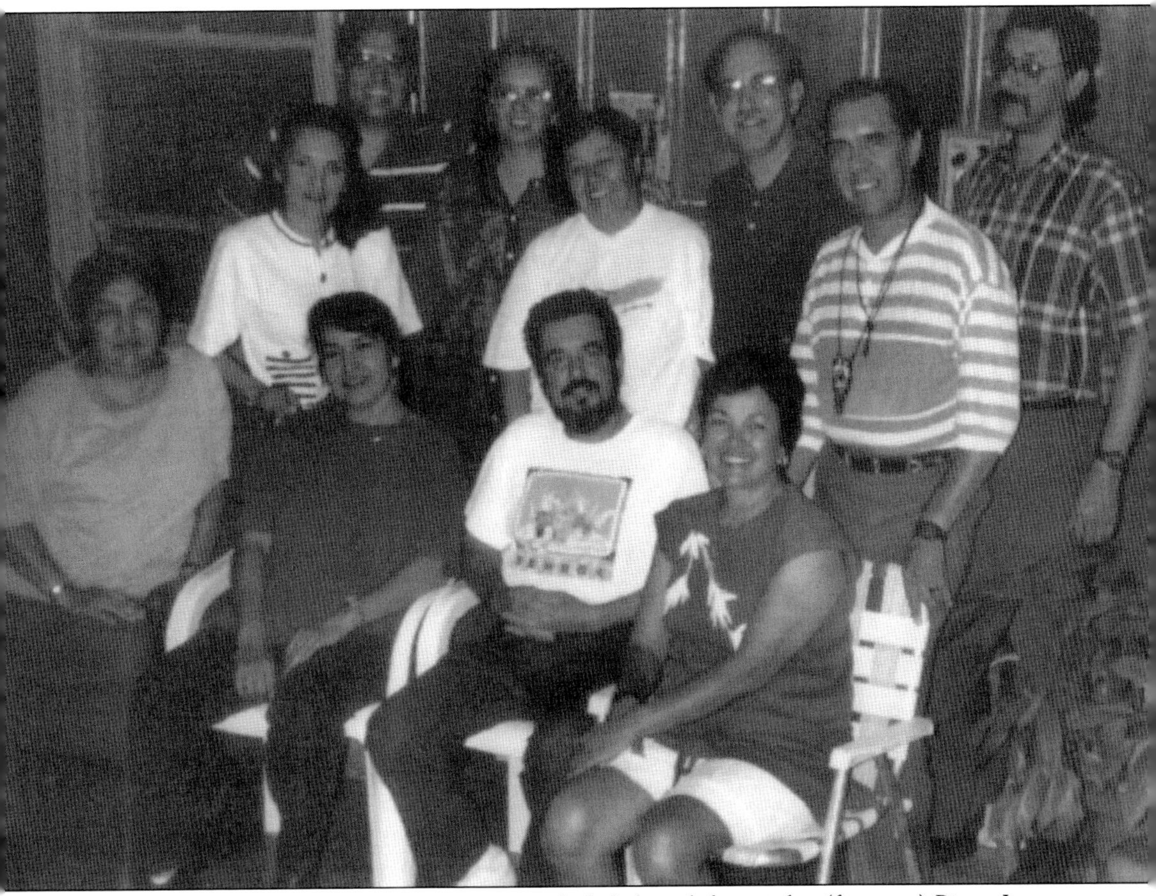

This Raza Unida group from San Antonio included, from left to right, (first row) Pietra Luera Bustamante, Juanita Bustamante, José Montalvo, and Lucille Benavides; (second row) Anna Riojas, Rosie Castro, and Ramón Vásquez y Sánchez; (third row) William Benavides, Irma Mireles, Daniel Meza, and Manuel Garza. Several of these people were candidates for public office under the Raza Unida banner, including Irma Mireles, who was elected to the San Antonio River Authority. Rosie Castro did not win her bid for a seat on the city council in 1969, but her sons have made it to public office; today, Julián Castro is the mayor of San Antonio and Joaquín Castro is a US representative. (Courtesy of Irma Mireles.)

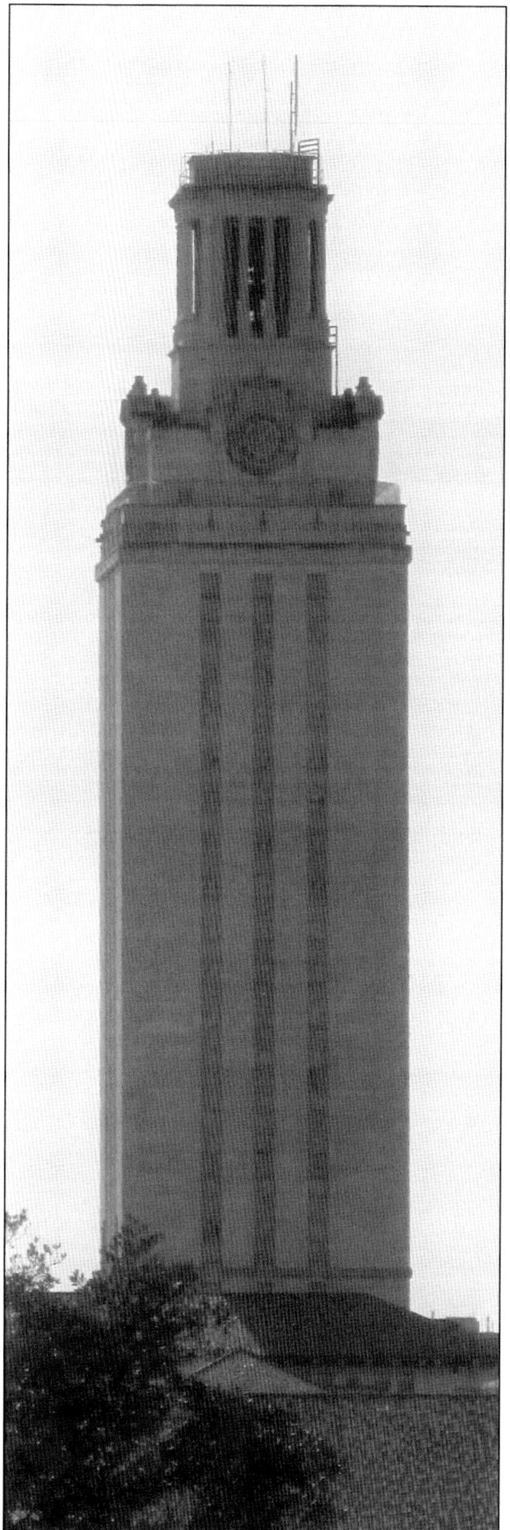

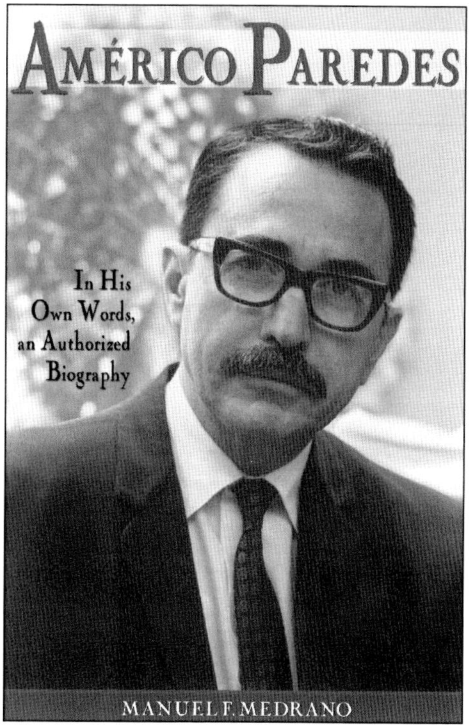

Central to students' demands were the addition of college preparation courses and the hiring of more Chicano teachers. The college enrollment of Chicanos in seven major national universities was pathetic: a mere 5,878 in the 1966–1967 school year. At the University of Texas at Austin (UT), Chicano students totaled only 771 out of 27,345 total students. By 1970, UT had established a Mexican American studies program with Dr. Américo Paredes (above) at the helm. Within a few years, he resigned in disgust over the lack of institutional support. Diana Serna Cantú, a TACHE cofounder, recalls that UT MAYO Chicano students, advised by Jessie Rangel, another TACHE cofounder, demanded a Chicano Night at the student union building in 1974. Rebuffed in their demand, MAYO members occupied the iconic University of Texas tower (left), in the center of campus. According to Diana Serna, the headline of the campus newspaper, the *Longhorn*, read, "Takeover of the tower by Chicano students." (Above, courtesy of Diana Serna Aguilera; left, courtesy of Natalia Verjat Gutiérrez.)

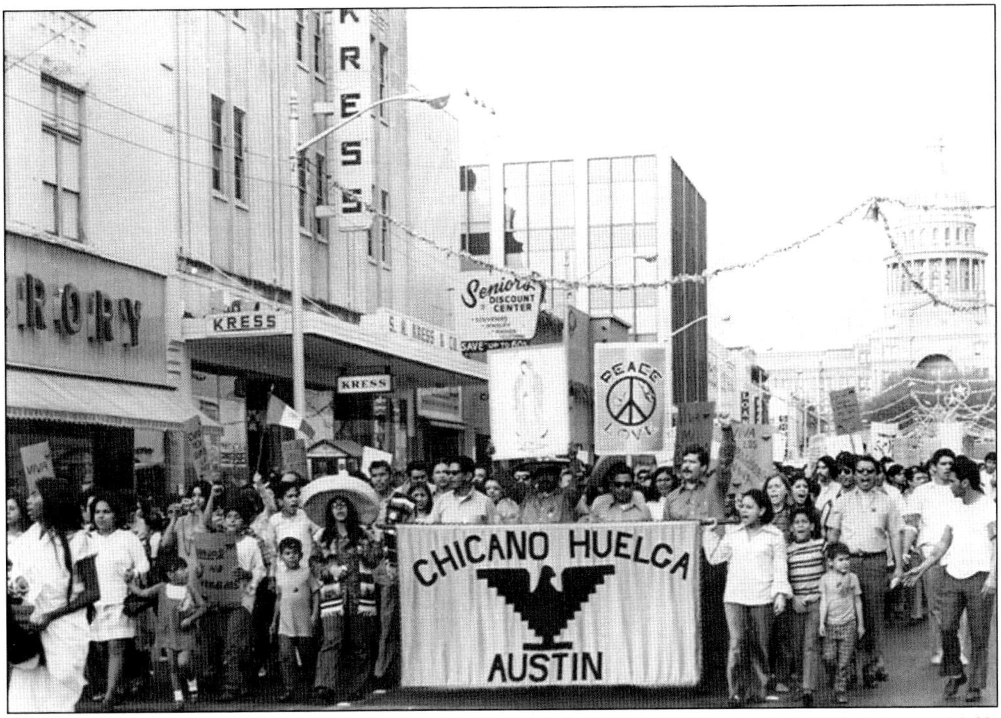

Chicano workers went on strike against the Economy Furniture Company in Austin in 1969. The cause of urban labor became a part of the Chicano movement. Youth joined Chicano workers in marching on Congress Avenue. The state capitol is in the background. (Courtesy of Alfredo Santos.)

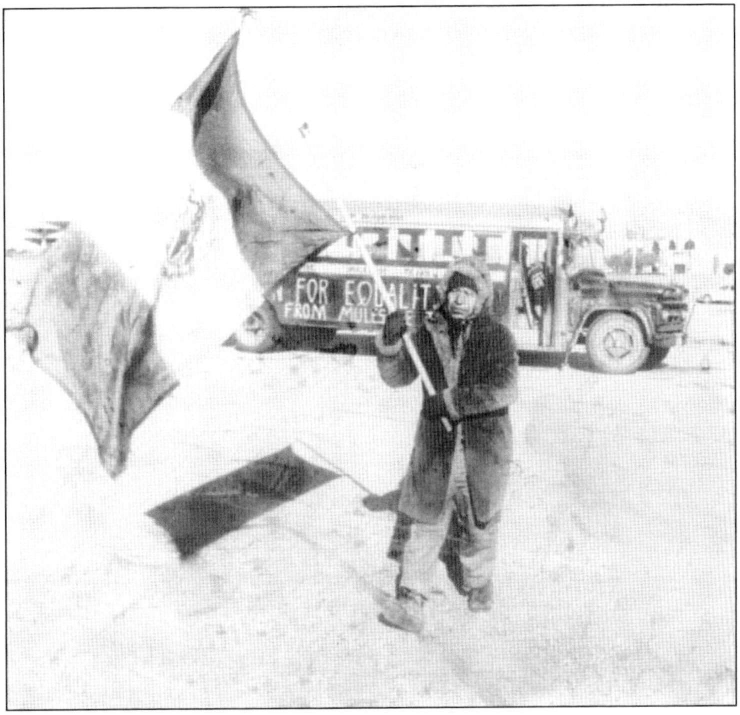

Chicano farmworkers went on strike in Muleshoe, in the Texas panhandle, in 1975. María Beltrán, of Women for Equality in Muleshoe, carries the Mexican flag to the protest. (Courtesy of Olga Aguero.)

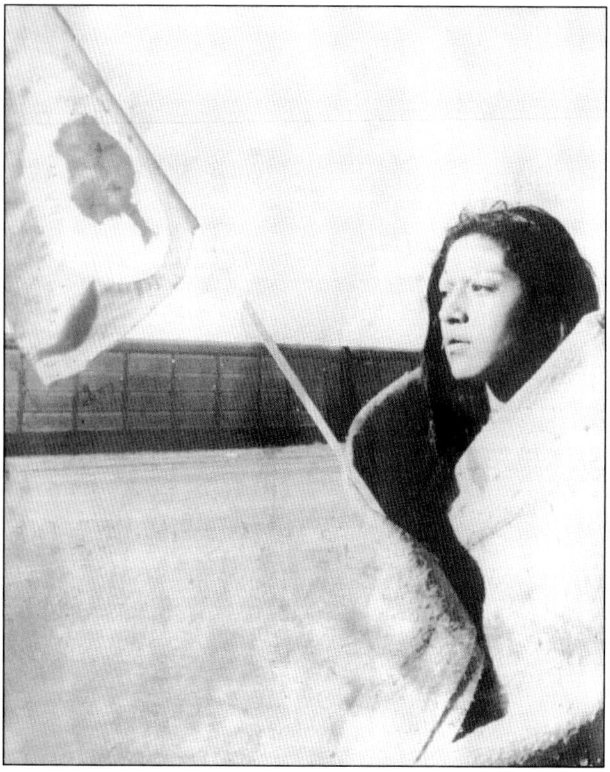

A young woman draped in a heavy blanket and carrying a Texas Farm Worker Union flag near the railroad loading dock protests the low wages paid to farmworkers in the fields of the Texas Panhandle in 1975. (Courtesy of Olga Aguero.)

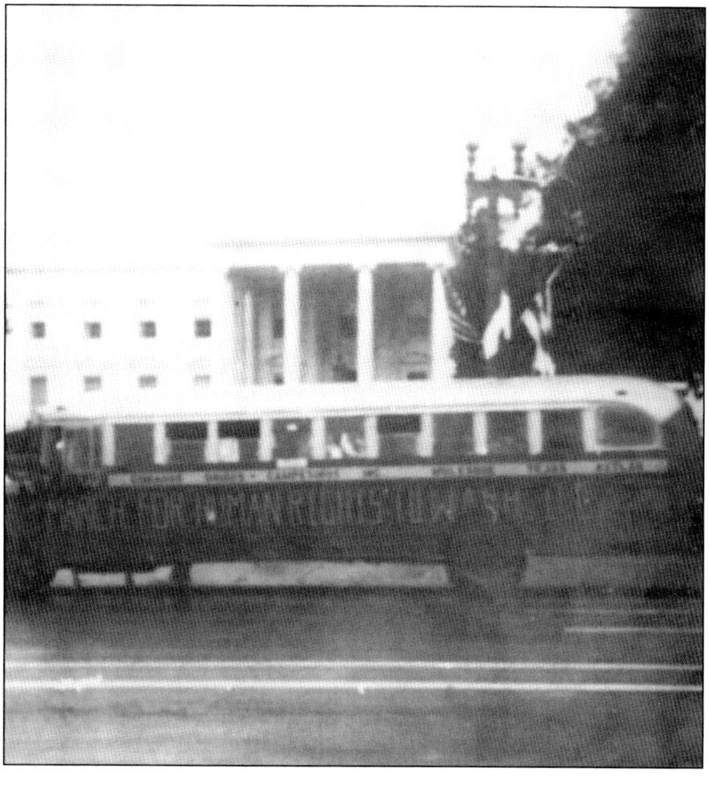

Led by Antonio Orendian, members and supporters of the Texas Farm Workers Union marched 1,600 miles from Texas to Washington, DC, protesting the right-to-work laws that were prevalent in nonunion states. They left on June 18, 1977, and arrived at the White House on September 5. After Pres. Jimmy Carter refused to meet with them to discuss their issues, they waged a hunger strike and chained themselves to the fence of the White House, demanding an audience with their president, and were arrested. (Courtesy of Olga Aguero.)

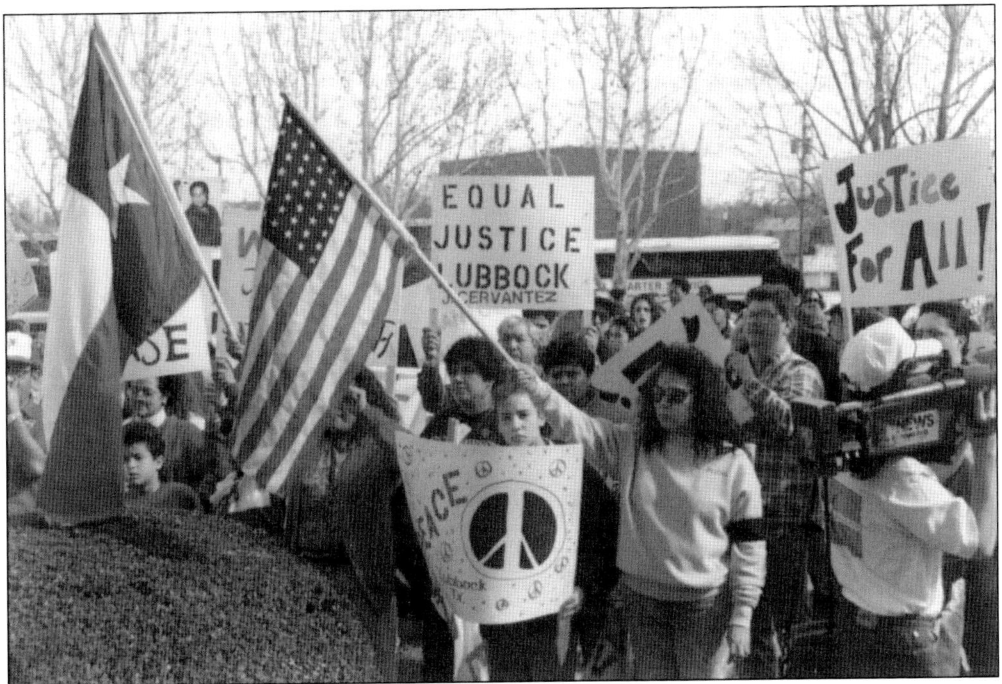

Police brutality was also a focus of the Chicano movement. Here, protesters gathered at the Lubbock police station in 1979 to demand an inquiry into the beating of José Cervántez by local police. (Courtesy of Olga Aguero.)

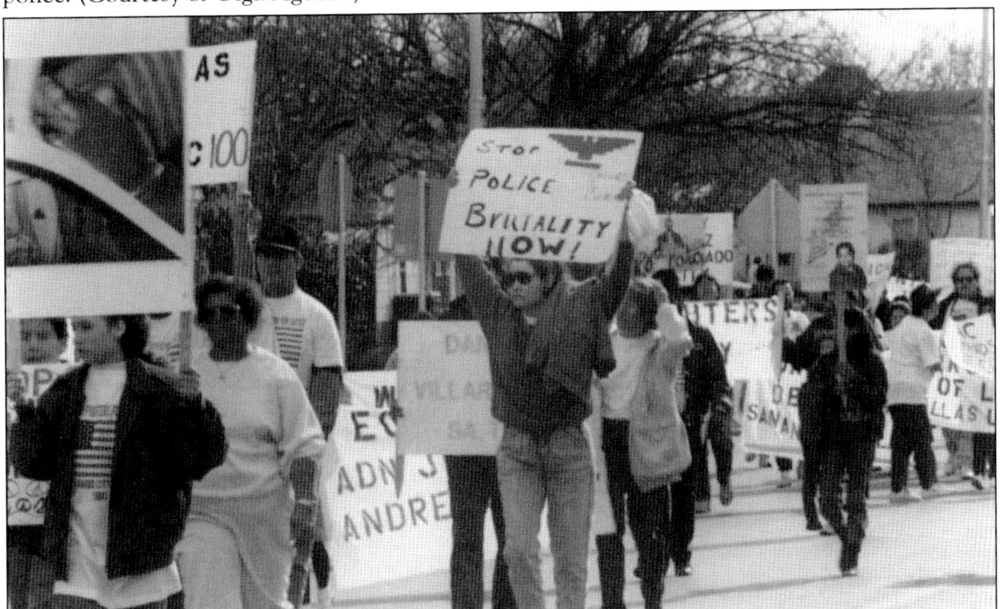

Chicano protestors march in the streets of Austin's east side en route to the capitol, carrying signs with the names, affiliation, location, and images of victims of police brutality. (Courtesy of Olga Aguero.)

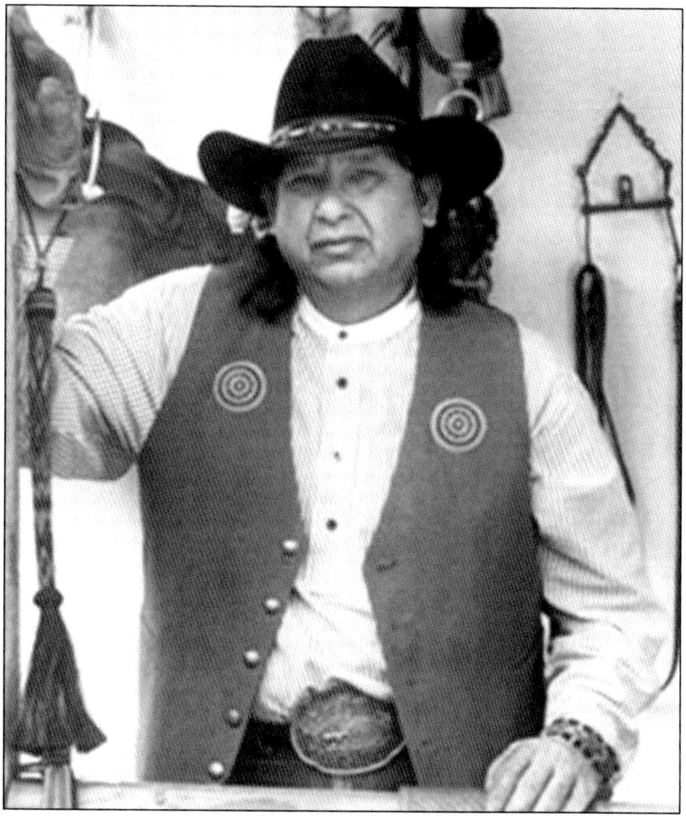

Chicano art began with protest art. Among the pioneers was Amado Peña (at left), who donated much of his work to help raise funds for Chicano groups, including TACHE. He was honored by TACHE at the 1992 annual conference with the Meritorious Service Award, for this work and for funding scholarships. The first award in this category was given to Dr. Américo Paredes in 1979. (Both courtesy of José Angel Gutiérrez.)

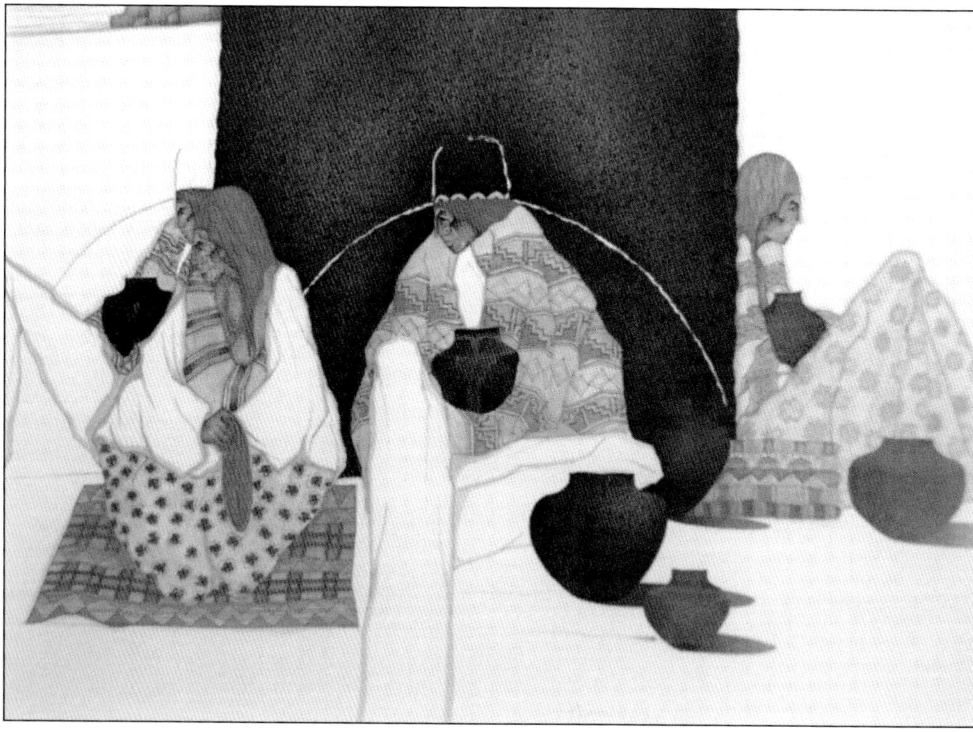

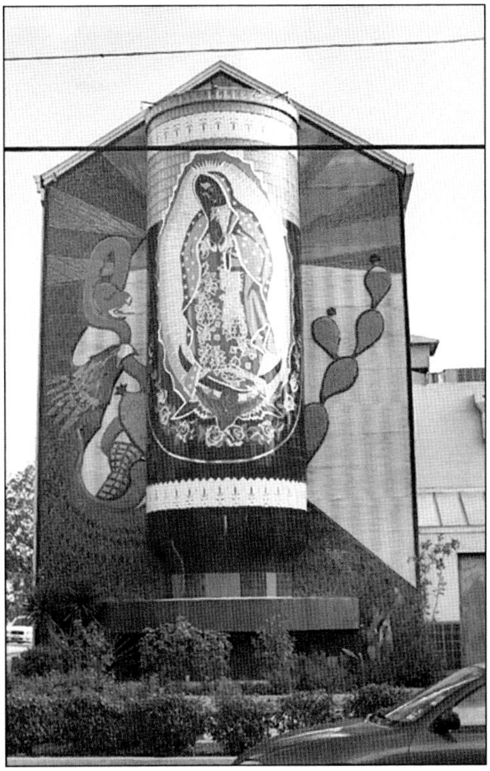

The second floor of this building on Guadalupe Street was decorated by Jesse Treviño and housed the offices of the Mexican American Youth Organization (MAYO) and the Mexican American Unity Council, the tax-exempt entity for MAYO. Other artists who made a name for themselves with Chicano art were Carmen Lomas Garza, César Martínez, Malaquías Montoya, and Margaret Garza. Other examples of the influence of Chicano art include Cheech Marin's Chicano Collection, which features 26 artists and their work and is often on national tour, and San Diego's Chicano Park, which has several murals with Chicano themes. Dr. Gilbert Cárdenas, Notre Dame University's Chicano studies program director, also has a collection of Chicano art. Seen below is the work of Malaquías Montoya. (Both courtesy of José Angel Gutiérrez.)

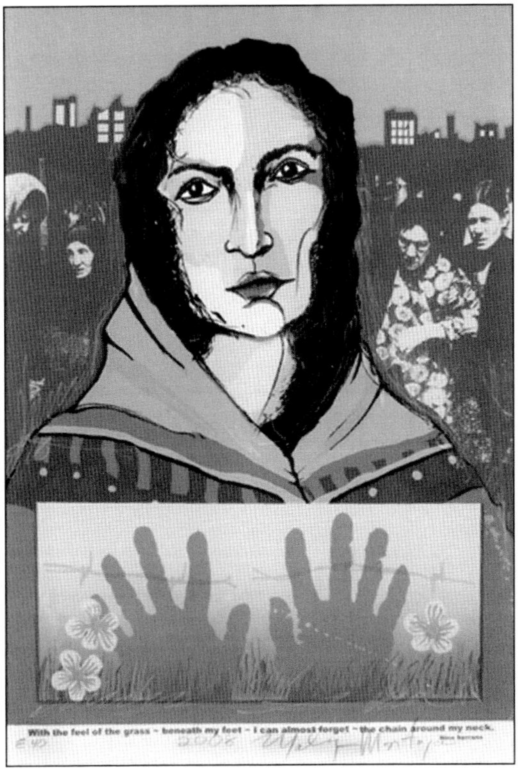

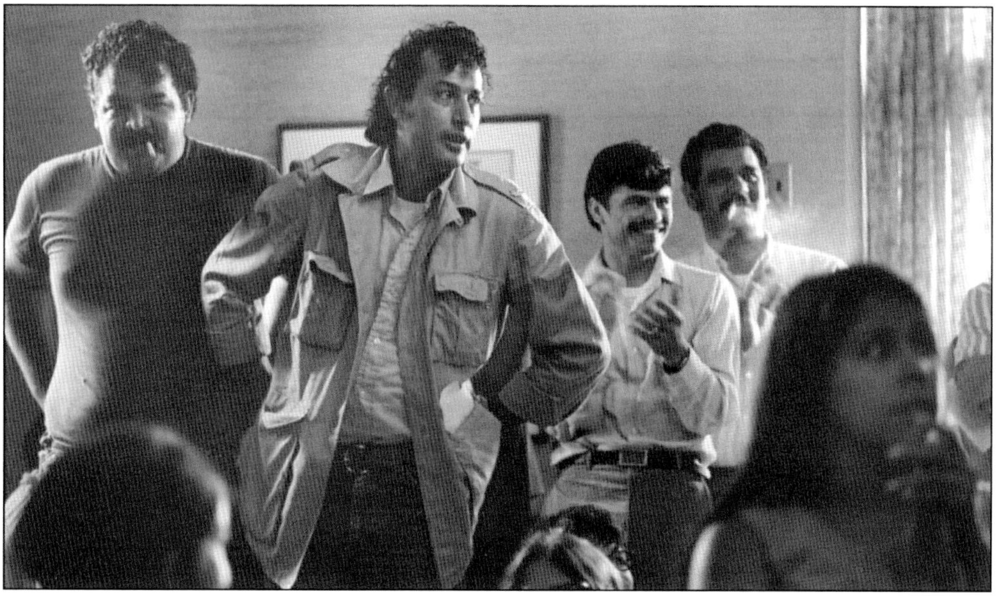

Roberto Hernández (far left) and Ernesto Chacón (second from left) instruct protestors on tactics just before the 1970 Chapman Hall takeover by Chicano students at the University of Wisconsin-Milwaukee. They were protesting the lack of Chicano students enrolled at UW-Milwaukee—less than a dozen, with no faculty members. Hernández passed away in 1994. Today, the Chicano Latino studies program at UW-Milwaukee carries his name. In the background on the far right is Miguel Delgado, who went on to become a professor at Palo Alto College in San Antonio and a TACHE member. In 2010, UW-Milwaukee had more than 1,300 Chicano Latino students enrolled, 30 Chicano Latino faculty members, and a Latino chancellor. (Courtesy of Ernesto Chacón.)

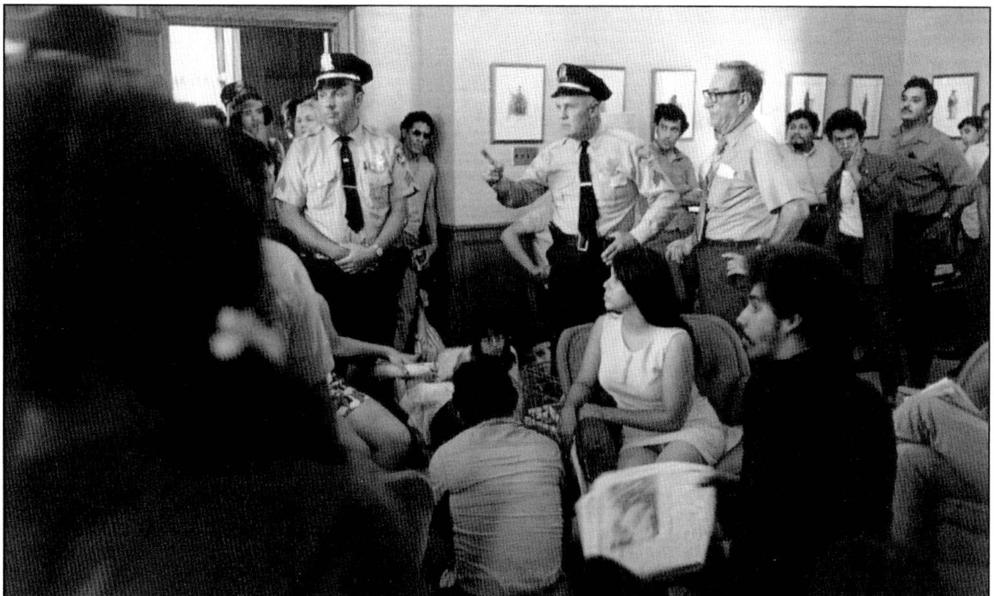

City and campus police admonished Chicano students to vacate the UW-Milwaukee building or be arrested. The students refused, and police forcibly removed them. Several of the protest leaders and supporting parents were jailed. (Courtesy of Ernesto Chacón.)

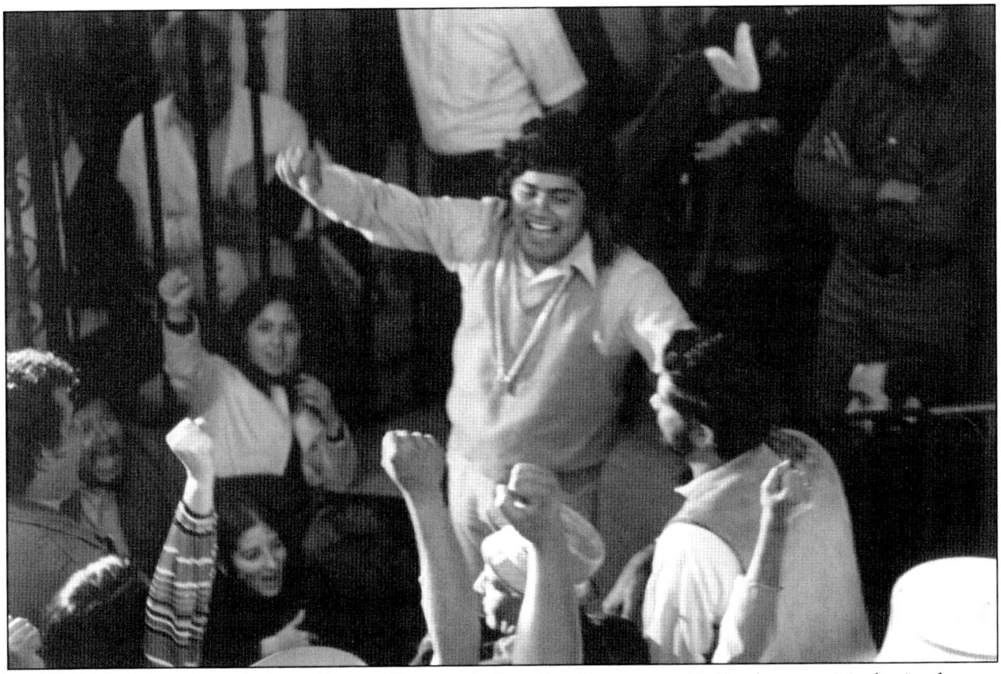

Jesús Salas is seen here being released from jail after the Chapman Hall takeover. Marla Anderson and Dante Navarro were also jailed, along with two others. Navarro passed away in April 2013. In 2000, Salas was appointed to serve as a regent of the University of Wisconsin system of higher education. Ernesto Chacón, before he retired, served as the deputy director of Gov. Jim Doyle's Milwaukee office. (Courtesy of Ernesto Chacón.)

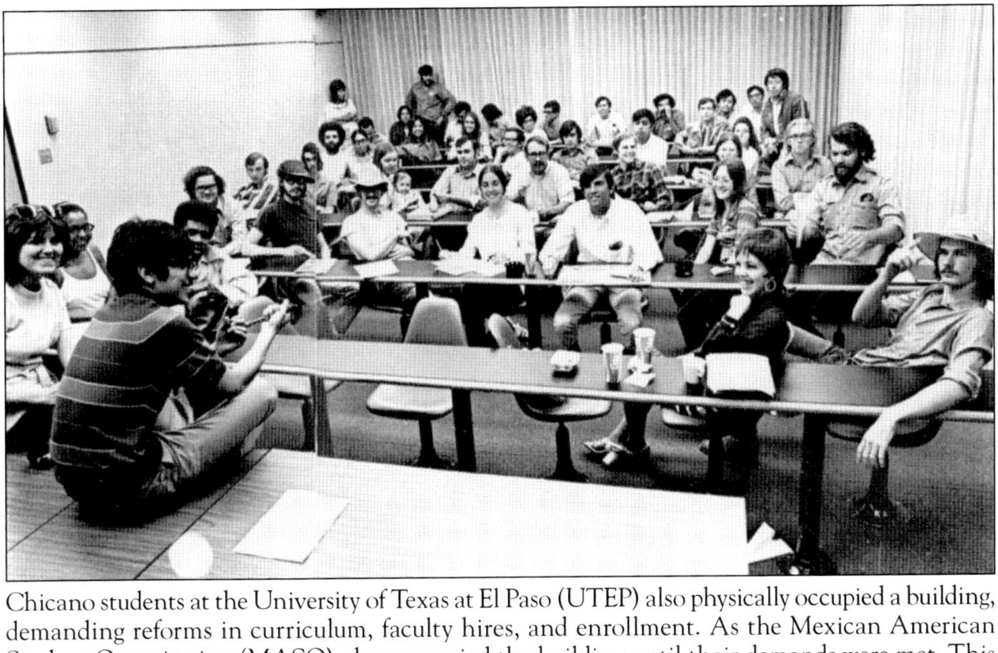

Chicano students at the University of Texas at El Paso (UTEP) also physically occupied a building, demanding reforms in curriculum, faculty hires, and enrollment. As the Mexican American Student Organization (MASO), they occupied the building until their demands were met. This was the beginning of the Chicano studies program at UTEP. (Courtesy of *El Paso Herald-Post* records, MS 348. University of Texas at El Paso Library, Special Collections Department.)

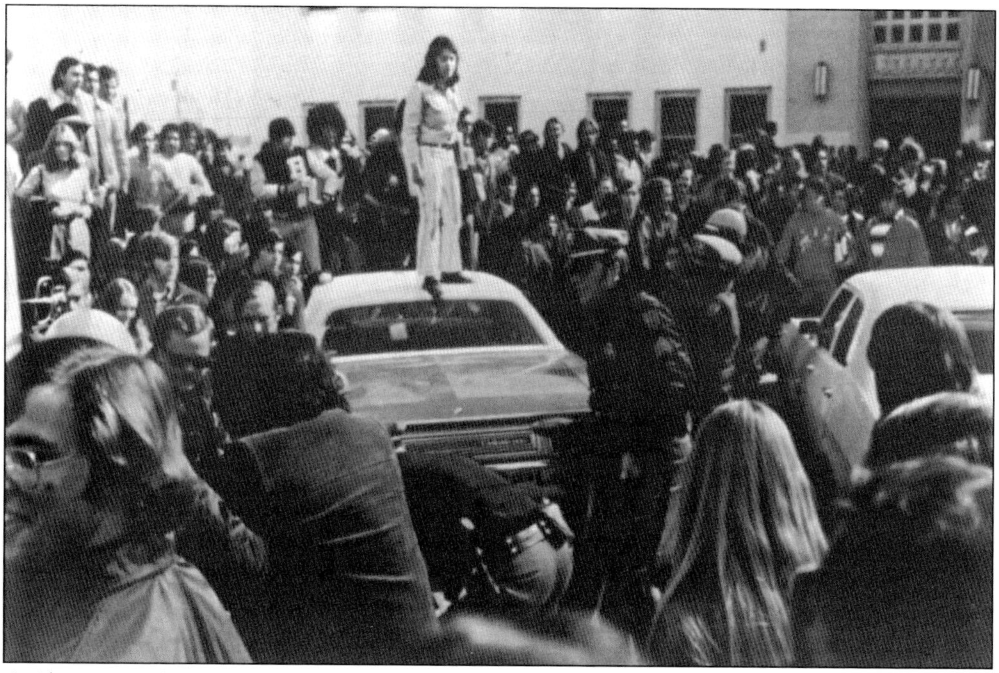

A Chicana student at UTEP exhorts people to join the others inside the building to protest the lack of Chicano student admissions, the need for Chicano studies and more Chicano faculty members, and the insensitivity of administrators. (Courtesy of *El Paso Herald-Post* records, MS 348. University of Texas at El Paso Library, Special Collections Department.)

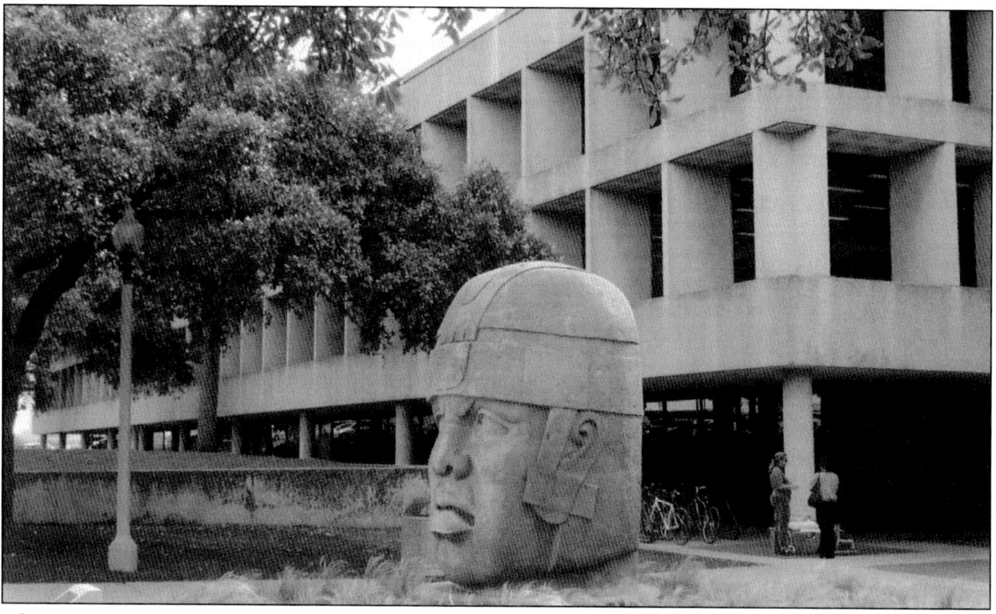

This pre-Hispanic replica of the Olmec head is located on the east side of the Sid Richardson Building, the first offices for the Center for Mexican American Studies at the University of Texas at Austin. This program came about as a result of Chicano student protests as well, after students threatened to rearrange books in the specialized libraries of the campus. (Courtesy of Natalia Verjat Gutiérrez.)

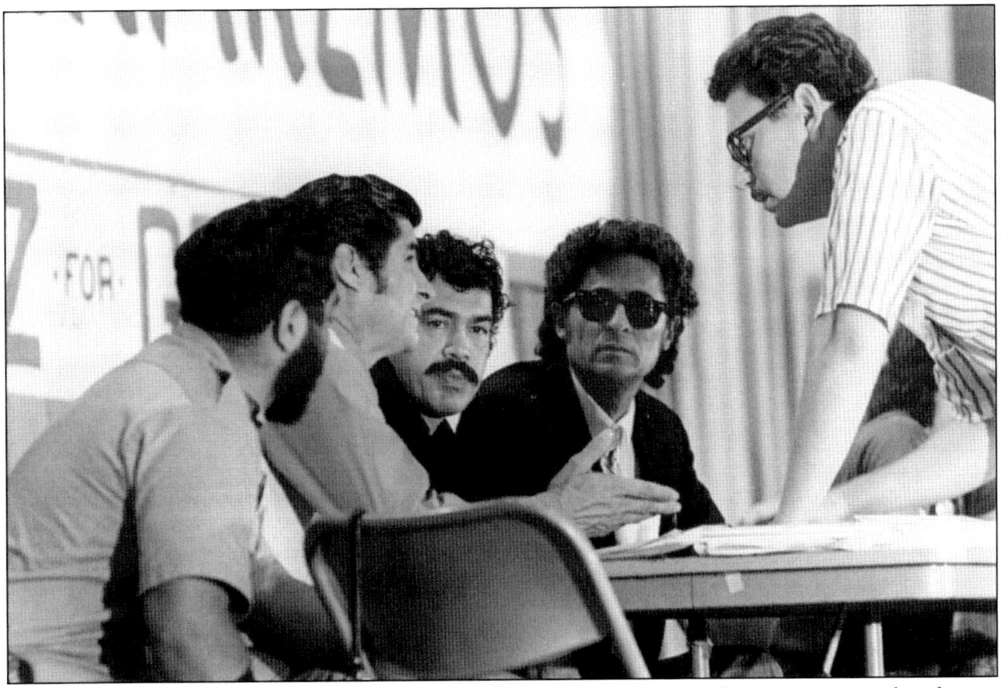

At the Denver Chicano Liberation Youth Conference in 1969, a resolution was passed to form a Chicano political party. MAYO activists in Texas, led by José Angel Gutiérrez, formed the Raza Unida Party (RUP) on January 10, 1970, and called for a national convention in El Paso on Labor Day weekend in 1972. Seen here from left to right are Juan José Peña (New Mexico), Reies López Tijerina (New Mexico), Rodolfo "Corky" González (Colorado), Ramón Tijerina (Texas), and José Angel Gutiérrez (Texas). Gutiérrez was elected the national chair of the Raza Unida Party over González in 1972. (Courtesy of *El Paso Herald-Post* records, MS 348. University of Texas at El Paso Library, Special Collections Department.)

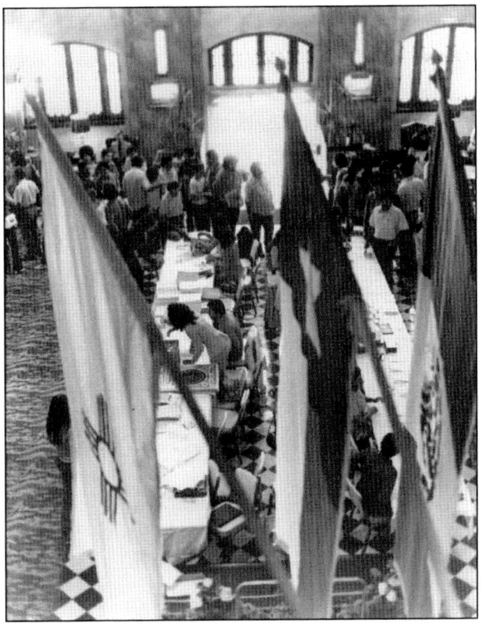

This photograph shows the registration of delegates, guests, press, and observers during the 1972 national Raza Unida Party convention held in El Paso. Delegates attended from 18 states and the District of Columbia. (Courtesy of *El Paso Herald-Post* records, MS 348. University of Texas at El Paso Library, Special Collections Department.)

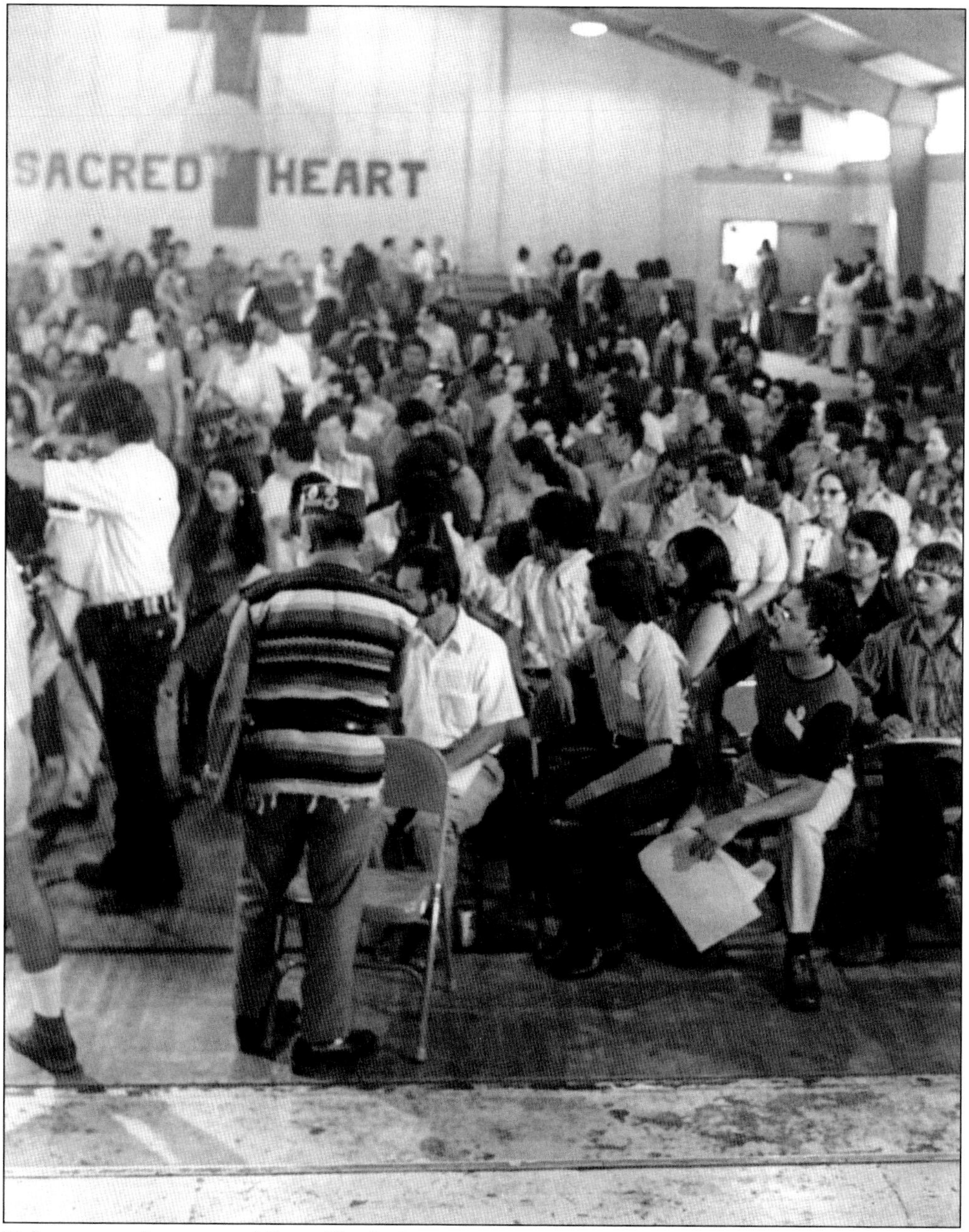

Delegates at the national Raza Unida Party convention gathered at this location and in the Auditorio Municipal of Ciudad Juárez before moving into the El Paso Convention Center. Tragedy struck early, just as participants began arriving from across the country, when Ricardo Falcón was murdered by Perry Munson in Oro Grande, Arizona, en route to the convention. Falcón was seeking water for an overheated car radiator. Across the border in Juárez, a half-brother of noted author Rudolfo Anaya was also found dead; some claimed he was also coming to the convention. (Courtesy of *El Paso Herald-Post* records, MS 348. University of Texas at El Paso Library, Special Collections Department.)

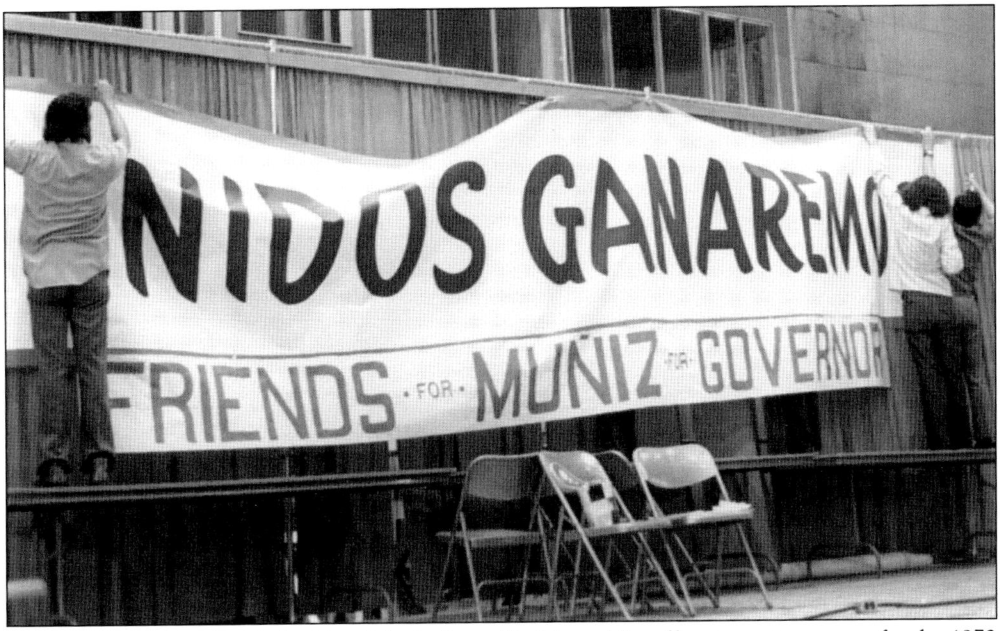

Candidates affiliated with the Raza Unida Party filed for public office in various states for the 1972 general elections. In Texas, Ramsey Muñiz filed for governor. Supporters at the El Paso Convention Center during the RUP convention posted this banner on a back wall. (Courtesy of *El Paso Herald-Post* records, MS 348. University of Texas at El Paso Library, Special Collections Department.)

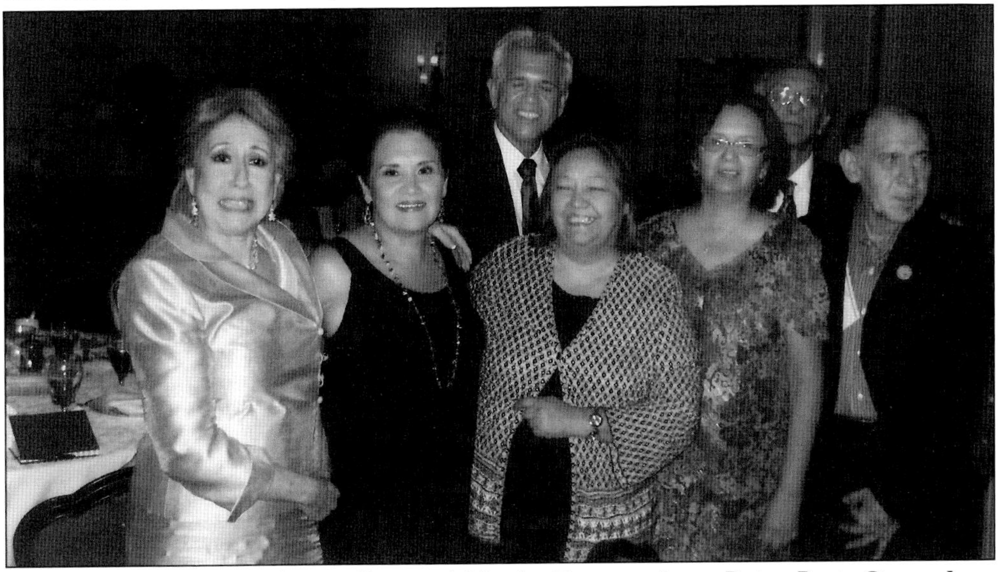

Seen here from left to right are (first row) Martha Tijerina, Anna Rojas, Rosie Castro, Irma Mireles, and Ignacio Pérez; (second row) Edgar Lozano and Manuel Garza. Castro and Compean ran unsuccessful campaigns for the San Antonio City Council in 1969. Mireles was elected to the San Antonio River Authority and became the first Chicana to win countywide office in Bexar County. Compean was the RUP gubernatorial candidate in 1978. The RUP ran candidates for public office in 17 states and the District of Columbia between 1969 and 1980, electing some to boards of education, such as Frank Shafer Corona, in the Adams Morgan school district in Washington, DC. (Courtesy of Irma Mireles.)

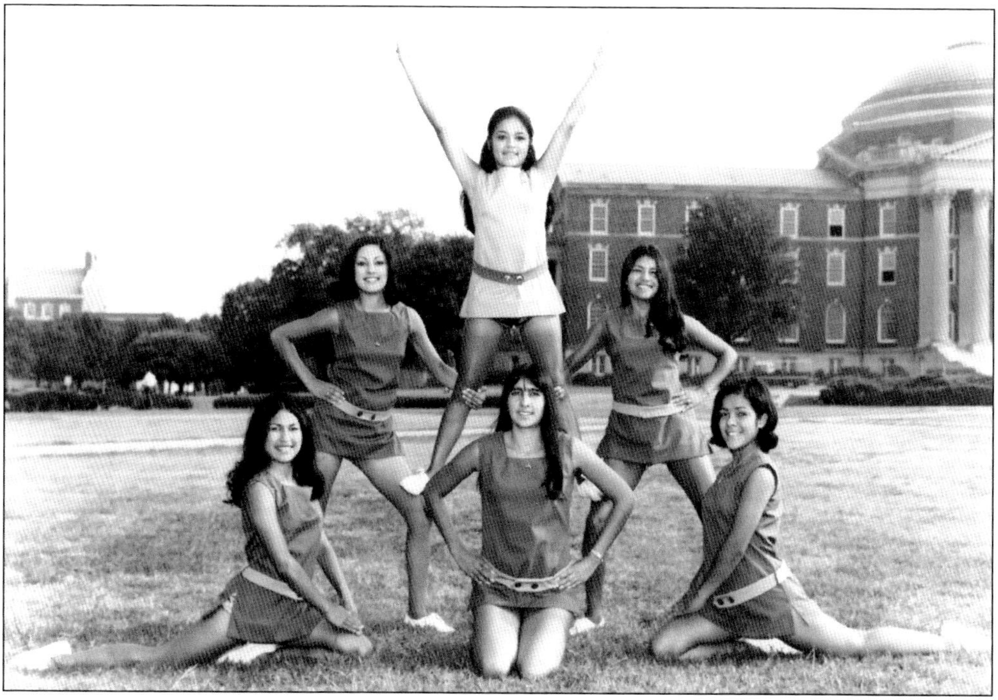

After the successful 1969 walkout and 1970 school board election, Crystal City Independent School District students were able to elect their cheerleaders. The all-Chicano squad seen here was elected. It included, from left to right, (first row) Mary Ochoa, Diana Serna, and Yolanda Torres; (second row) Gloria Ramírez, Diana Palacios, and Maggie Heredia. Each year before the 1969 walkout, only one Chicana was selected as a cheerleader and one as a twirler for the band. (Courtesy of Diana Serna Aguilera.)

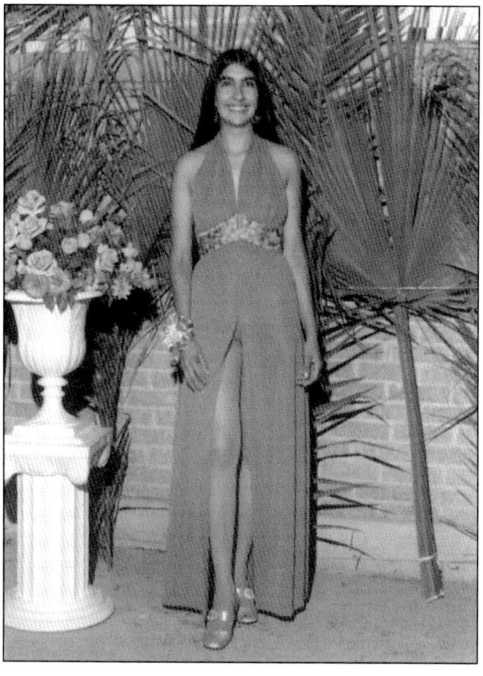

Dr. Leonard Valverde and Dr. Teresa Herrera Escobedo formed the Chicano Faculty Association at the University of Texas at Austin in 1974. The first order of business was to find others like them across the state and organize a statewide conference. The group included a steering committee of Oscar Valadez (Dallas), Jessie Rangel (Lubbock), Gloria Ann López and Lydia Linares (Laredo), Juan Gonzáles (Houston), Alice G. Chacón (San Antonio), and Diana Serna Cantú (pictured here on prom night) and Angie del Cueto Quiros, who were both UT undergraduate students. They held a statewide conference titled "Chicanos in Higher Education" on March 8, 1975. (Courtesy of Diana Serna Aguilera.)

Two

ORGANIZING TACHE

The Chicano movement, with its action agenda, assertive youthful leadership, and new vision for attracting new members, created in many followers and adherents a need for personal contribution. The few Chicanos in higher education at the national and state levels sought out each other and began organizing their groups as vanguard reformers. In California, as the Chicano Coordinating Committee on Higher Education, a steering committee led the initiative to formulate *El Plan de Santa Barbara*, named for the city where they met. The list of participants included many who are icons today, including Rodolfo Acuña, Ana Nieto Gómez, Carlos Muñoz, Rosalba Méndez, Monte Pérez, Luís Nogales, and Jesús Chavarría.

El Plan became the blueprint for many other efforts across the nation to institute Chicano studies programs and curriculums. At the national level, early pioneers included Tomás Rivera, Frank Angel, John Aragón, Simón González, Tomás Arciniéga, José Angel Cárdenas, Rupert Trujillo, Ignacio Córdova, Solomón Flores, Atilano Valencia, Usvaldo Palomares, Feliciano Rivera, and Steve Arvizu, who were the founders of the National Task Force de la Raza. The task force also funded organizing efforts at the state and local levels, such as helping Angel Noé González to address inequalities in the education of Chicano children in Crystal City.

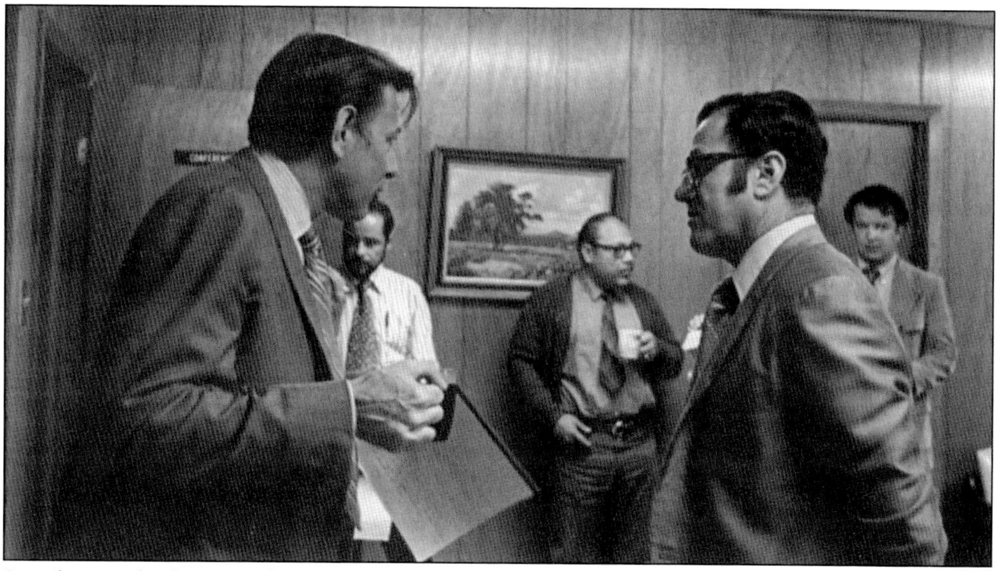

Seen here in the foreground in 1974 are Dr. Simón González (left), an associate professor of education at the University of California, Los Angeles, and Angel Noé González, the superintendent of the Crystal City Independent School District. Dr. Simón González was chosen by his peers to head up the National Task Force de la Raza. Funding for the work of the task force was obtained by the group under the Education Professions Development Act of 1967. The task force sought educational equality and expanded employment opportunities for Chicanos in higher education and in public schools. (Courtesy of Angel Noé González.)

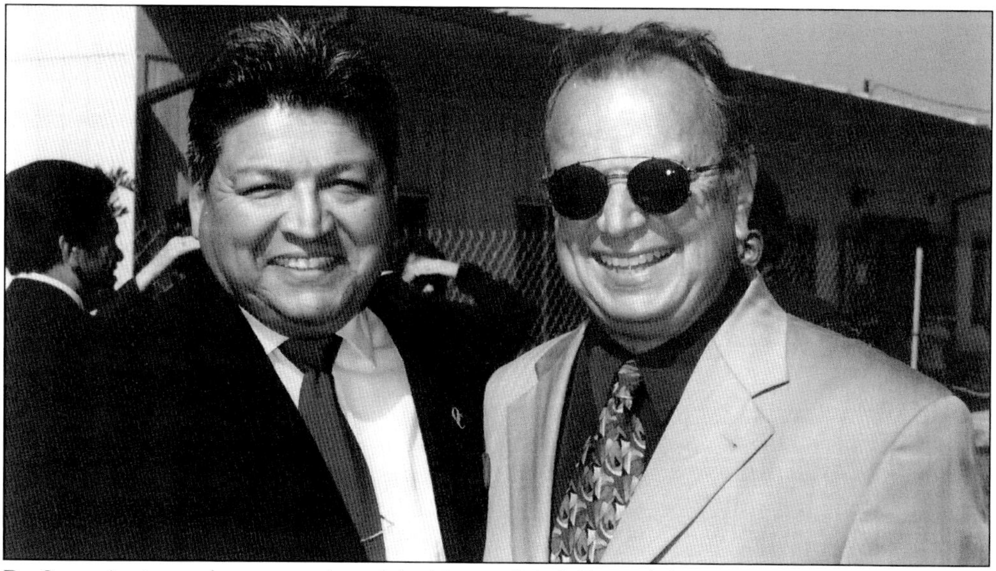

Dr. Steve Arvizu, a charter member of the National Task Force de la Raza and its regional director for western states, recalls, "Ours was a lively and courageous group willing to bite the hand that fed us in order to make everyone more responsive . . . I was one of the younger and more aggressive in patrolling the boundaries and pressuring federal bureaucrats and school administrators." Dr. Arvizu (left) retired in 2001 as president of Oxnard College in California. Pete Tafoya, the chair of the board of trustees of Ventura County Community College, is on the right. (Courtesy of Dr. Steve Arvizu.)

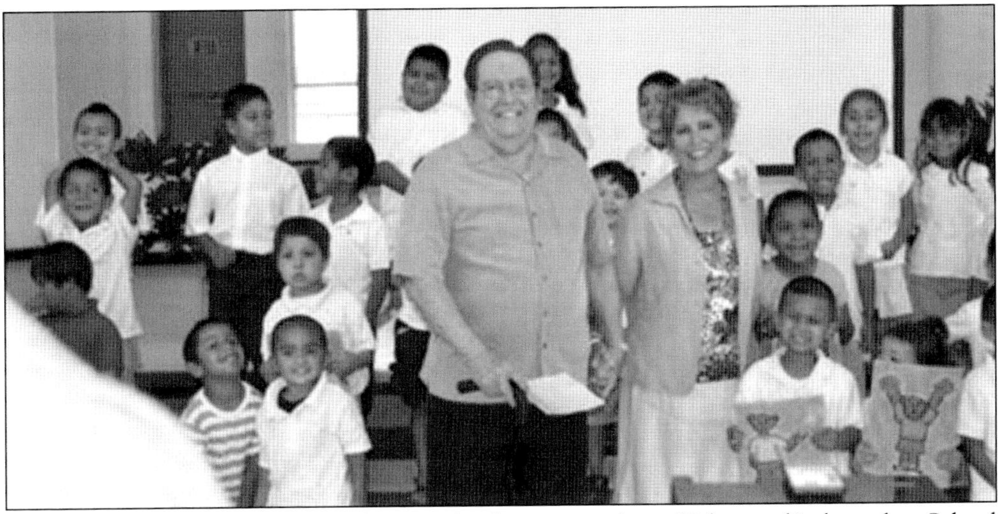

Dr. José Angel Cárdenas, the first Chicano school superintendent of Edgewood Independent School District in San Antonio, also served as the regional director for the National Task Force de la Raza. Dr. Cárdenas reached out to groups such as the Chicano Faculty Association in Austin, the Texas Association for Bilingual Education (TABE), the Mexican American School Board Members Association, and the Texas Association of Mexican American Educators (TAMAE) to attend a statewide conference titled "The Education of Mexican Americans" in Austin on February 8–9, 1975. Funding from the National Task Force de la Raza made these organizing conferences possible. (Courtesy of the International Development Research Association of San Antonio.)

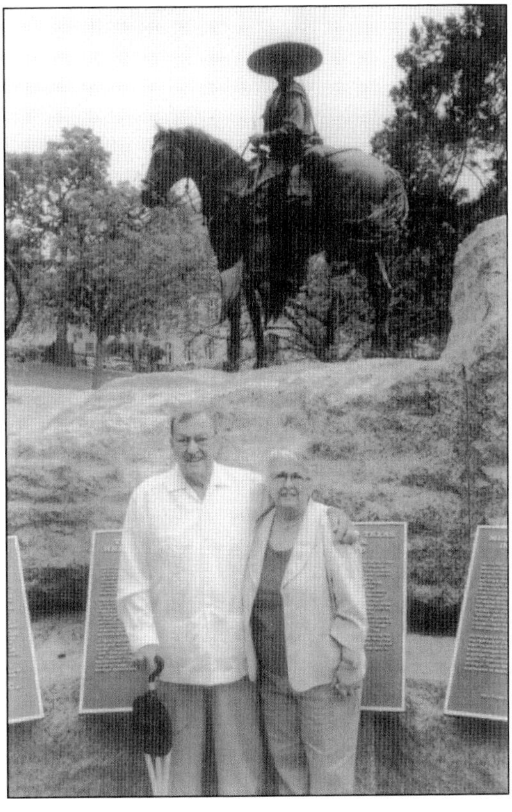

Angel Noé González and Diola González became the first Chicano school superintendent and supervisor/teacher of bilingual education, respectively, in the Crystal City Independent School District, after the 1969 school walkout. They are seen here visiting the Tejano Monument on the capitol grounds in Austin in 2012. It took a decade of legislative efforts on the part of several Chicano state representatives, beginning with Ismael "Kino" Flores in 2001, as well as state senators Mario Gallegos and Juan "Chuy" Hinojosa, to authorize and fully fund the monument. (Courtesy of Angel Noé González.)

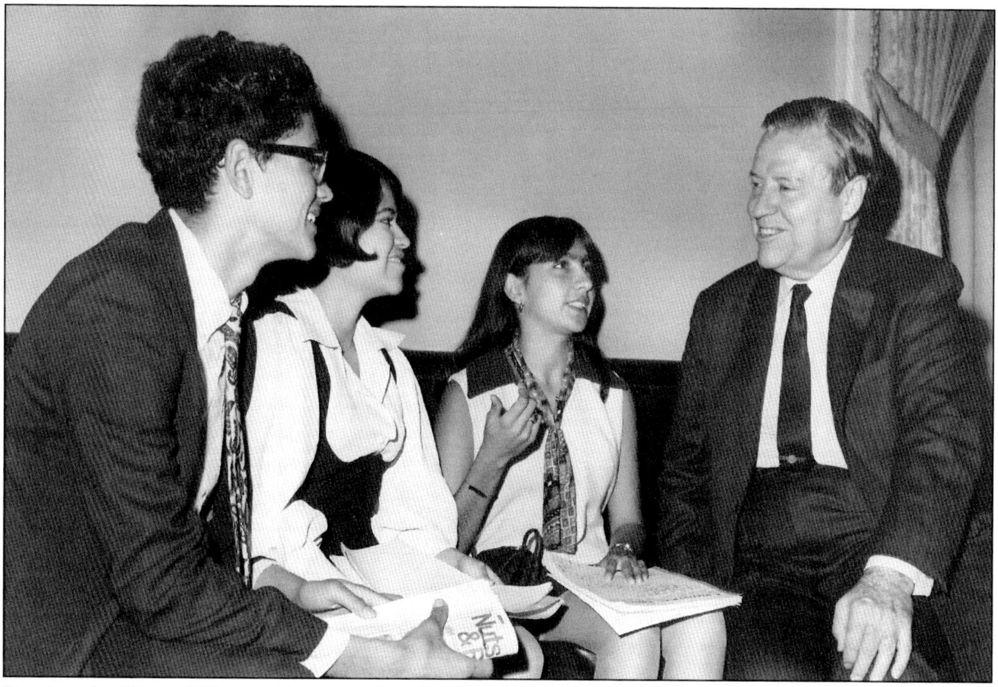

During the Crystal City walkout, student leaders (from left to right) Mario Treviño, Severita Lara, and Diana Serna, met with Sen. Ralph Yarborough (D–Texas) to discuss their walkout petition demands. The students also met with future president George H.W. Bush, a Texas congressman at the time, and officials at the department of justice and the department of health, education, and welfare to demand an investigation into the unequal practices of their school district. (Courtesy of Diana Serna Aguilera.)

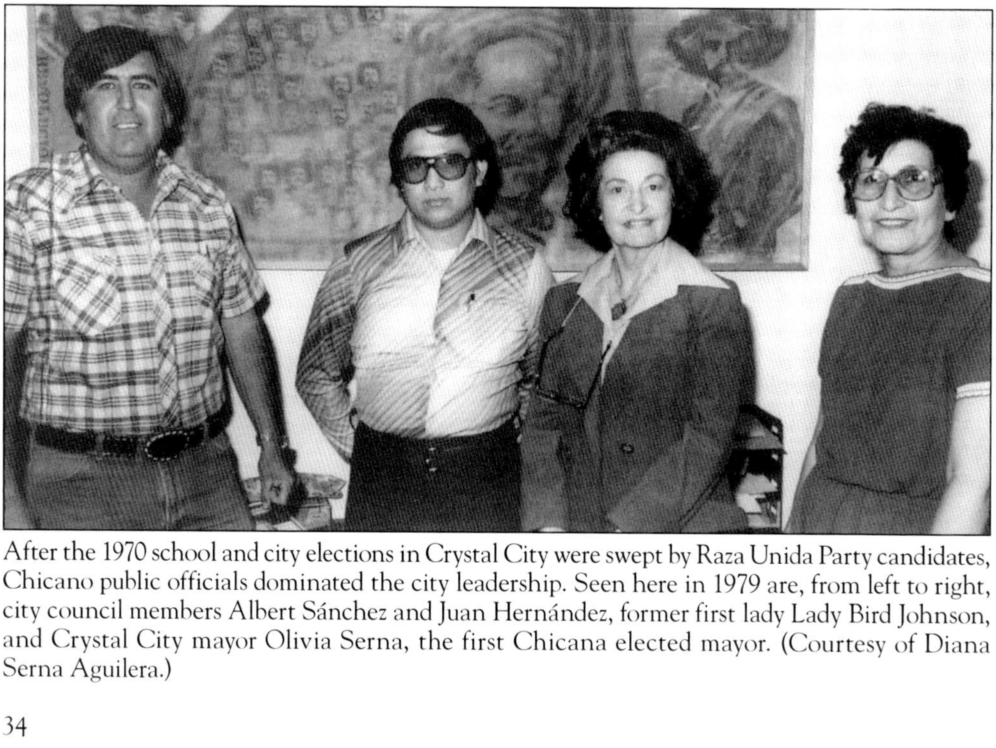

After the 1970 school and city elections in Crystal City were swept by Raza Unida Party candidates, Chicano public officials dominated the city leadership. Seen here in 1979 are, from left to right, city council members Albert Sánchez and Juan Hernández, former first lady Lady Bird Johnson, and Crystal City mayor Olivia Serna, the first Chicana elected mayor. (Courtesy of Diana Serna Aguilera.)

In the first progress letter, seen here, Dr. Leonard Valverde reported on meetings and new steering committee members. A draft of the constitution and bylaws were reviewed and the place and date for the founding convention were set. Another steering committee meeting was called for May 17. In the second progress letter, in June 1975, two keynote speakers were listed: Dr. Tomás Arciniéga and Dr. Alfredo de los Santos. The survey for the organization's name received 64 responses, with 29 people choosing Mexican American Coalition for Higher Education, 20 choosing Chicano Higher Education Association, and the remaining votes split between other names. (Both, courtesy of Jesse Rangel.)

PROGRESS LETTER

No. 1 May 1975

This progress letter is a means of informing you of a statewide planning effort by existing organizations and representatives from various campuses to unite Mexican Americans in higher education into a state organization. The general purpose of the organization will be to provide a forum for the discussion of issues related to Chicanos in higher education and to cooperate in providing workable solutions to these concerns.

The UT Chicano Faculty Association at Austin obtained funds from the National Education Task Force de La Raza to hold a statewide convention to formalize the organization of Mexican American faculty, professional staff, and students. UT CFA was one of the four joint sponsors of the "Education of the Mexican American" conference held in Austin, February 8-9, 1975. At the session set aside for higher education, approximately forty persons met for the first time to discuss the feasibility of a state organization for Chicanos in higher education. A steering committee was formed at this meeting and assigned the responsibility to (1) plan and implement a state convention, (2) prepare a tentative constitution and bylaws, and (3) compile a limited list of tentative names for the organization. Items 2 and 3 are to be voted upon by the attending participants at the planned organizational convention.

The steering committee met on March 8, 1975 on the University of Texas, Austin campus to begin preliminary planning. Compilation of a master mailing list was started by dividing all the state institutions of higher education (both two and four year) among the members. The committee considered a list of suggested names for the organization and agreed to present the following three at the planned convention with participants having the option of adding other names for consideration: Raza Council on Higher Education (RACHE), Mexican American Coalition for Higher Education (MACHE), and Chicano Higher Education Association (CHEA). A criterion for identifying major speakers at the convention

MEXICAN AMERICANS
IN HIGHER EDUCATION

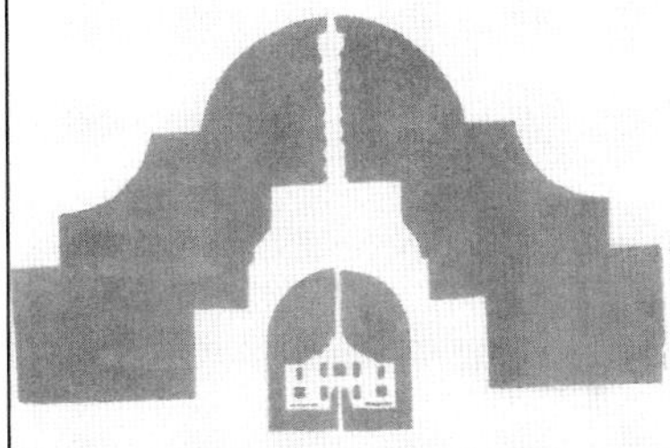

A Mission for
Mexican American Educators
in Higher Education
in Texas

El Tropicano Motor Hotel
San Antonio, Texas
August 8 - 9, 1975

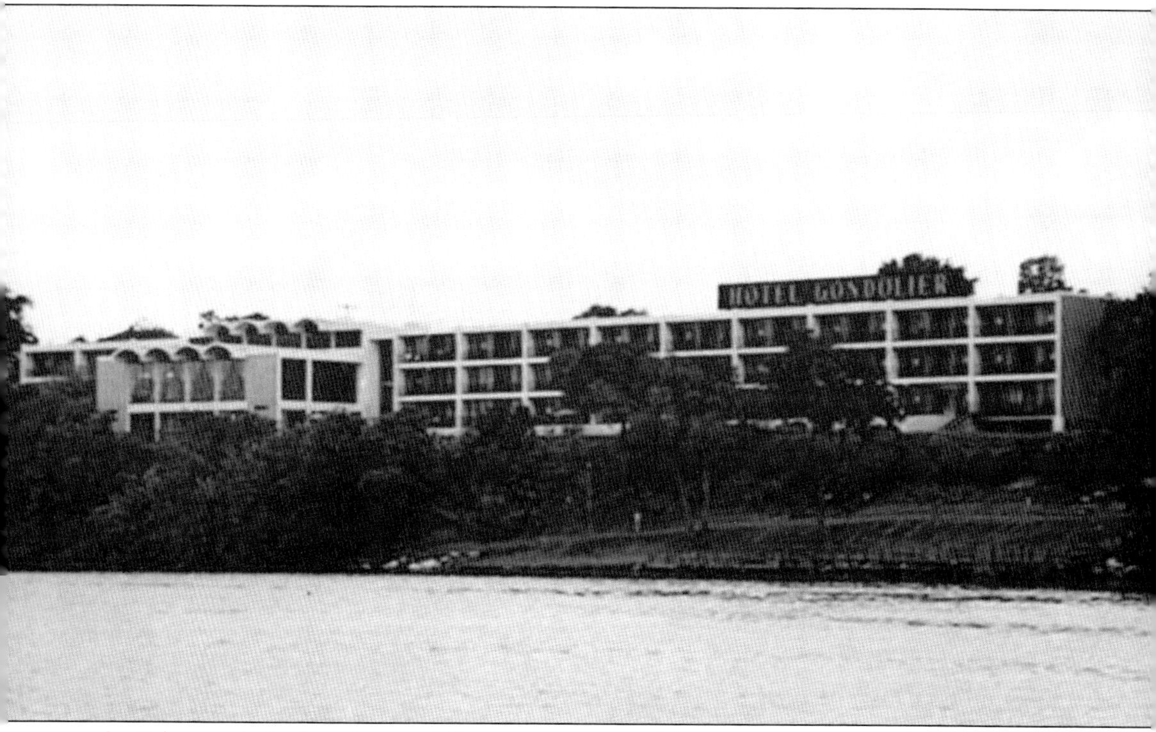

On February 8, 1975, Dr. Leonard Valverde approached Dr. José Angel Cárdenas with a proposal written by Dr. Teresa H. Escobedo, Dr. Efraím P. Armendáriz, and himself for funding a conference in Austin at the Hotel Gondolier. The mail-out inviting all Chicano faculty and staff listed Gustavo García as the master of ceremonies and Ed Baca, the regional commissioner for the office of education in the department of health, education, and welfare, and Dr. Marlin Brockette, the commissioner of education of the Texas Education Agency, as speakers. College faculty, students, and staff met in the Canaletto Room East. Several Chicano community college presidents were in attendance, including Dr. Domingo Arechiga of Laredo; Dr. Alfredo de los Santos of El Paso; and Dr. Leonard Maestas and André Guerrero of Austin, the codirectors of the Juárez-Lincoln Center, a Chicano effort to build a college. (Courtesy of Jesse Rangel.)

Name	Title	College or University
Rodolfo Arevalo (Dr.)	Assistant Dean of Students	UT
L.R. Ables	Director	Bee County College
Efraim P. Armendariz (Dr.)	Professor	UT
Rebecca M. Banera (sic)		San Antonio College
George M. Blanco (Dr.)	Professor	UT
Alice G. Chacon		San Antonio College
Evey Chapa	Instructor	UT
Herman Curiel	Graduate Student	University of Houston
Ruth del Cueto	Instructor	San Antonio College
Angie del Cueto Quiros		UT
Leonardo de la Garza	Dean	Austin Community College
Ramon H. Dovalina	Registrar	Austin Community College
Teresa H. Escobedo (Dr.)	Professor	UT
Augustine Garza	Administrative Officer	UT
Raquel Gavia		Austin Community College
Alberto Garza		Grand Valley State College
Juan Gonzalez (Dr.)		University of Houston
Armando Gutiérrez		UT
Belinda Herrera	Graduate Students (sic)	UT
Lydia Linares		Laredo Community College
Ernesto Luna	Administrative Officer	Houston Community College
John Martinez	Graduate Student	UT
Cervaner (sic) Martinez (Dr.)	Professor	UT San Antonio
Raul Murguia	Professor	San Antonio College
Ernest O'Neill (Dr.)	Professor	UT
Roberto C. Perez	Administrative Officer	UT
Roy Rodriguez	Graduate Student	UT
Imelda Ramos	Research Assistant	UT
Jesus J. Rubio, Jr.	Research Assistant	UT
Robert Reyes (Dr.)		San Antonio College District
Santos Reyes, Jr.	Professor	UT
Roque Segura	Faculty	El Paso Community College
John Soto (Dr.)	Professor	UT
Isabel Treviño	Librarian	San Antonio College
Eudelia Talamantez	Graduate Student	UT
Maria Alicia Travelle		Texas Woman's University
Jude Valdez	Graduate Student	UT
Oscar R. Valadez	Assistant to Vice Chairman	Dallas Community College
Leonard A. Valverde (Dr.)	Assistant Professor	UT

This is a list of the faculty and staff members of colleges and universities who attended the first meeting, on February 8, 1975. (Courtesy of Jesse Rangel.)

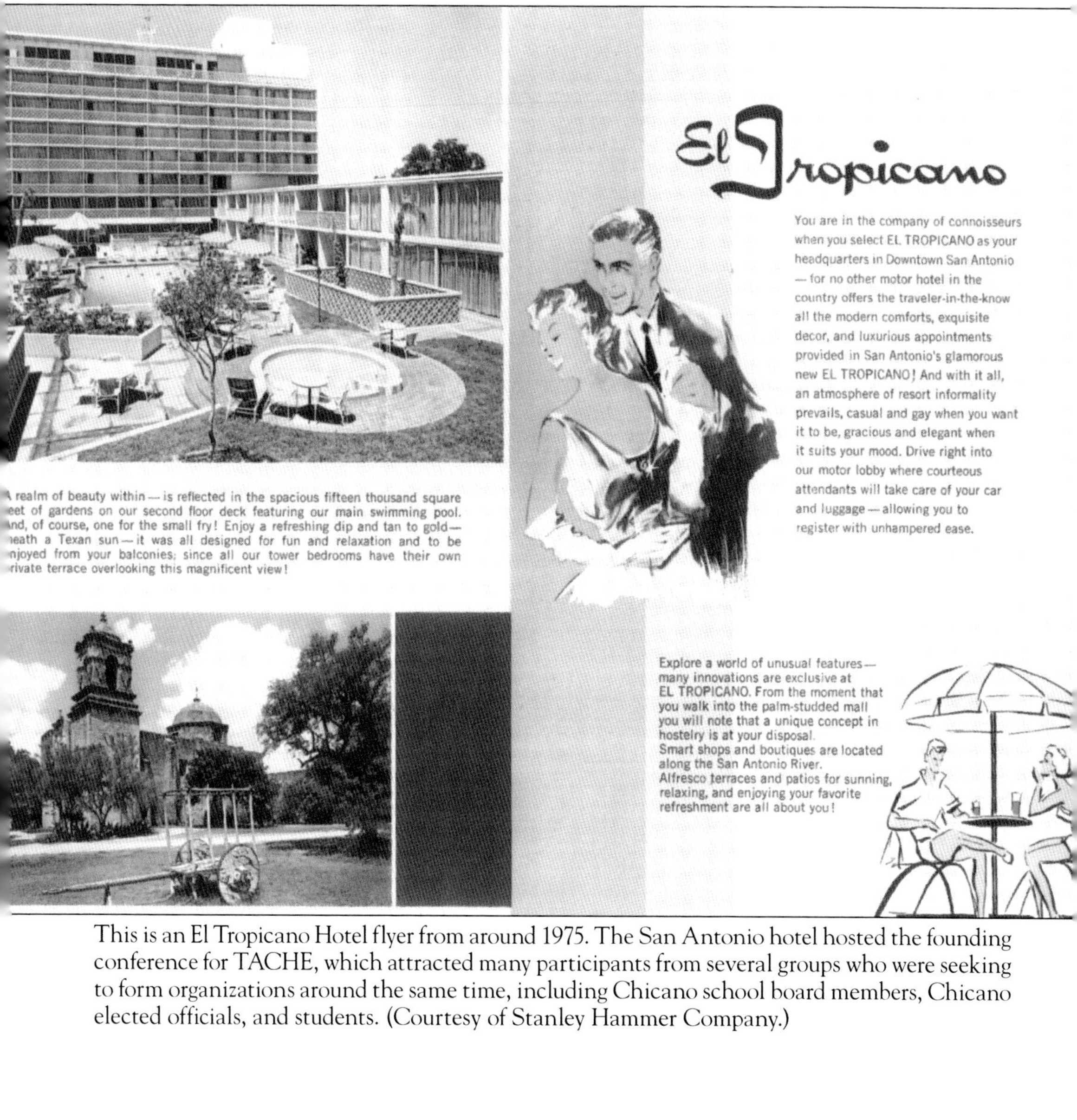

This is an El Tropicano Hotel flyer from around 1975. The San Antonio hotel hosted the founding conference for TACHE, which attracted many participants from several groups who were seeking to form organizations around the same time, including Chicano school board members, Chicano elected officials, and students. (Courtesy of Stanley Hammer Company.)

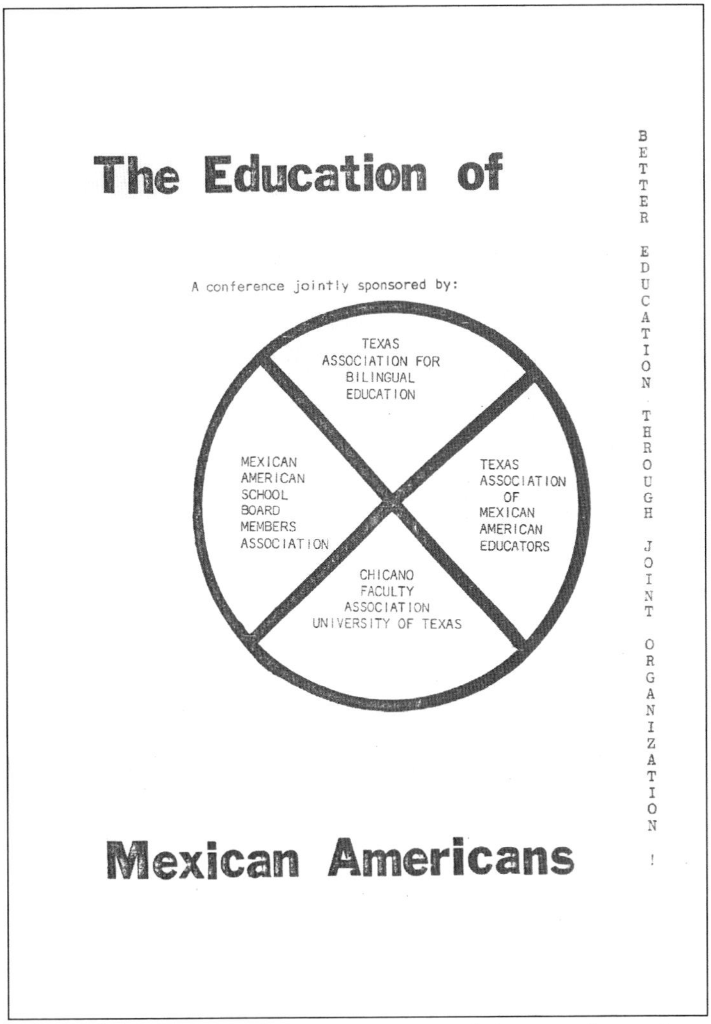

The UT Chicano Faculty Association began organizing and planning the conference, which also included Ernesto Ramírez Jr. and Santos Reyes Jr., the acting director of the Mexican American Studies Center, both of whom were at UT. The conference was held at the El Tropicano Hotel in San Antonio on August 8–9, 1975. The keynote speakers were Dr. Tomás Arciniéga, the dean of the school of education at California State University, Fresno; Dr. Henry Casso, an associate professor at the University of New Mexico; and Dr. Alfredo de los Santos, the president of El Paso Community College. Facilitators and panelists included Jesse Rangel, Daniel Meza, Dr. Leonard de la Garza, Dr. Tomás Rivera, Dr. Robert Reyes, Elsie Sánchez, Salvador Gómez, and state representative Gonzalo Barrientos. Steering committee members Diana Serna Cantú, Vicky Gómez, Lydia Linares, and Margaret Garza recorded the work sessions and published the proceedings. On August 9, 1975, the 160 people present voted to adopt the first TACHE constitution and elect statewide officers and six regional representatives. Roberto Reyes was elected the temporary president until formal elections were held, at which time Dr. Leonard Valverde was elected. Gloria Ann López was elected secretary, Dr. Teresa Herrera Escobedo as publication editor, and Adolph López III as treasurer. The six regional representatives were Dr. José Juárez (south Texas), Jessie Rangel (the Panhandle), Oscar Valadez (northeast), Margaret Garza (central), Fidel De León (far west), and Enrique Medrano (Gulf area). The organization also voted to adopt the name Texas Association of Chicanos in Higher Education. (Courtesy of Natalia Verjat Gutiérrez.)

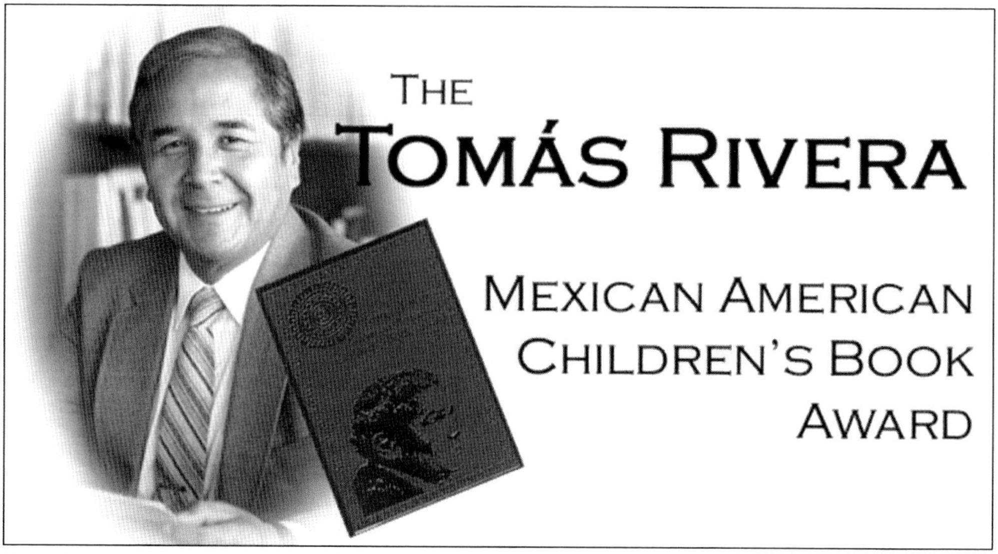

Seen here is the logo of the children's book award named in honor of Dr. Tomás Rivera, a native of Crystal City. Dr. Rivera became the first Chicano associate dean at the newly formed University of Texas at San Antonio and attended the founding TACHE conference. He and Dr. Leonard de la Garza chaired the work session on curriculum at the conference. Dr. de la Garza later became chancellor of the Tarrant County Community College District in 1997, a position he held until 2009. Dr. Rivera became known for his writings and was chancellor of the University of California, Riverside, until his untimely death on May 16, 1984. (Courtesy of Jaime Chahín.)

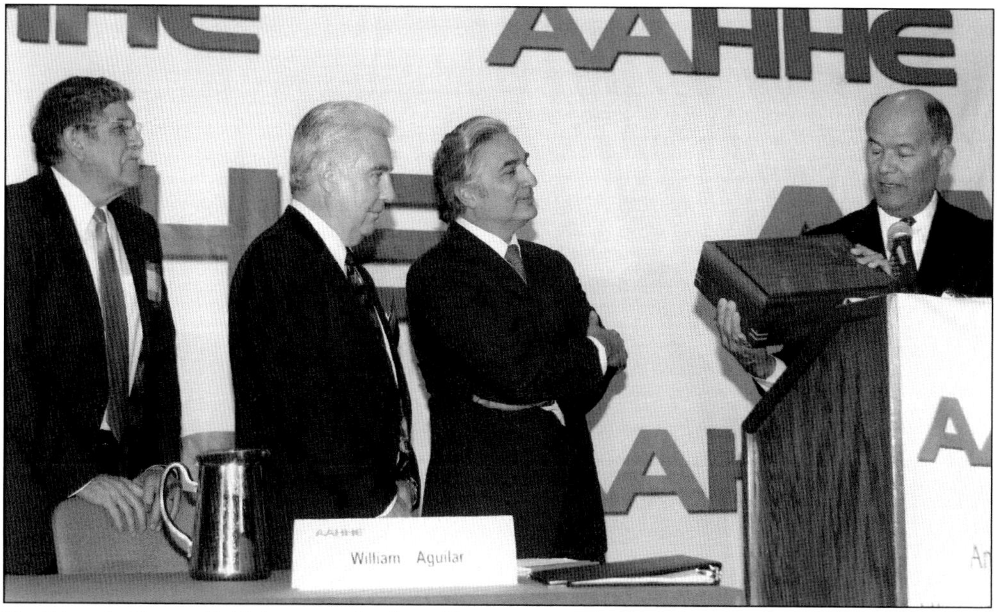

Dr. Ricardo Romo (left) became the first Chicano president of the University of Texas at San Antonio in 1999. The downtown campus, which was more accessible to inner-city Chicano students, opened in 1997 and is located at 501 César E. Chávez Boulevard. With him are Dr. William Aguilar (second from left), the chairman of the board of the American Association of Hispanics in Higher Education, and Dr. Francisco Cigarroa (third from left), the University of Texas chancellor. The speaker on the far right is Dr. Louie Olivos. (Courtesy of Rudy Ornelas.)

Proceedings of the conference were compiled and edited by Dr. Leonard Valverde and Dr. Teresa Herrera Escobedo and printed with funding from the National Task Force de la Raza's regional office in San Antonio. On the last pages of the publication are 155 names of participants at the founding of TACHE, including, among others, Carmen M. Tafolla, the director of Mexican American studies at Texas Lutheran College in Seguín; Fernando Oaxaca, with the White House's office of the president, management and operations, in Washington, DC; Manuel F. Medrano, an instructor at Texas Southmost College in Brownsville; Margaret Garza, the director of student financial aid at St. Mary's University in San Antonio; Neftali G. García, a professor at St. Mary's; Roberto Galván, a professor at Southwest Texas State University in San Marcos; Arnoldo de León, an assistant professor at Angelo State University in San Angelo; Leonel J. Castillo, the city comptroller for Houston; Manuel D. Berriozabal, a professor at the University of New Orleans; Joe J. Bernal, a researcher at the International Development Research Association (IDRA) of San Antonio; Rebecca M. Barrera, an education specialist at IDRA; and Oscar R. Valadez, the assistant to the vice chancellor of academic affairs at Dallas Community College. (Both courtesy of Jesse Rangel.)

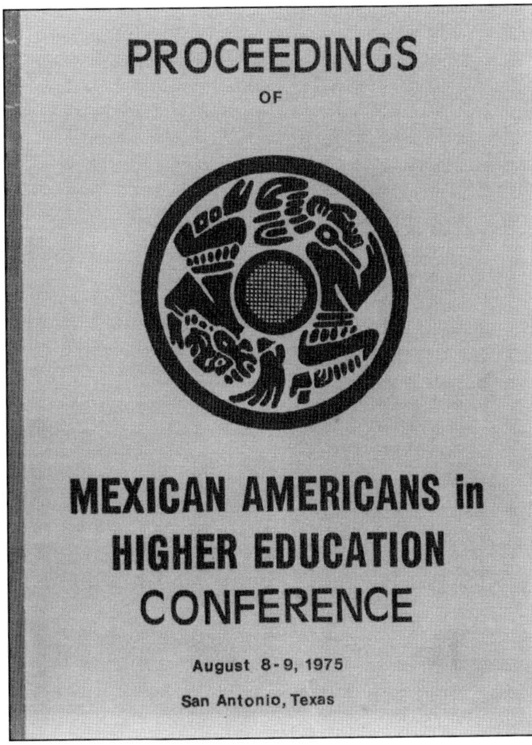

PROCEEDINGS

OF

MEXICAN AMERICANS in HIGHER EDUCATION CONFERENCE

August 8-9, 1975

San Antonio, Texas

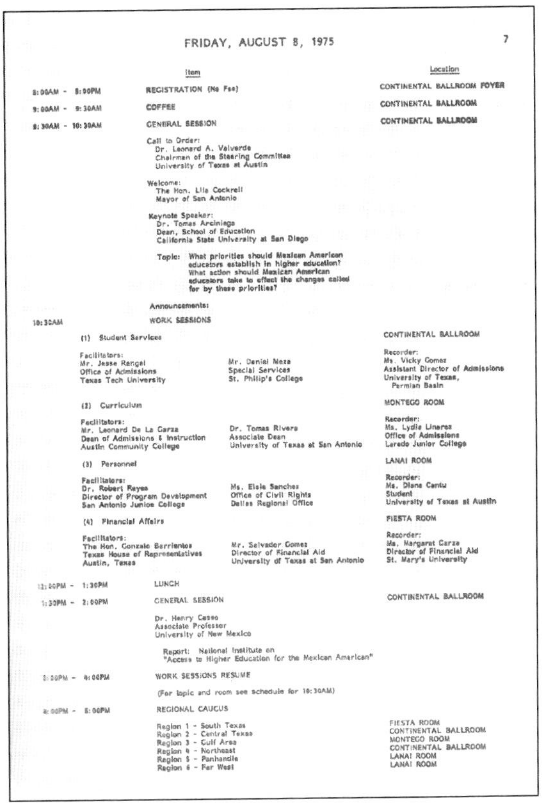

FRIDAY, AUGUST 8, 1975 — 7

	Item		Location
8:00AM - 5:00PM	REGISTRATION (No Fee)		CONTINENTAL BALLROOM FOYER
9:00AM - 9:30AM	COFFEE		CONTINENTAL BALLROOM
9:30AM - 10:30AM	GENERAL SESSION Call to Order: Dr. Leonard A. Valverde Chairman of the Steering Committee University of Texas at Austin Welcome: The Hon. Lila Cockrell Mayor of San Antonio Keynote Speaker: Dr. Tomas Arciniega Dean, School of Education California State University at San Diego Topic: What priorities should Mexican American educators establish in higher education? What action should Mexican American educators take to effect the changes called for by these priorities? Announcements:		CONTINENTAL BALLROOM
10:30AM	WORK SESSIONS		
	(1) Student Services Facilitators: Mr. Jesse Rangel Office of Admissions Texas Tech University	Mr. Daniel Meza Special Services St. Philip's College	CONTINENTAL BALLROOM Recorder: Ms. Vicky Gomez Assistant Director of Admissions University of Texas, Permian Basin
	(2) Curriculum Facilitators: Mr. Leonard De La Garza Dean of Admissions & Instruction Austin Community College	Dr. Tomas Rivera Associate Dean University of Texas at San Antonio	MONTEGO ROOM Recorder: Ms. Lydia Linarez Office of Admissions Laredo Junior College
	(3) Personnel Facilitators: Dr. Robert Reyes Director of Program Development San Antonio Junioe College	Ms. Elsie Sanchez Office of Civil Rights Dallas Regional Office	LANAI ROOM Recorder: Ms. Diana Cantu Student University of Texas at Austin
	(4) Financial Affairs Facilitators: The Hon. Gonzalo Barrientos Texas House of Representatives Austin, Texas	Mr. Salvador Gomez Director of Financial Aid University of Texas at San Antonio	FIESTA ROOM Recorder: Ms. Margaret Garza Director of Financial Aid St. Mary's University
12:00PM - 1:30PM	LUNCH		
1:30PM - 2:00PM	GENERAL SESSION Dr. Henry Casso Associate Professor University of New Mexico Report: National Institute on "Access to Higher Education for the Mexican American"		CONTINENTAL BALLROOM
2:00PM - 4:00PM	WORK SESSIONS RESUME (For topic and room see schedule for 10:30AM)		
4:00PM - 5:00PM	REGIONAL CAUCUS Region 1 - South Texas Region 2 - Central Texas Region 3 - Gulf Area Region 4 - Northeast Region 5 - Panhandle Region 6 - Far West		 FIESTA ROOM CONTINENTAL BALLROOM MONTEGO ROOM CONTINENTAL BALLROOM LANAI ROOM LANAI ROOM

The UT Chicano Faculty Association first used the image in 1974, and it then became the logo of TACHE. Dr. Leonard Valverde, the founder of TACHE, remembers that Chicano faculty and students wanted to identify with their indigenous roots, that they loved their hybrid identity as *mestizos*. The year 1974 is slightly misleading because the organization was not officially voted into existence until August 1975. (Courtesy of Javier Olguín.)

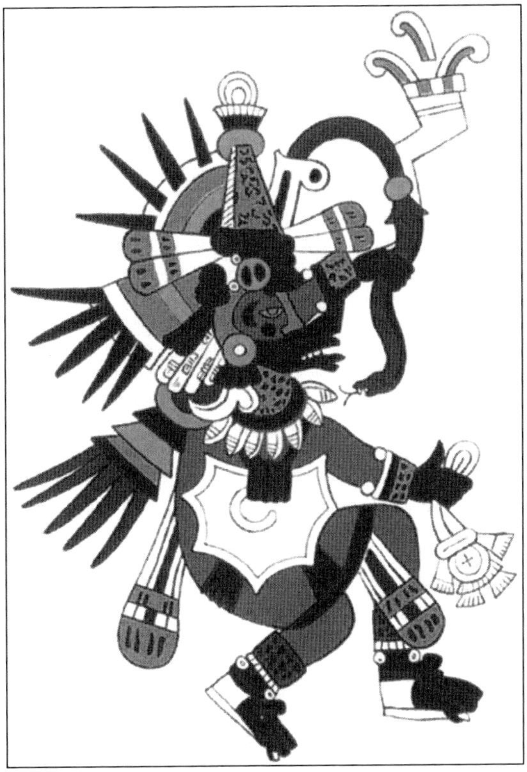

Dr. Jude Valdez believes that the images in the logo represent the gods Quetzalcoatl (right) and Tezcatlipoca (below), the deities for knowledge and education of the *Meshica* tribe of Aztecs in central Mexico. Rafael Jesús González, a noted Mexican anthropologist, claims that the two images most resemble the twin Mayan gods Hanahpu and Xbalanque, the sun and moon, respectively. TACHE members initiated a contest for an official logo in 1975. A total of 16 sketches were submitted, and three were awarded prizes. None were selected, however, as TACHE leaders instead chose the original UT Chicano Faculty Association logo. (Both courtesy of the TACHE Archive, University of Texas at Austin, Benson Library.)

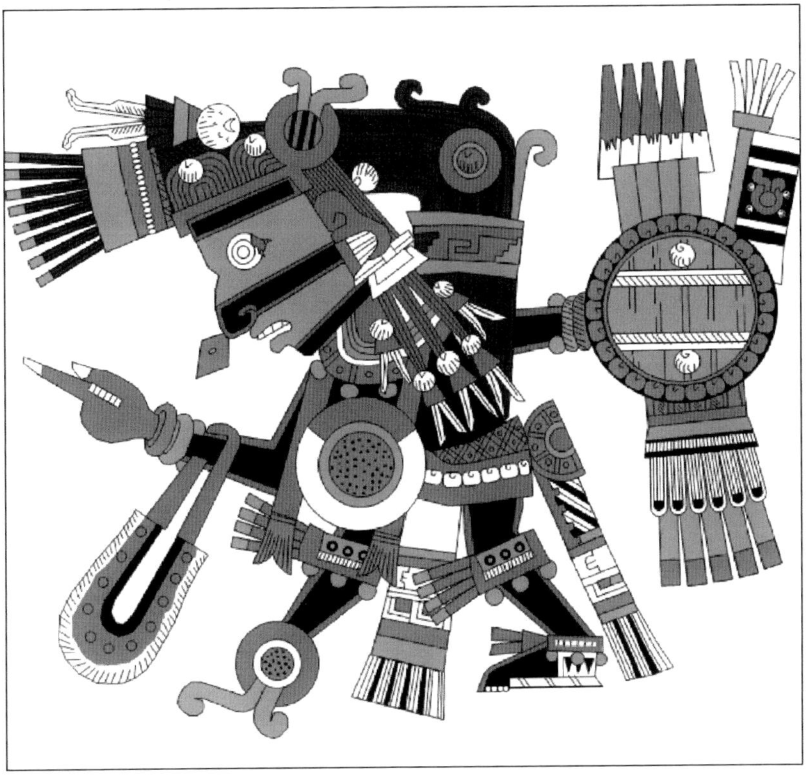

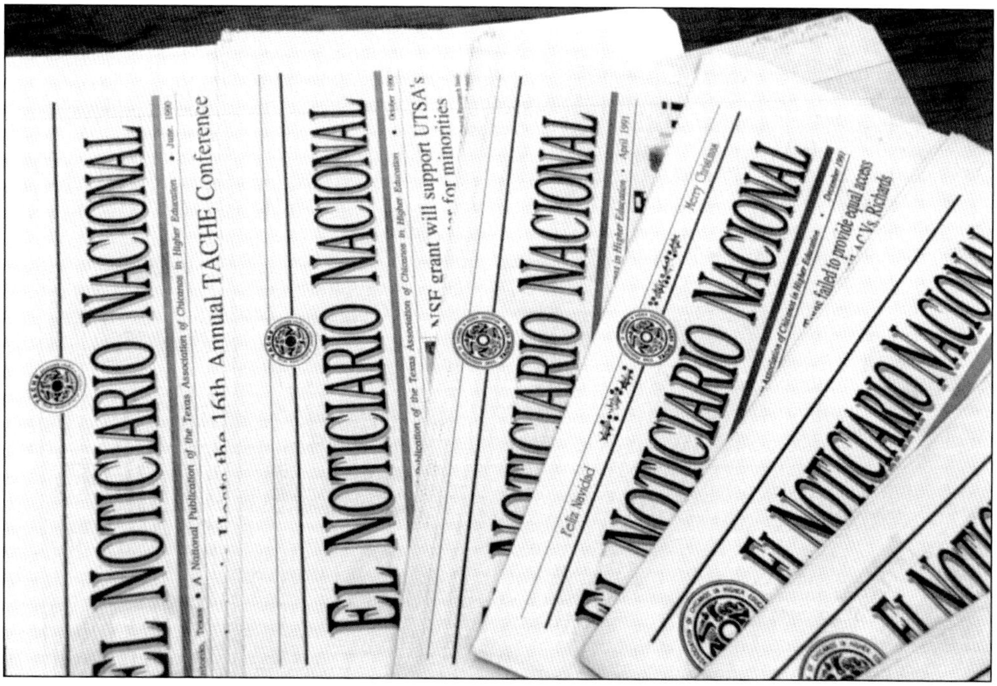

In November 1975, after the convention, Dr. Teresa Herrera Escobedo sent out the first TACHE newsletter, which became the *Noticiario*. Over the decades, the newsletter adopted several names, including *El Noticiario de TACHE* and, in the 1990s, *El Noticiario Nacional*. Finally, in the 2000s, under the direction of Javier Olguín, the TACHE vice president of communications, the name was changed to just *Noticiario*. It is now available in an electronic format. (Courtesy of the TACHE Archive, University of Texas at Austin, Benson Library; photograph by Natalia Verjat Gutiérrez.)

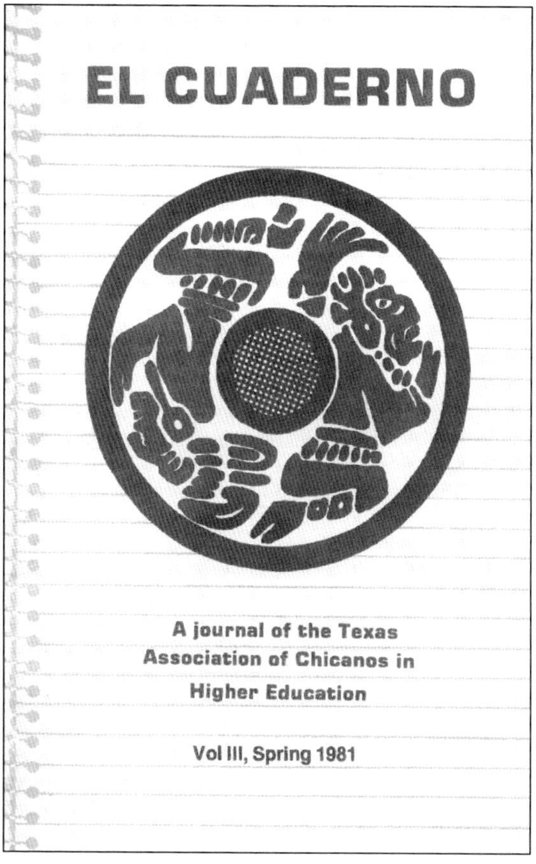

At the founding convention, keynote speakers Dr. Alfredo De los Santos and Dr. Tomás Arciniéga made several recommendations, including the development of a national journal to address Chicano concerns. (Courtesy of TACHE Archive, University of Texas at Austin, Benson Library; photograph by Natalia Verjat Gutiérrez.)

Dr. Tomás Arciniéga addressed the founding members of TACHE on "What Priorities Should Mexican American Educators Establish in Higher Education?" and "What Action Should Chicano Educators Take to Affect the Changes Needed?" Dr. Arciniéga became the dean of the school of education at California State University, Fresno, and then the president of California State University, Bakersfield. Today, he continues his activism and advocacy with the Hispanic Association of Colleges and Universities (HACU). (Courtesy of Tomás Arciniéga.)

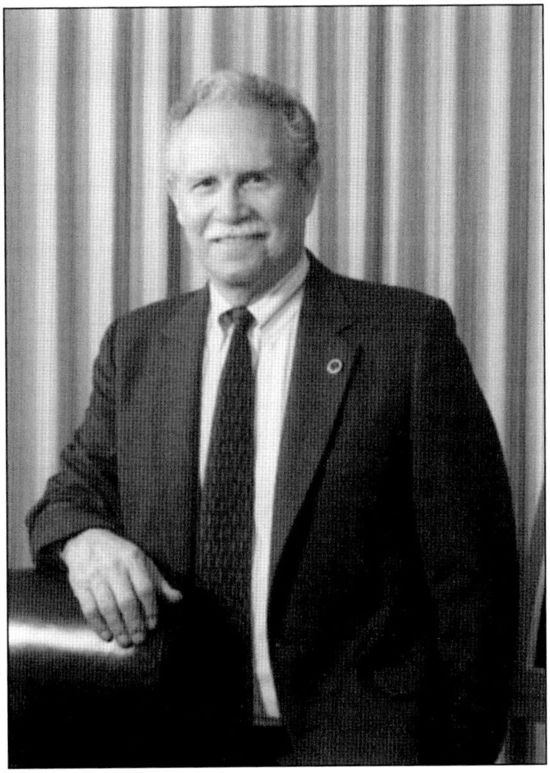

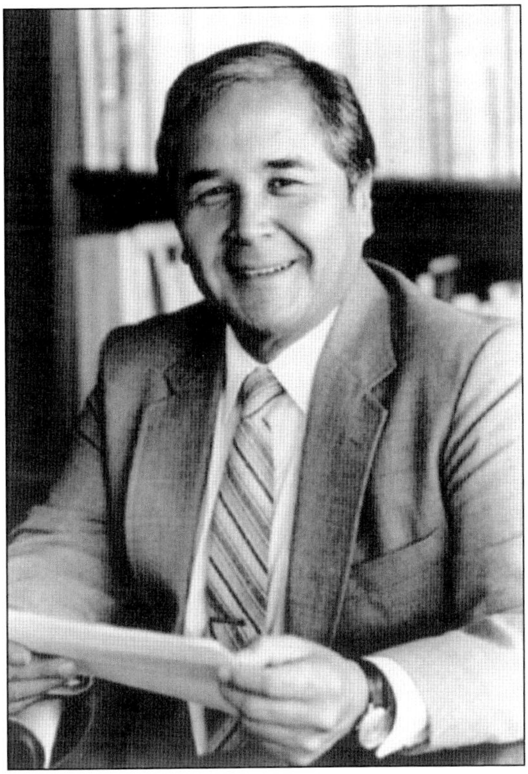

Dr. Tómas Rivera, a Spanish teacher, became one of the first Chicano faculty members at the new University of Texas at San Antonio campus. He rose through the ranks of academia to become chancellor of the University of California, Riverside, before his untimely death. He is best known for his award-winning storybook *. . . y no se lo tragó la tierra*, which translates into English as *. . . and the Earth Did Not Part*. (Courtesy of Dr. Leonard Valverde.)

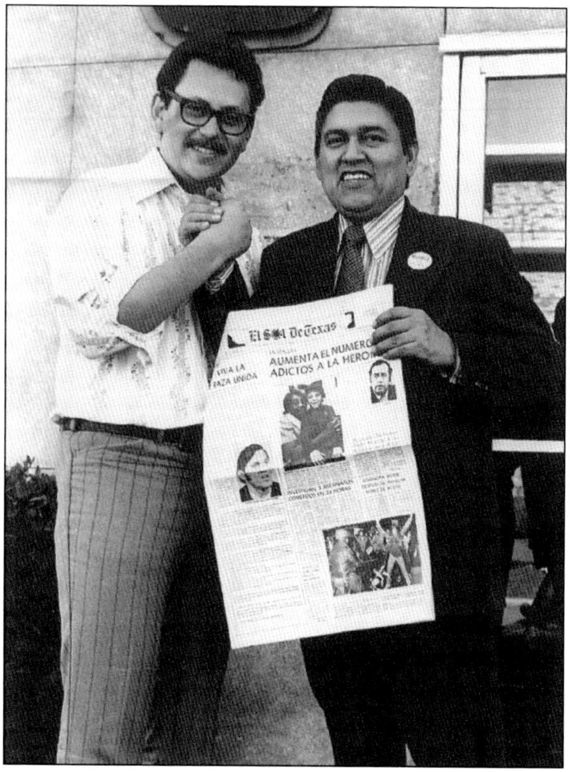

Jesús Gutiérrez and Sara Suárez began the first Spanish-language newspaper in northern Texas, *El Sol de Texas*, in 1966, selling copies at church gatherings for 10¢. The newspaper was eventually sold, and competitors emerged to reach the growing Spanish-speaking population of the Dallas-Fort Worth area, including *El Extra* and *El Hispano News* in 1986, the *Heraldo News* in 1992, and more. Jesús Gutiérrez (right) is seen here with José Angel Gutiérrez holding up the newspaper showing the 1974 gubernatorial candidate of the Raza Unida Party, Ramsey Muñiz. (Courtesy of Jesús Gutiérrez.)

Dr. Rudy Rodríguez, a longtime activist in the trenches for bilingual education, produced the documentary *The Texas Bilingual Story*. He was the TACHE president in 2001 and is a member of the Denton Independent School District's board of trustees. (Courtesy of Rudy Rodríguez.)

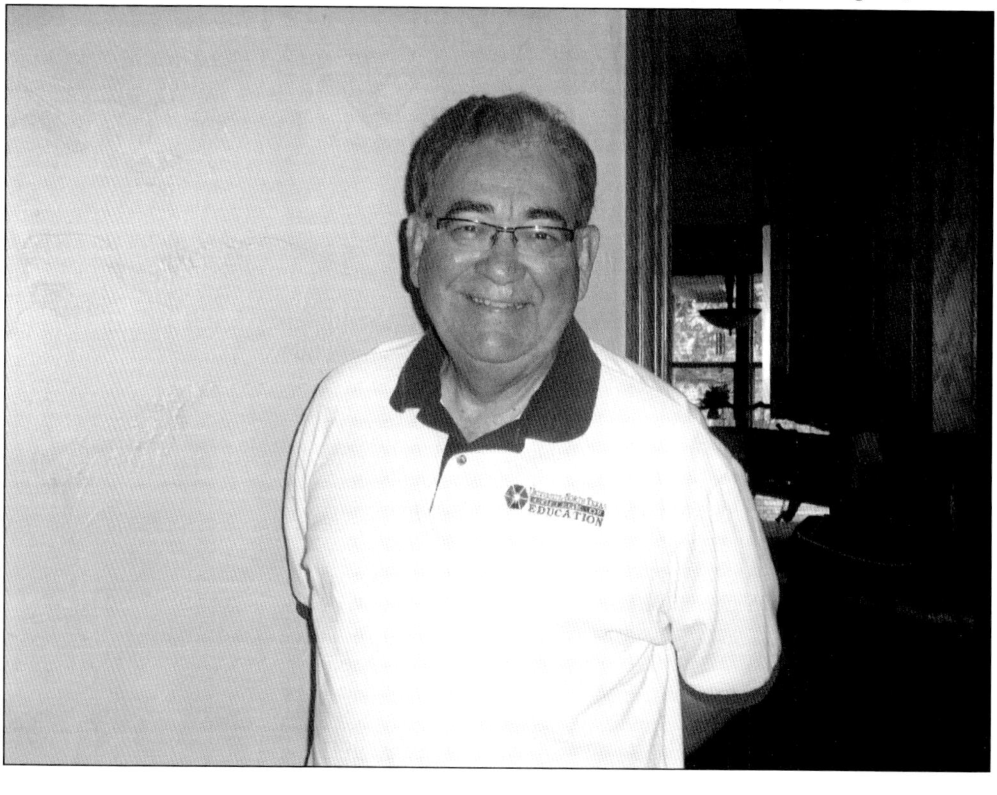

Three

Annual Conferences

In the 1970s and into the 1980s, Texas was among many states with a history of segregation in public schools, including in higher education, that sought full compliance with Title VI of the 1964 Civil Rights Act and an end to "dual systems of higher education." Unfortunately, the five "Texas Plans" that have been developed through the years have failed to find a final solution to "dual systems of higher education," including the fifth and current plan, called the Recruitment and Retention Strategy.

TACHE members find it surprising and unfortunate that with the talent and resources that exist in Texas, a solution cannot be found. Each TACHE annual conference is themed to fit the issue or goal for the year; typically, the themes focus on aspects of the Texas Plan that have yet to be realized.

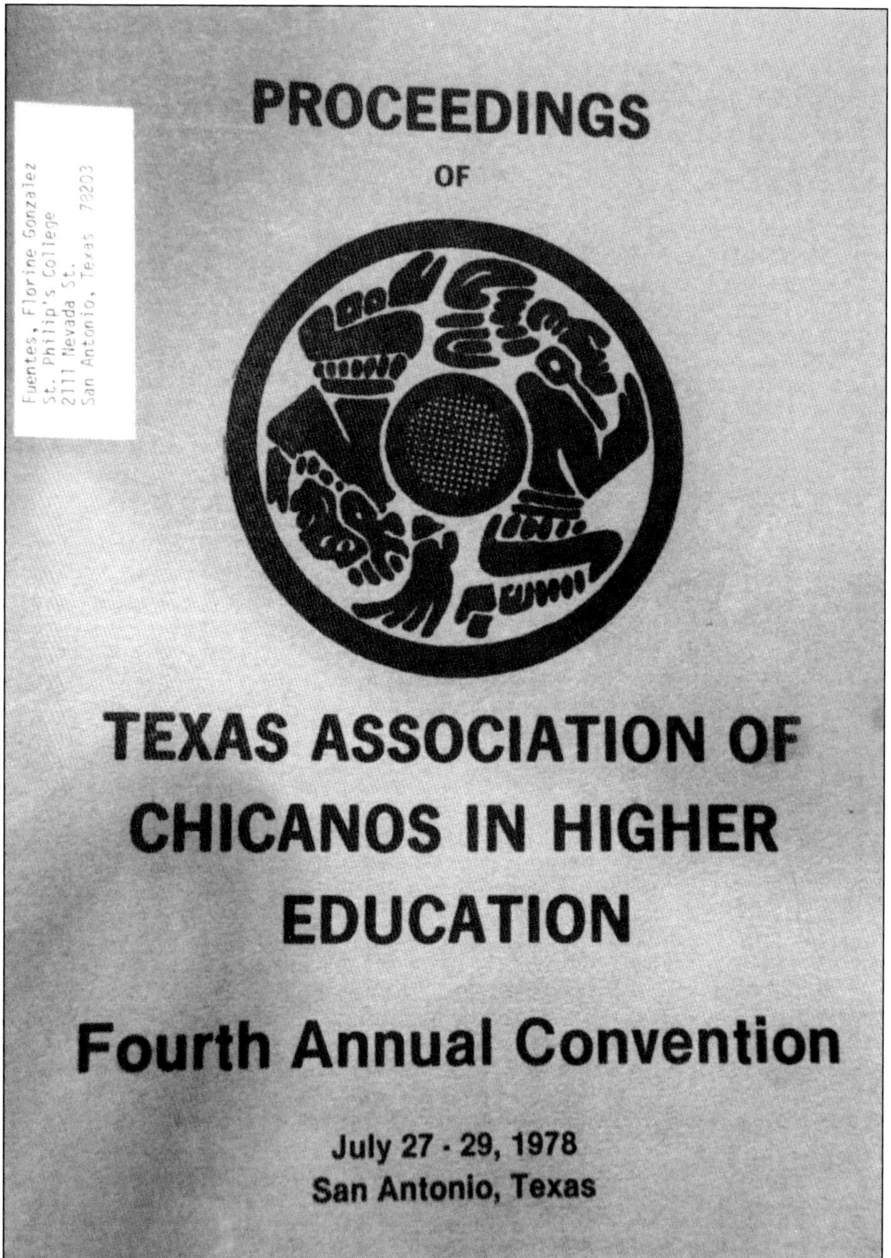

The first annual conference, held in 1975 at San Antonio and presided over by Dr. Leonard Valverde, featured many Chicano luminaries of the time, including Dr. Henry Casso of Albuquerque and Richard E. Pesqueira, the president of the University of Southern Colorado (now Colorado State University-Pueblo). The commissioner of the Texas Higher Education Coordinating Board, Dr. Kenneth H. Ashworth, addressed the participants. The early conferences were held in the summer months. At the founding conference, the membership and registration fee was $10; by 2013, the membership fee was $40, and early registration for the conference was $325. Student registration fees remained the same until 1998. (Courtesy of Dr. Rudy Rodríguez; photograph by Natalia Verjat Gutiérrez.)

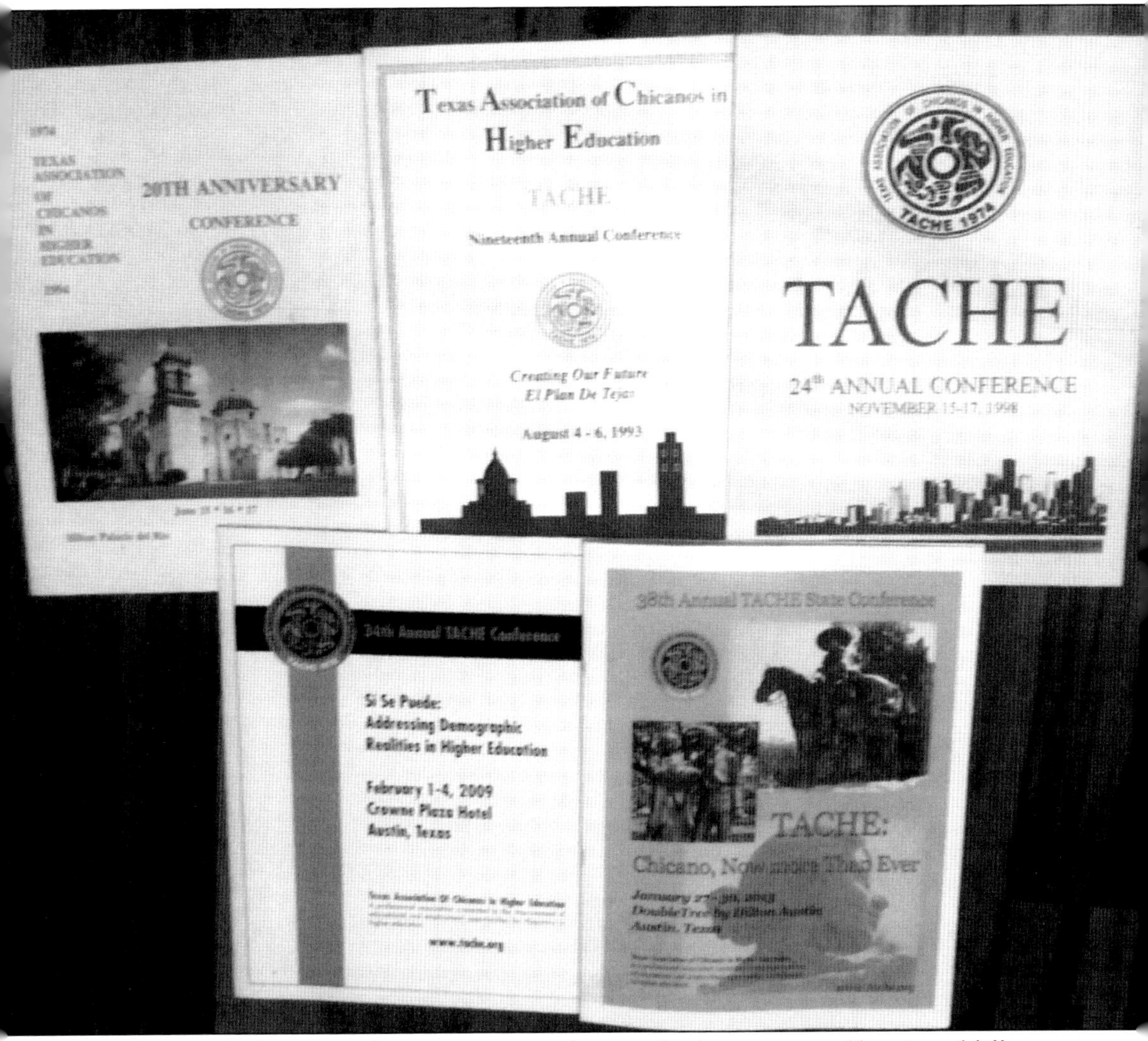

This photograph shows several program covers indicating the theme, year, and location of different conferences. Within a few years, the members realized they should solicit and receive institutional funding for TACHE from their colleges and universities. The annual conference date was then changed to be during the academic year. The program booklet, which costs a substantial amount to print, raises more money than is spent because it features advertisements from donor universities and corporations. The program booklet also becomes a collector's item for members, particularly those who are featured in it as benefactors, presenters, or recipients of meritorious service, lifetime achievement, or distinguished faculty awards. (Courtesy of the TACHE Archive, University of Texas at Austin, Benson Library; photograph by Natalia Verjat Gutiérrez.)

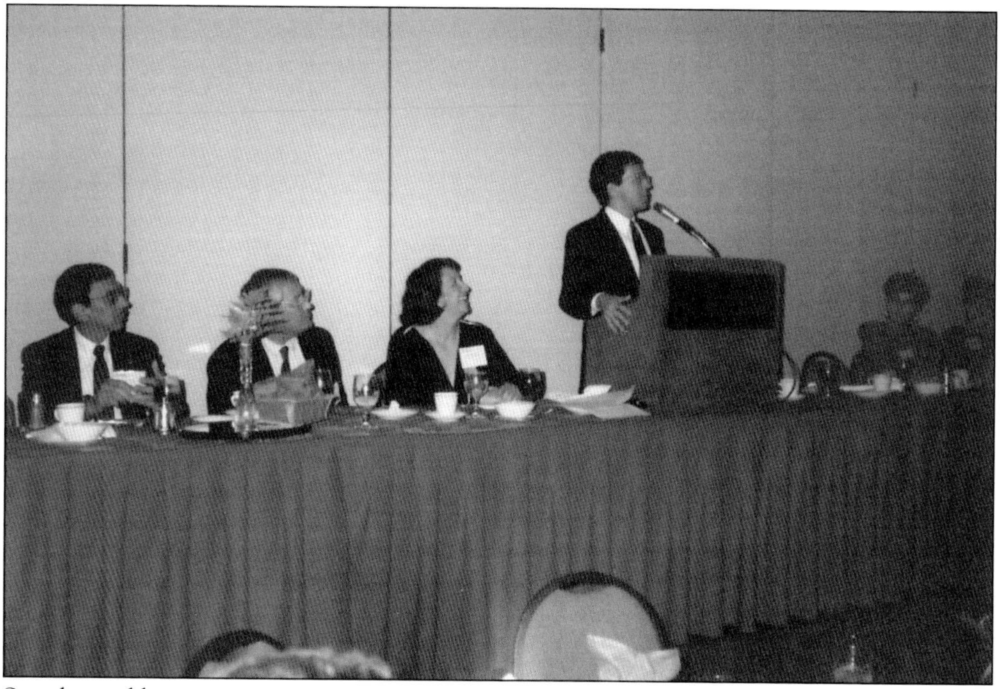

Seen here addressing convention participants in 1991 are, from left to right, Dr. Jude Valdez, Rey Elizondo, TACHE president Linda Rodríguez, and Texas attorney general Dan Morales. (Courtesy of Linda Rodríguez.)

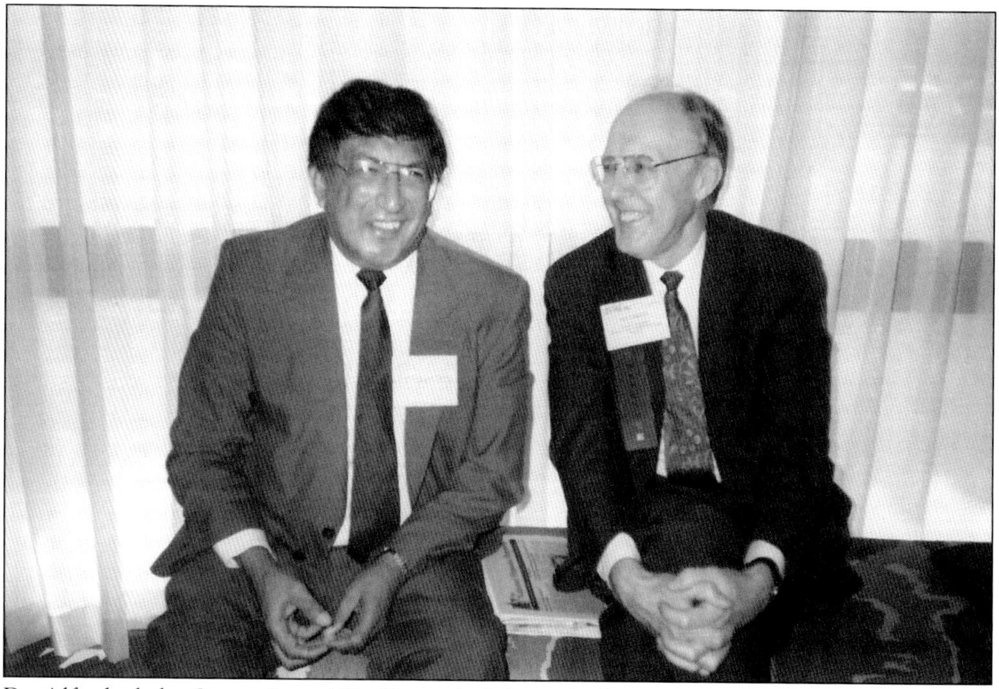

Dr. Alfredo de los Santos Jr. and Dr. Kenneth Ashworth, the commissioner of the Texas Higher Education Coordinating Board, are seen here at the 1991 conference, held in El Paso. (Courtesy of Linda Rodríguez.)

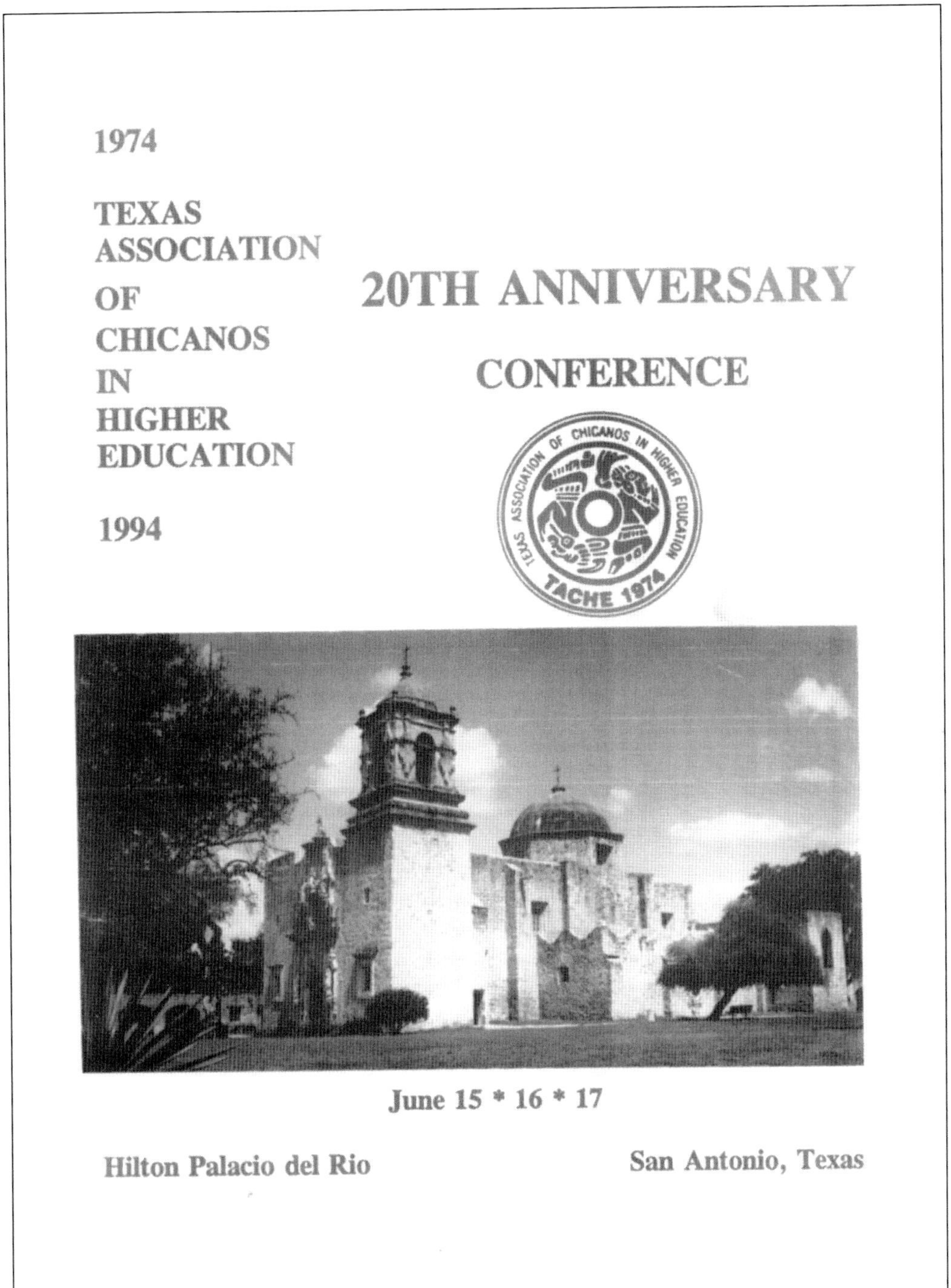

It is the duty of the president-elect to organize the annual conference to comply with the TACHE constitution, which states, "The Association shall provide a forum for the discussion of issues related to Chicanos in Higher Education." The annual conference has five main foci: issues, fundraising, networking, awards and scholarships, and electing new officers. Each conference has a theme, which often dictates the choice of keynote speakers, special guests, presenters, sessions, and issue focus. (Courtesy of Dr. Rudy Rodríguez; photograph by Natalia Verjat Gutiérrez.)

1974 Austin	1984 San Antonio	1994 San Antonio	2004 Corpus Christi	2014 Fort Worth
1975 San Antonio	1985 McAllen	1995 Dallas	2005 Austin	
1976 Austin	1986 Houston	1996 Corpus Christi	2006 Houston	
1977 San Antonio	1987 Dallas	1997 Laredo	2007 Dallas	
1978 San Antonio	1988 Austin	1998 Houston	2008 Austin	
1979 San Antonio	1989 Corpus Christi	1999 San Antonio	2009 Austin	
1980 Austin	1990 San Antonio	2000 Dallas	2010 San Antonio	
1981 Dallas	1991 El Paso	2001 Austin	2011 Austin	
1982 El Paso	1992 Corpus Christi	2002 NONE HELD	2012 Galveston	
1983 San Antonio	1993 Austin	2003 Austin	2013 Austin	

Seen here is a list of conference locations by year. (Courtesy of Dr. Rudy Rodríguez.)

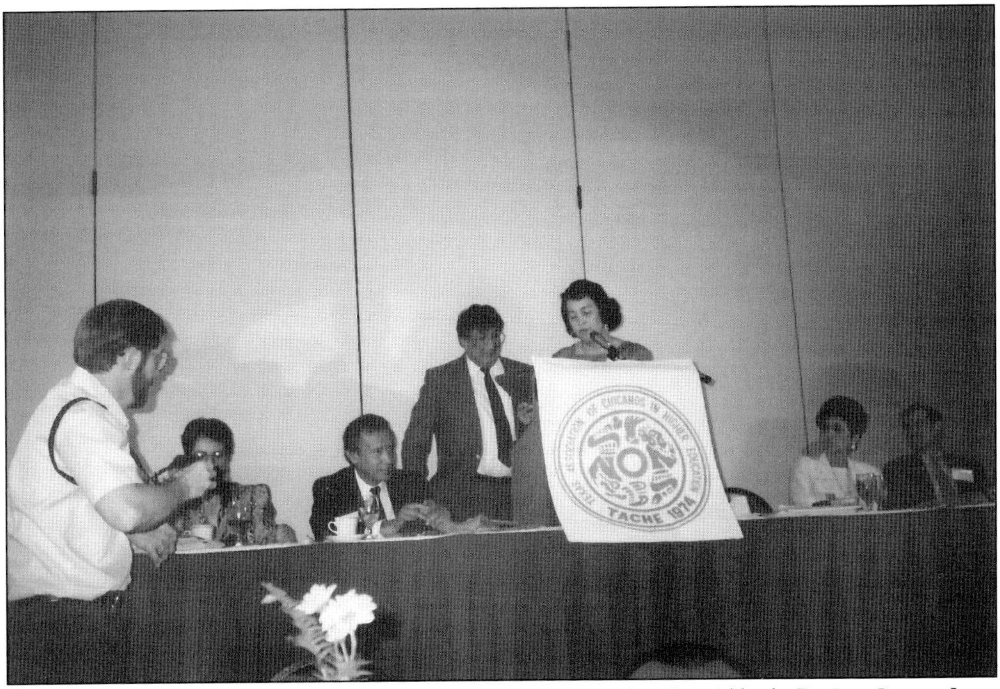

TACHE president Linda Rodríguez introduces keynote speaker Dr. Alfredo De Los Santos Jr. at the 1991 conference. (Courtesy of Linda Rodríguez.)

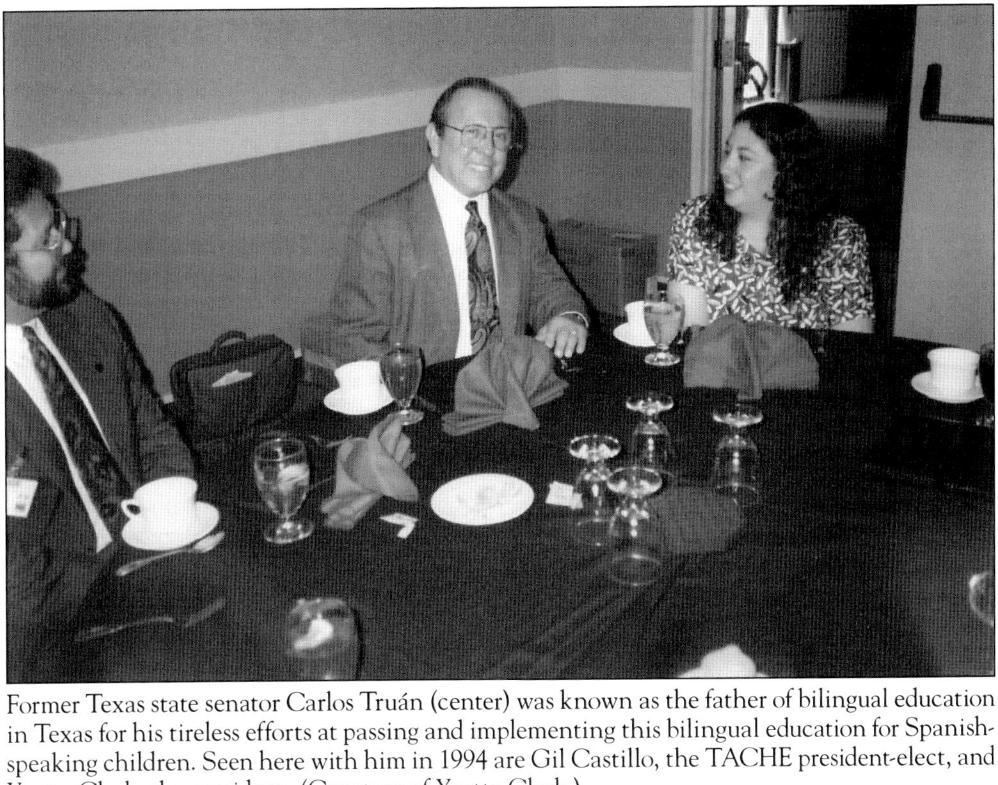

Former Texas state senator Carlos Truán (center) was known as the father of bilingual education in Texas for his tireless efforts at passing and implementing this bilingual education for Spanish-speaking children. Seen here with him in 1994 are Gil Castillo, the TACHE president-elect, and Yvette Clark, the president. (Courtesy of Yvette Clark.)

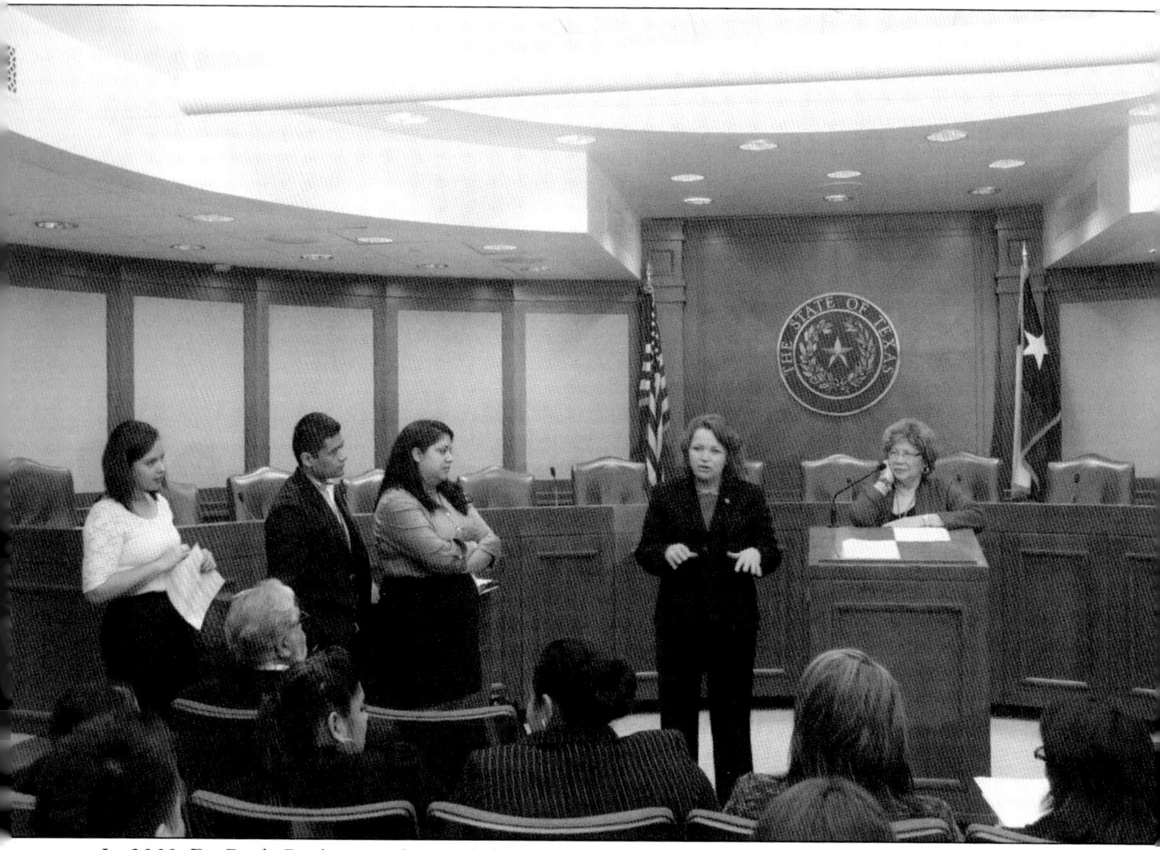

In 2002, Dr. Rudy Rodríguez changed the conference meeting date to coincide with the legislative session. In odd-numbered years, TACHE members bus over to the capitol and visit with legislators on issues of importance to TACHE. The 2013 policy initiatives were: reauthorization and funding of the Doctoral Incentive Loan Repayment program (a previous TACHE initiative); restoration of funding for public colleges and universities to previous levels; increase in funding for the Texas Grant and Texas Educational Opportunity Grant programs; and for Texas public college and university faculties and staffs to reflect each institution's student population. TACHE wants the Texas Coordinating Board for Higher Education to require each public college and university to report on diversity. TACHE president Linda Contreras Bullock (foreground) and president-elect Julie Arias (background, far right) lead this role-playing session before meeting with legislators in January 2013. (Courtesy of Natalia Verjat Gutiérrez.)

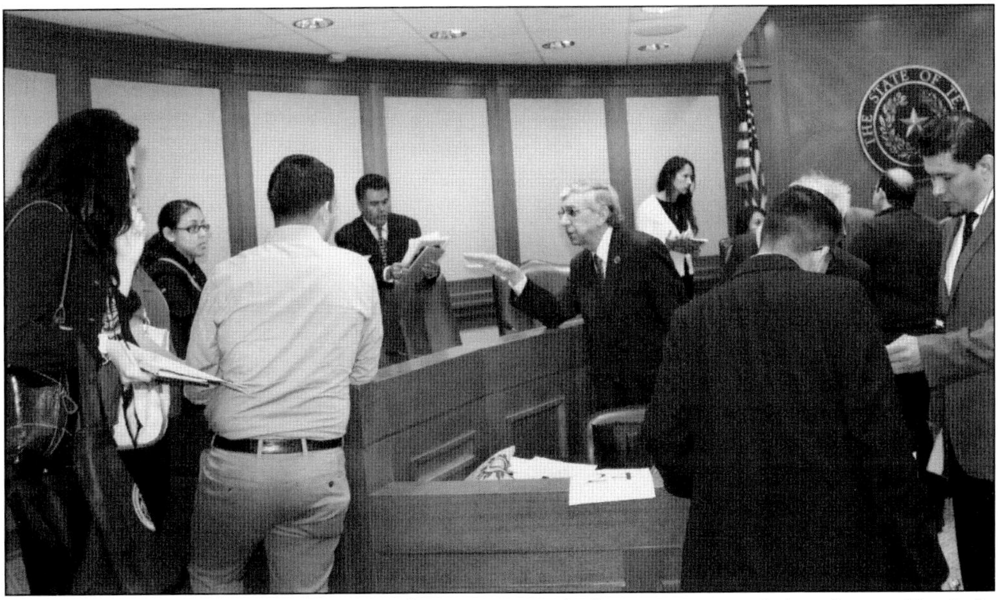

Role-playing is part of TACHE members' training before visiting with legislators. Dr. Jude Valdez organized this activity during the 2013 legislative session visit. (Courtesy of Natalia Verjat Gutiérrez.)

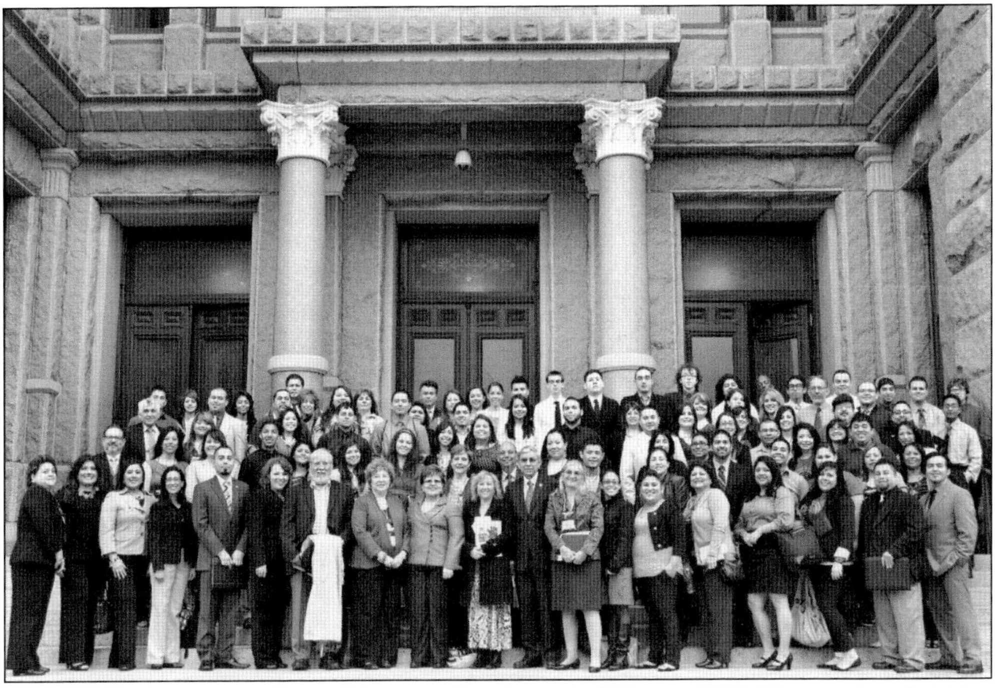

TACHE members pose in front of the capitol in Austin in February 2013. The practice of visiting legislators early in the session and presenting testimony before state legislative committees to advocate TACHE's agenda was initiated by Dr. Leonard Valverde and Ernesto Medrano to "prepare legislation and identify individuals and means of introducing said legislation at the fore coming legislative session." (Courtesy of Arturo Martínez.)

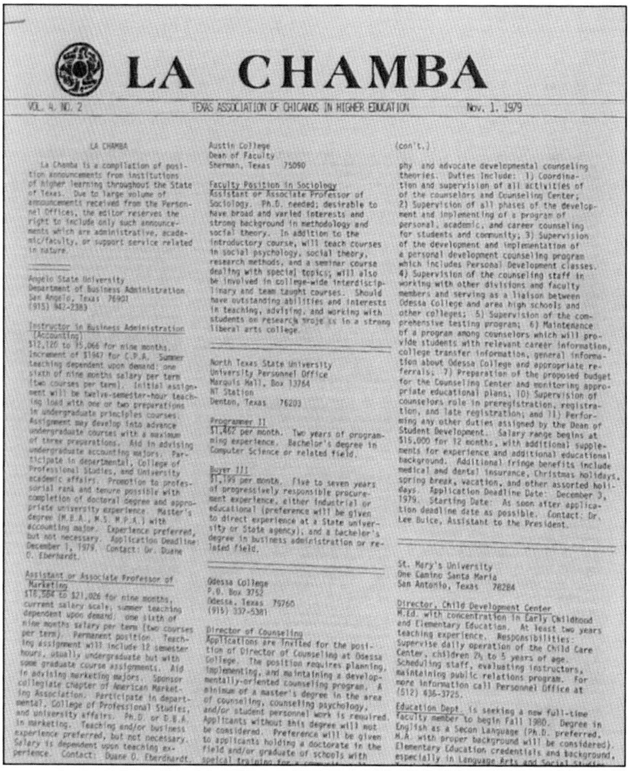

LA CHAMBA

VOL. 4, NO. 2 TEXAS ASSOCIATION OF CHICANOS IN HIGHER EDUCATION Nov. 1, 1979

LA CHAMBA

La Chamba is a compilation of position announcements from institutions of higher learning throughout the State of Texas. Due to large volume of announcements received from the Personnel Offices, the editor reserves the right to include only such announcements which are administrative, academic/faculty, or support service related in nature.

Angelo State University
Department of Business Administration
San Angelo, Texas 76901
(915) 942-2383

Instructor in Business Administration (Accounting)
$12,120 to 15,066 for nine months. Increment of $1947 for C.P.A. Summer teaching dependent upon demand: one sixth of nine months salary per term (two courses per term). Initial assignment will be twelve-semester-hour teaching load with one or two preparations in undergraduate principles courses. Assignment may develop into advance undergraduate courses with a maximum of three preparations. Aid in advising undergraduate accounting majors. Participate in departmental, College of Professional Studies, and University academic affairs. Promotion to professorial rank and tenure possible with completion of doctoral degree and appropriate university experience. Master's degree (M.B.A., M.S. M.P.A.) with accounting major. Experience preferred, but not necessary. Application Deadline: December 1, 1979. Contact: Dr. Duane O. Eberhardt.

Assistant or Associate Professor of Marketing
$16,584 to $21,026 for nine months, current salary scale; summer teaching dependent upon demand: one sixth of nine months salary per term (two courses per term). Permanent position. Teaching assignment will include 12 semester hours, usually undergraduate but with some graduate course assignments. Aid in advising marketing majors. Sponsor collegiate chapter of American Marketing Association. Participate in departmental, College of Professional Studies, and university affairs. Ph.D. or D.B.A. in marketing. Teaching and/or business experience preferred, but not necessary. Salary is dependent upon teaching experience. Contact: Duane O. Eberhardt.

Austin College
Dean of Faculty
Sherman, Texas 75090

Faculty Position in Sociology
Assistant or Associate Professor of Sociology. Ph.D. needed; desirable to have broad and varied interests and strong background in methodology and social theory. In addition to the introductory course, will teach courses in social psychology, social theory, research methods, and a seminar course dealing with special topics; will also be involved in college-wide interdisciplinary and team taught courses. Should have outstanding abilities and interests in teaching, advising, and working with students on research proje is in a strong liberal arts college.

North Texas State University
University Personnel Office
Marquis Hall, Box 13764
NT Station
Denton, Texas 76203

Programmer II
$1,467 per month. Two years of programming experience. Bachelor's degree in Computer Science or related field.

Buyer III
$1,199 per month. Five to seven years of progressively responsible procurement experience, either industrial or educational (preference will be given to direct experience at a State university or State agency), and a bachelor's degree in business administration or related field.

Odessa College
P.O. Box 3752
Odessa, Texas 79760
(915) 337-5381

Director of Counseling
Applications are invited for the position of Director of Counseling at Odessa College. The position requires planning, implementing, and maintaining a developmentally-oriented counseling program. A minimum of a master's degree in the area of counseling, counseling psychology, and/or student personnel work is required. Applicants without this degree will not be considered. Preference will be given to applicants holding a doctorate in the field and/or graduate of schools with speical training [illegible]

(con't.)

phy and advocate developmental counseling theories. Duties Include: 1) Coordination and supervision of all activities of of the counselors and Counseling Center; 2) Supervision of all phases of the development and implementing of a program of personal, academic, and career counseling for students and community; 3) Supervision of the development and implementation of a personal development counseling program which includes Personal Development classes. 4) Supervision of the counseling staff in working with other divisions and faculty members and serving as a liaison between Odessa College and area high schools and other colleges; 5) Supervision of the comprehensive testing program; 6) Maintenance of a program among counselors which will provide students with relevant career information, college transfer information, general information about Odessa College and appropriate referrals; 7) Preparation of the proposed budget for the Counseling Center and monitoring appropriate educational plans. 10) Supervision of counselors role in preregistration, registration, and late registration; and 11) Performing any other duties assigned by the Dean of Student Development. Salary range begins at $15,000 for 12 months, with additional supplements for experience and additional educational background. Additional fringe benefits include medical and dental insurance, Christmas holidays, spring break, vacation, and other assorted holidays. Application Deadline Date: December 3, 1979. Starting Date: As soon after application deadline date as possible. Contact: Dr. Lee Buice, Assistant to the President.

St. Mary's University
One Camino Santa Maria
San Antonio, Texas 78284

Director, Child Development Center
M.Ed. with concentration in Early Childhood and Elementary Education. At least two years teaching experience. Responsibilities: Supervise daily operation of the Child Care Center, children 2½ to 5 years of age. Scheduling staff, evaluating instructors, maintaining public relations program. For more information call Personnel Office at (512) 436-3725.

Education Dept. is seeking a new full-time faculty member to begin Fall 1980. Degree in English as a Secon Language (Ph.D. preferred, M.A. with proper background will be considered). Elementary Education credentials and background, especially in Language Arts and Social Studies [illegible]

The professional employment newsletter *La Chamba* was founded in 1979. Increasing the number of Chicanos employed in higher education was a goal, and the newsletter served to spread the word about opportunities. It did not last long in production, however. As a volunteer-based organization, TACHE could not maintain the various publications it had begun. Today, institutional members have an opportunity to post job announcements on the TACHE website as a benefit of membership. (Courtesy of TACHE Archive, University of Texas at Austin, Benson Library; photograph by Natalia Verjat Gutiérrez.)

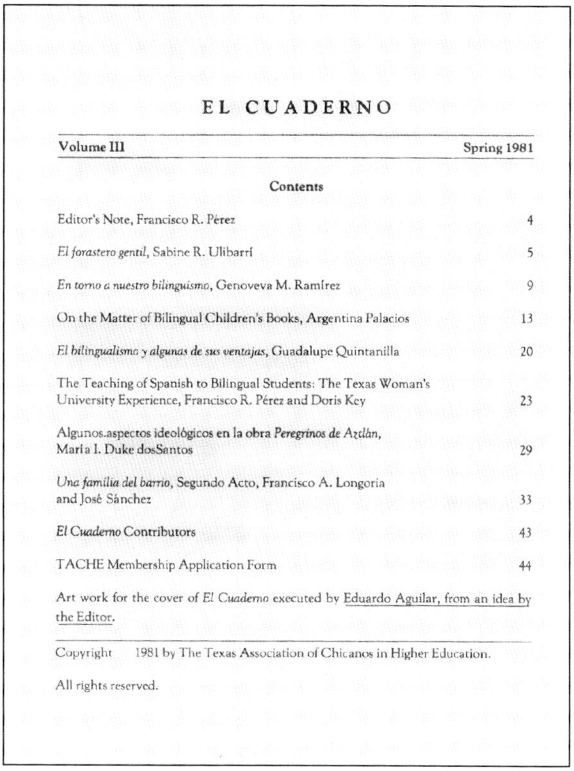

EL CUADERNO

Volume III Spring 1981

Contents

Art work for the cover of *El Cuaderno* executed by Eduardo Aguilar, from an idea by the Editor.

TACHE's academic journal, *El Cuaderno*, made its debut at the 1977 annual conference. Raúl Salvador Murguía, a cofounder of TACHE, served as editor. It was published twice a year and sold for $2. The journal continued for three more volumes until the spring of 1981, when Francisco R. Pérez was the editor. This issue of the notebook sold for $3 and was the last edition published. (Courtesy of Linda Rodríguez; photograph by Natalia Verjat Gutiérrez.)

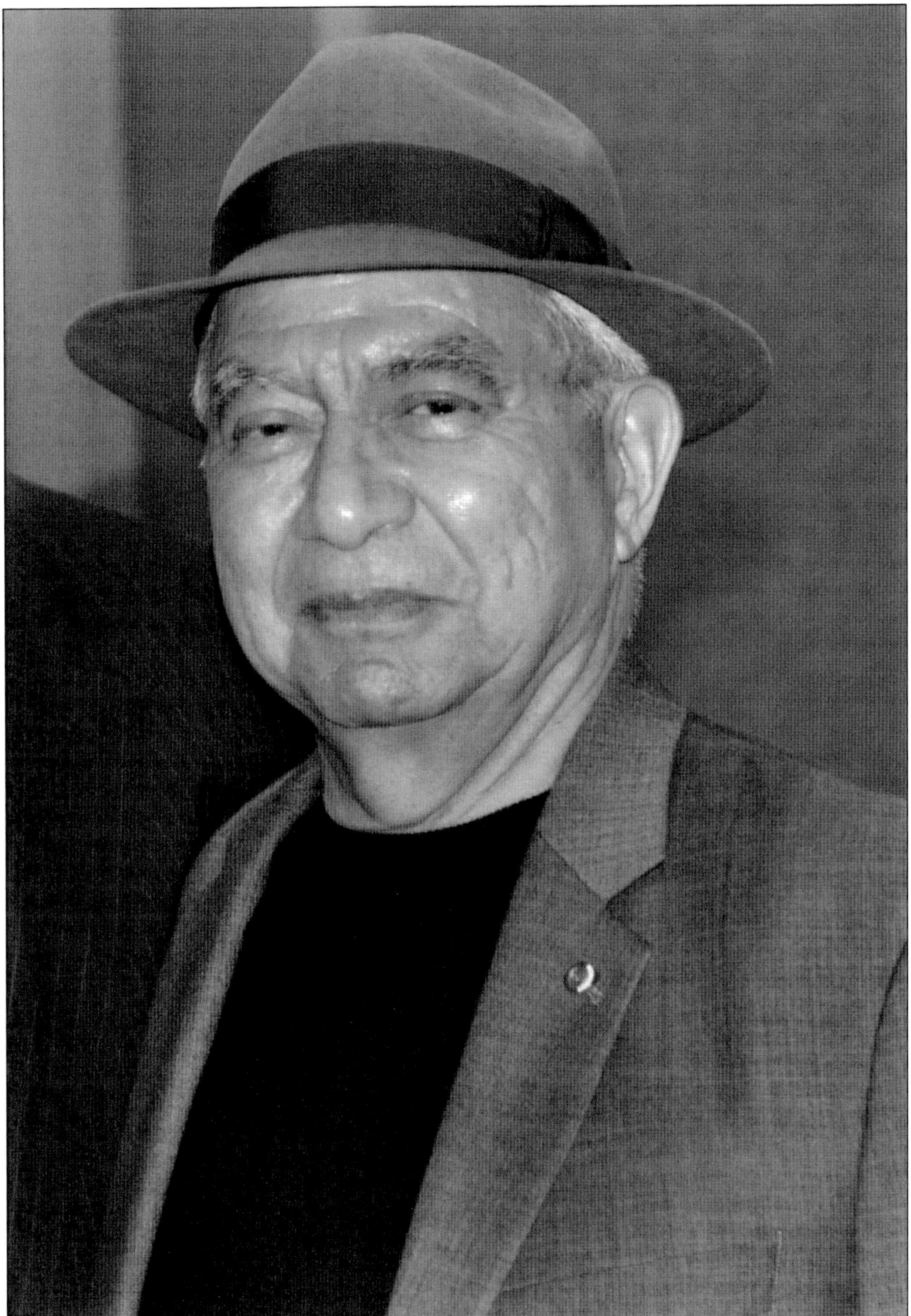

Dr. Arturo Madrid is the Norene and Frank T. Murchison Distinguished Professor of the Humanities and Literatures at Trinity University in San Antonio. A longtime TACHE member, he has been a frequent keynote speaker at the annual conferences. (Courtesy of Arturo Martínez.)

TACHE presents several awards annually, for lifetime achievement, meritorious service, distinguished faculty (both university and community college), and benefactor. In 1978, special recognition as a benefactor was given to Manuel L. Flores for securing funds from the H.E. Butt Company grocery chain in 1978. TACHE member Dr. Miguel Nevarez made the presentation. In 2000, Pearl Garza Fracchia received the Benefactor Award for her work with Southwestern Bell on behalf of TACHE. MALDEF was awarded the Meritorious Service Award in 1986, followed by the Rivera Center in 1988, H.E.B. once again in 1989, and the Texas Senate Hispanic Caucus and House Mexican American Caucus in 1993. (Courtesy of José Hernández.)

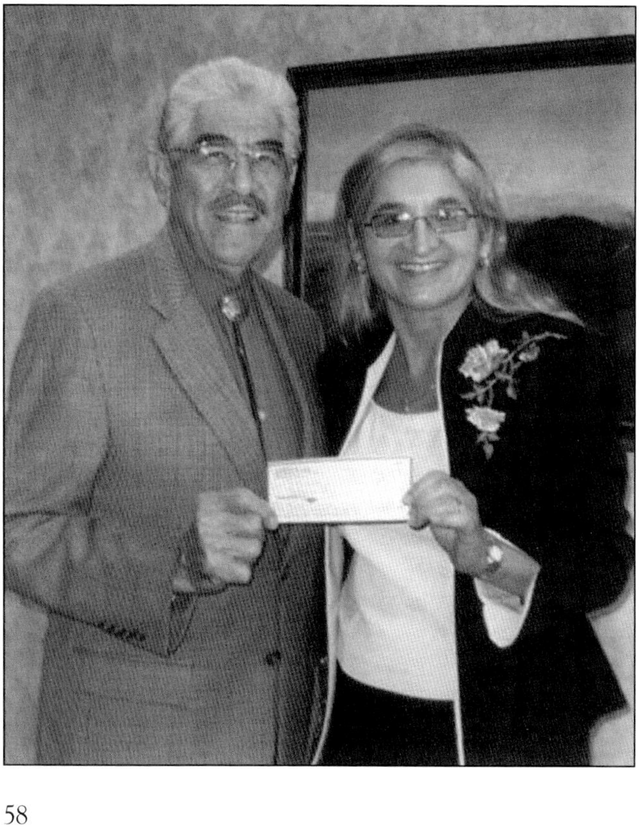

Dr. Leonardo de la Garza, chancellor of the Tarrant County Community College District, challenged TACHE to match his $5,000 contribution to endow the scholarship fund at the 33rd annual conference in Austin. (Courtesy of Magdalena de la Teja.)

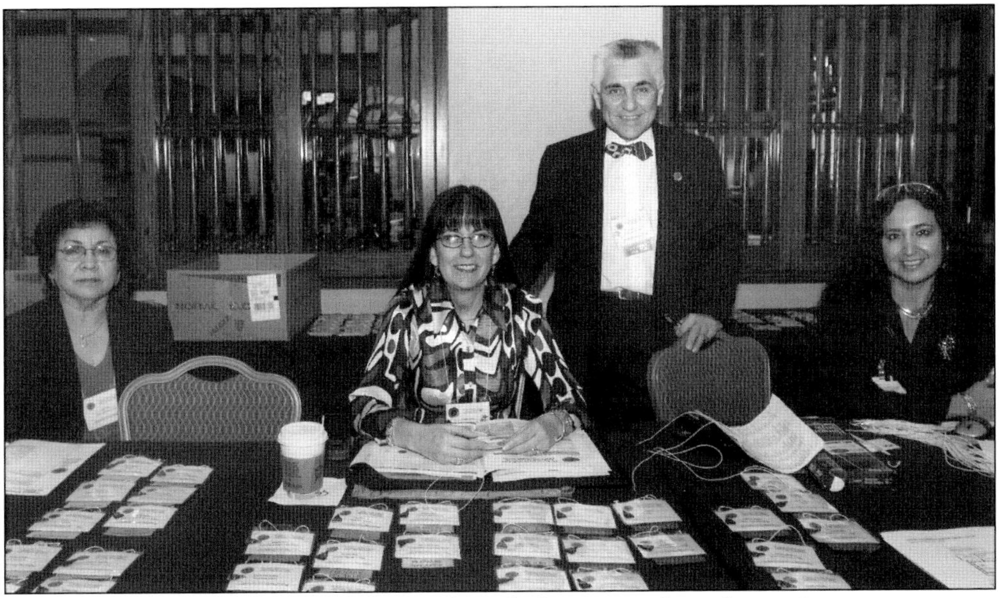

Individual membership fees have gone up through the years, as have the conference registration fees. By 1998, preregistration for the conference cost $175, with on-site registration costing $195. For students, the conference registration fee was also increased to $75. (Courtesy of Magdalena de la Teja.)

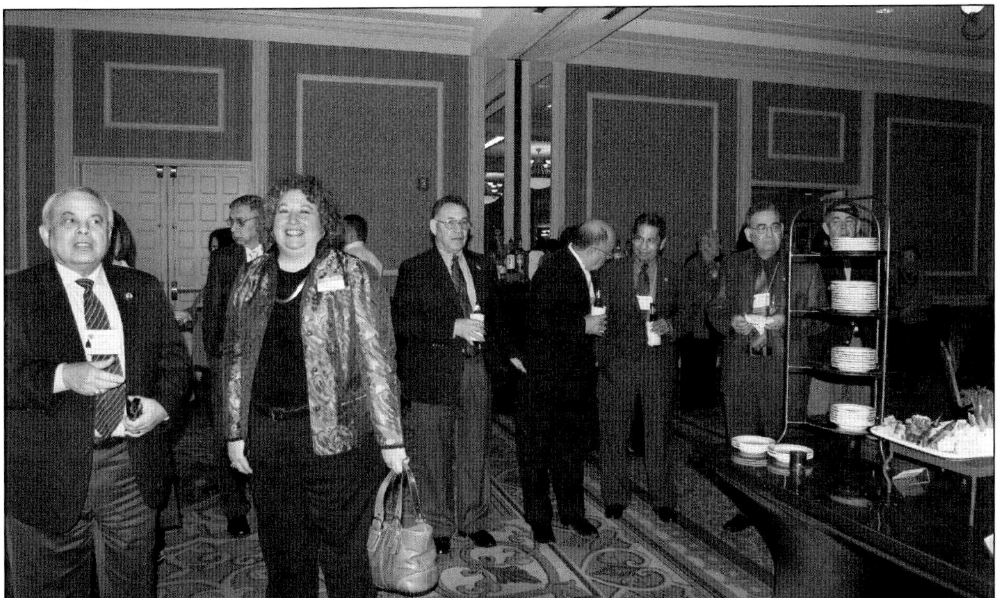

The annual conference is a moneymaker for TACHE, especially after it obtained federally tax-exempt status in 1982. Any donation to TACHE is tax-deductible for the donor. Money comes into the organizational coffers from various sources, primarily through sponsorships by institutions and corporations. Diamond sponsors contribute $10,000, platinum sponsors contribute $5,000, and gold and silver sponsors contribute $2,500 and $1,500, respectively. The 2013 conference featured 1 diamond, 2 platinum, 7 gold, and 12 silver sponsors, grossing $40,750 overall. (Courtesy of Natalia Verjat Gutiérrez.)

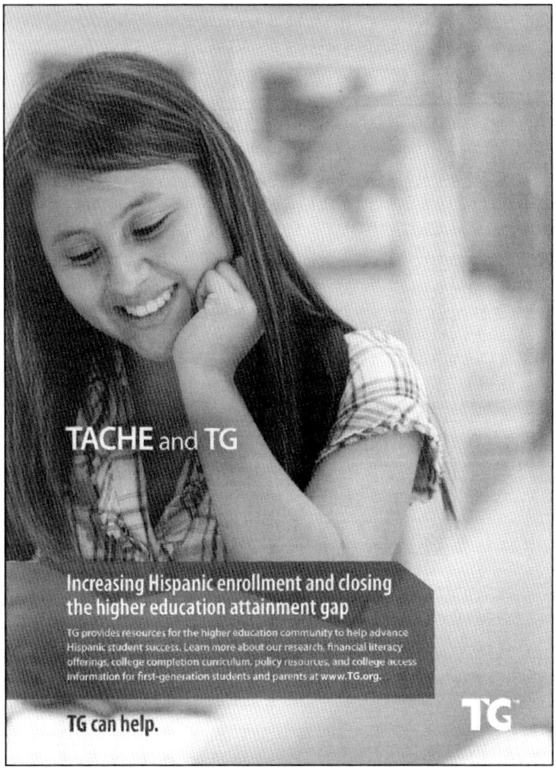

The 1994 annual conference program contained 13 full-page advertisements for colleges and universities as well as three for corporate and individual donors. For-profit groups can pay up to $300 per table, while tables for nonprofit groups go for $175. Institutional sponsors, colleges, and universities that are members of TACHE, pay $500 for a membership, which entitles them to paid memberships for five people. In 2000–2001, there were 49 institutional sponsors of TACHE. Registration fees at the 2013 annual conference amounted to $38,325. (Courtesy of Jacob Frairie.)

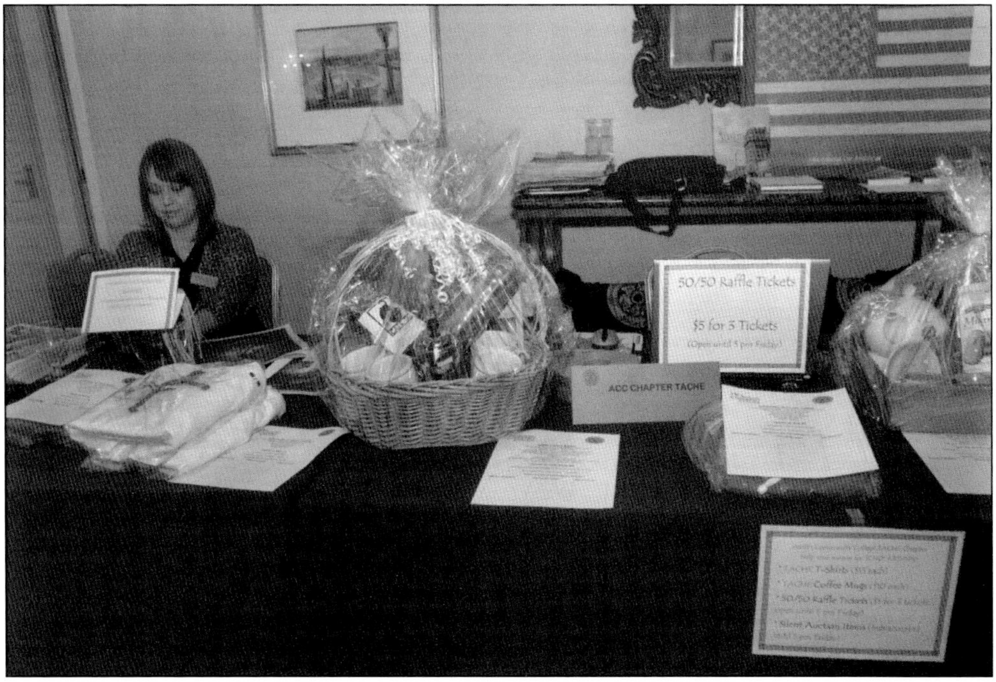

All kinds of goods and tickets are for sale at the silent auction. Exhibitors range from TACHE chapters and members to universities and merchants, and their monetary contributions to reserve space for the conference provide additional income to TACHE. (Courtesy of Javier Olguín.)

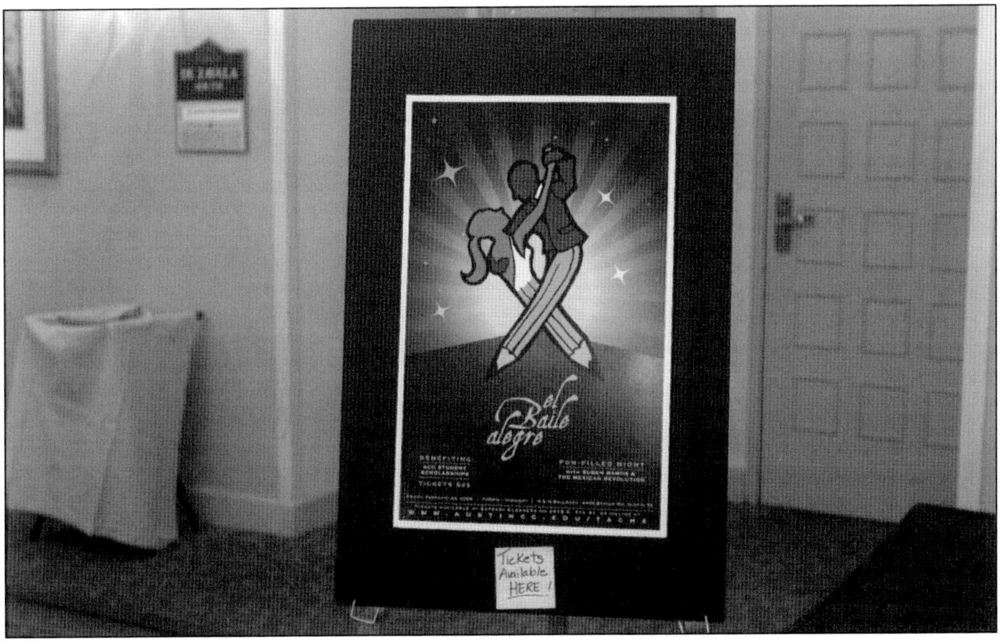

In addition to a youth track, each annual conference includes many receptions, social gatherings, and performances for listening and dancing. These social events are as important for networking and meeting potential friends as the many breakfast, lunch, and dinner activities are. (Courtesy of Javier Olguín.)

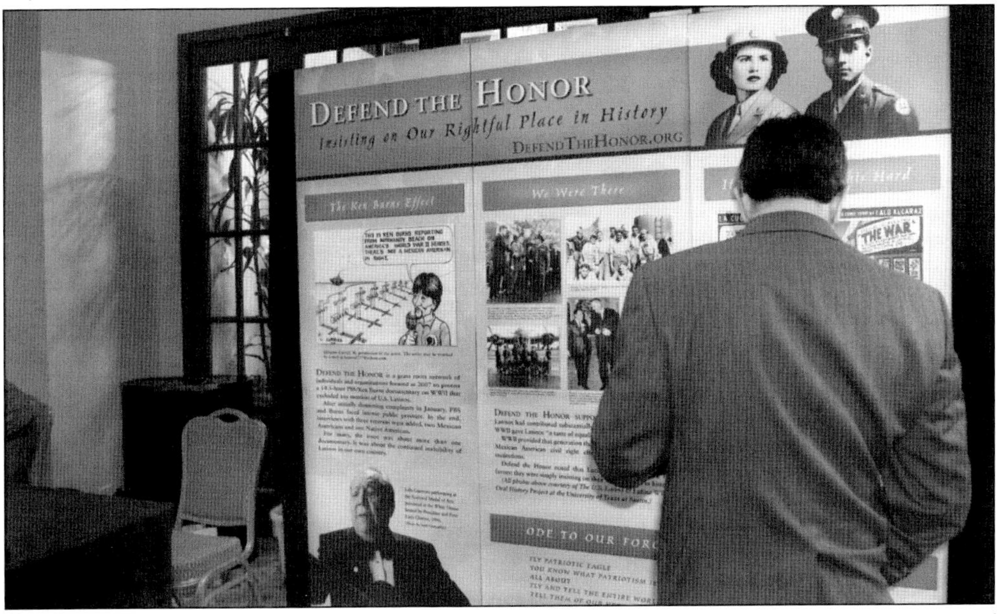

This tribute to World War II veterans of Mexican ancestry was begun by Dr. Maggie Rivas of UT-Austin. Several other TACHE members have also initiated oral history projects, including *Los Del Valle*, by Dr. Manuel Medrano at UT-Brownsville, and *Tejano Voices*, by José Angel Gutiérrez. UTEP is currently working on an archival project on the 1942–1964 bracero program, and Chicano activist Hermán Baca of National City, California, has just had his archives digitized and placed online by the University of California, San Diego. (Courtesy of Javier Olguín.)

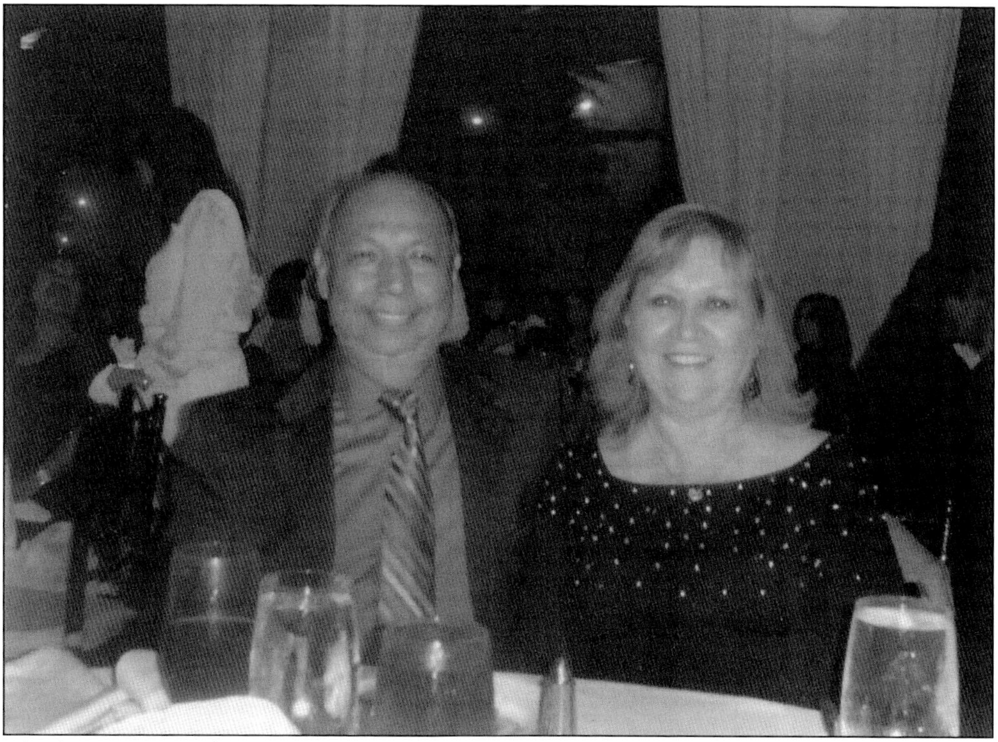

The first treasurer of TACHE, in 1975–1976, was Adolph López III, a counselor at San Antonio College. The treasurer for the organization in 2013 was Rosa María González (right), a longtime TACHE member. She reported TACHE's total assets, as of April 12, 2013, to be $175,975.05. González was among the first Chicano studies students at the University of Texas in the 1970s and is a member of the San Antonio chapter. Dr. Raúl "Rudy" Reyna is pictured at the left. (Courtesy of Rosa María González.)

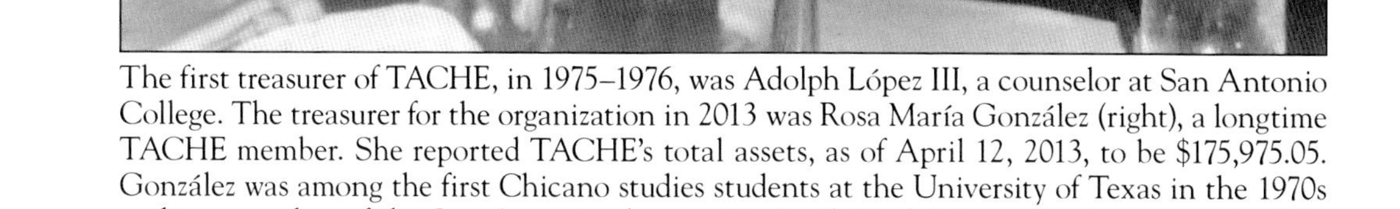

TACHE is financially healthy, according to certified public accountants R. Mendoza & Company, the husband-and-wife company of Richard and Rosie Mendoza, who are both CPAs. In 2011, TACHE had net assets of $151,449. They rose to $186,234 by the end of November 2012. Each incoming president prepares a budget in consultation with the other officers and board members and the treasurer. (Courtesy of Rosa María González.)

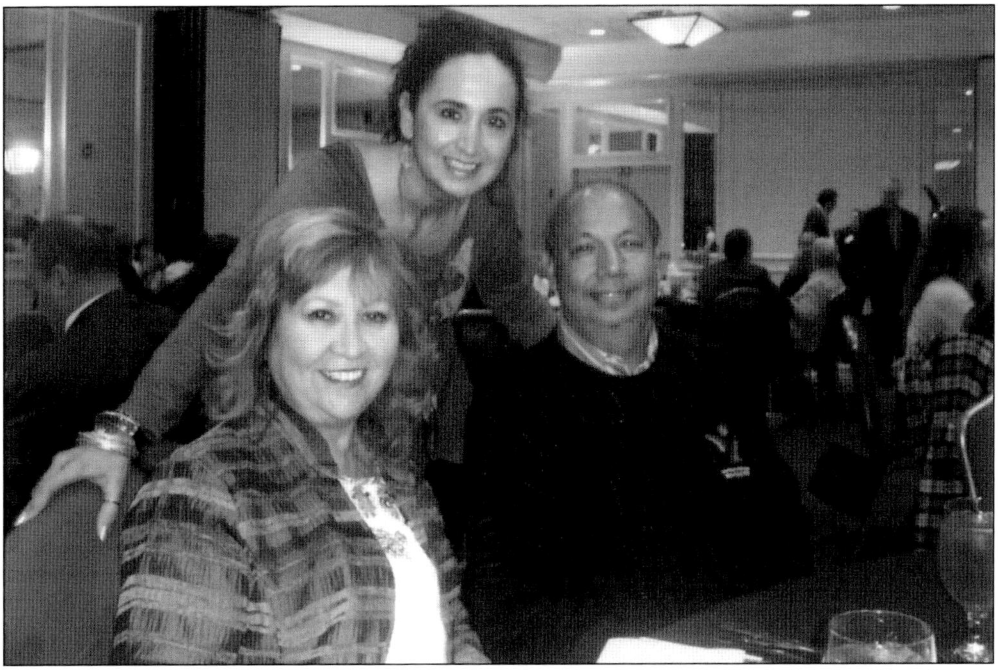

Seen here from left to right are Rosa María González of San Antonio TACHE, Ana Broadwater of Austin TACHE, and Dr. Raúl "Rudy" Reyna of University of Texas at San Antonio TACHE. Typically, TACHE budgets $30,000 for the conference and awards, $3,200 for chapter startup capital, and $15,000 for labor. Revenues come from the conference (usually about $40,000) and memberships (usually about $25,000). Exhibitors at the 2013 annual conference added $860 to the gross revenue from the event. (Courtesy of Rosa María González.)

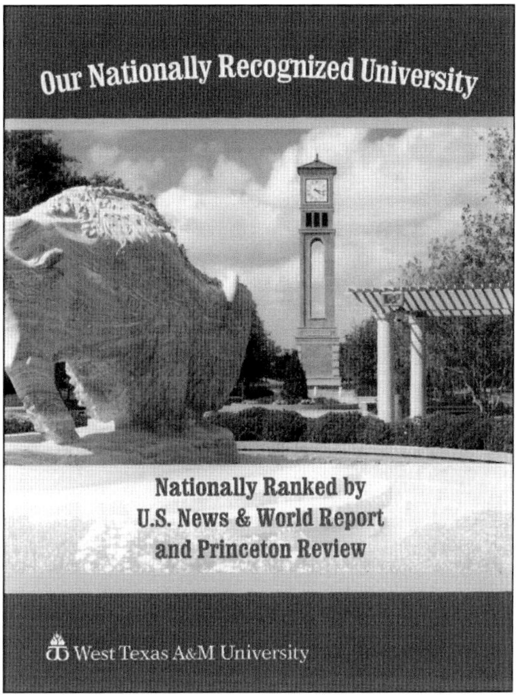

West Texas A&M University (WTAMU), in Canyon, has provided office space for TACHE in recent years, in addition to institutional and corporate support. WTAMU has a sizeable Hispanic student enrollment and is currently nearing Hispanic Serving Institution (HSI) status, which requires a 25-percent threshold of Hispanic students. (Courtesy of María Guerrero.)

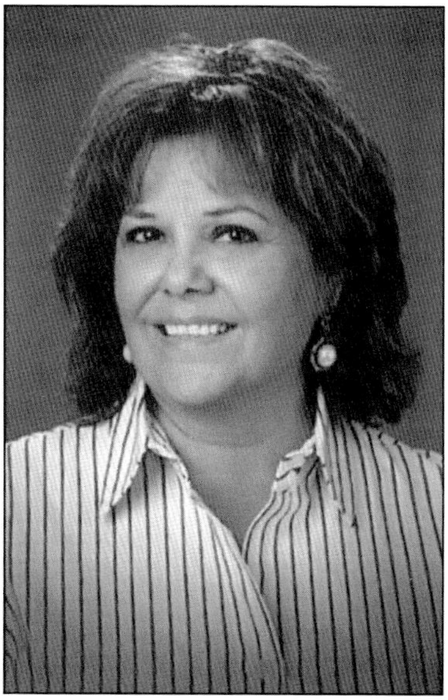

For years, María Guerrero has volunteered her time to assist Panhandle TACHE members. In particular, she has helped Julie Arias after Arias was elected TACHE president in 2009. As the operations manager for TACHE, Guerrero oversees and coordinates all major activities. She is employed part-time at the West Texas A&M University office. (Courtesy of María Guerrero.)

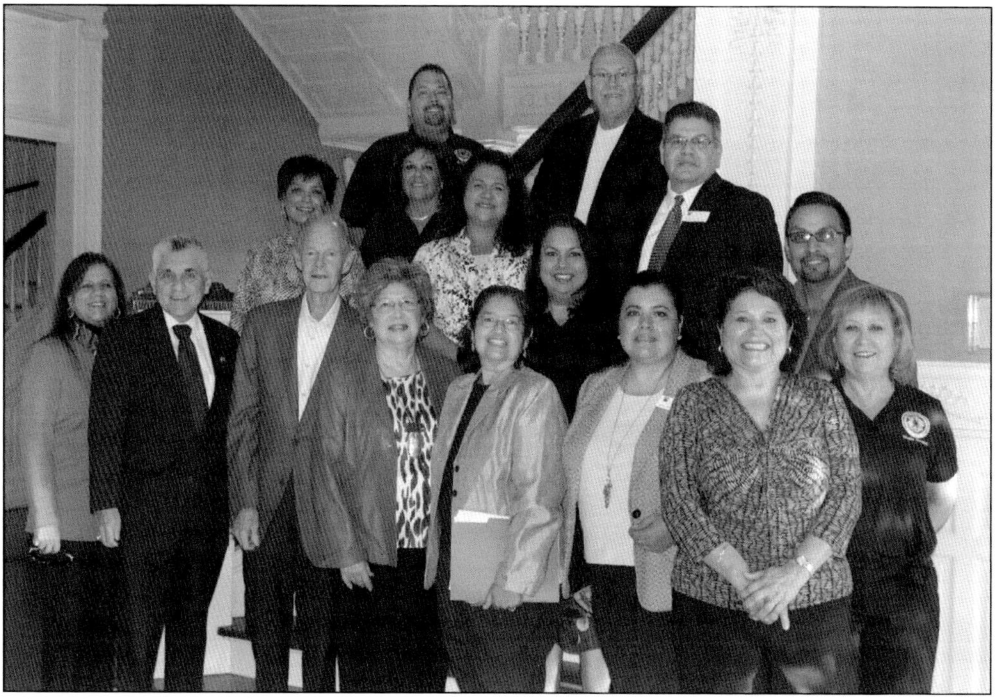

TACHE's organizational governance is headed by the state board of directors, led by the president and statewide officeholders as well as the representatives from each of the six regions. The board meets quarterly across the state, and at the annual conference. Typically, the board meetings are held beginning on Friday and then for a half-day on Saturday. The board members review reports from the officers and regional representatives. During the 2001 annual conference, Dr. Rudy Rodríguez, the president at the time, first pushed for annual reports from the regions and the development of a handbook of procedures. In 2012, president Linda Contreras Bullock submitted the first copy of the operations and procedures manual for TACHE, which was then adopted and implemented. (Courtesy of Natalia Verjat Gutiérrez.)

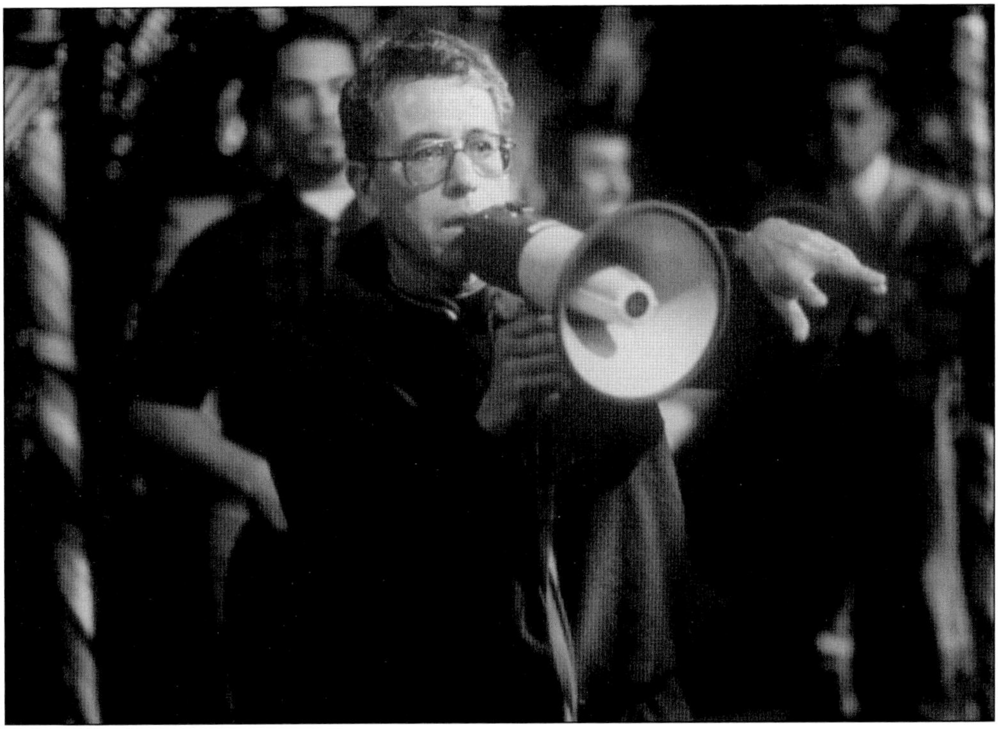

Sometimes, the TACHE annual conference features sessions with authors and their recent works. Other times, a session presents a short list of must-read books and must-see documentaries with description and analysis. Among these have been the works of Carmen Tafolla, Norma Cantú, Henry Ramos, Evelio Grillo, José Limón, David Montejano, and María Berriozabal. Seen above is Jesús "Chuy" Treviño, who is better known for his films than for his novels and autobiography, *Eyewitness* (at right). (Both courtesy of Jesús Treviño.)

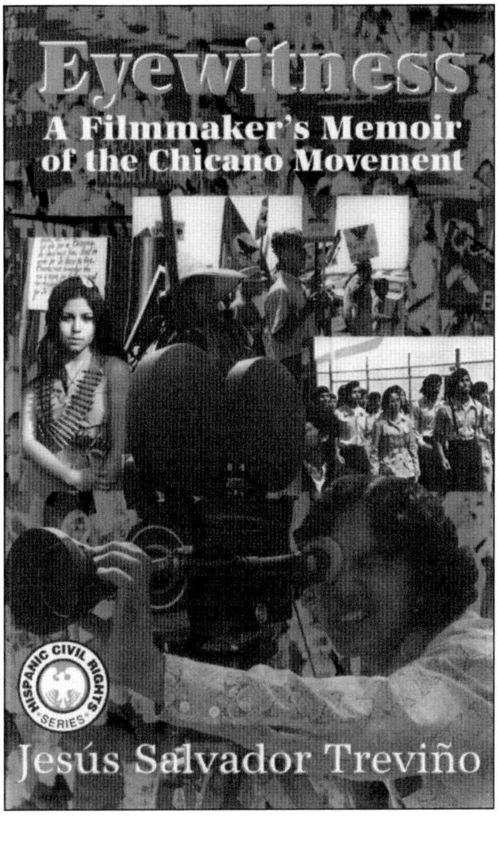

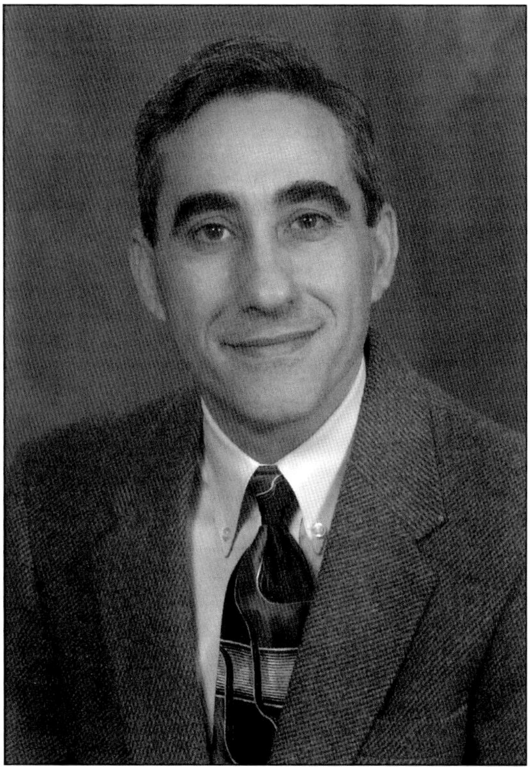

At the 36th annual conference, held in Austin in 2011, Dr. Jesús F. de la Teja, seen here, headlined the author's Tea Panel, along with Dr. Rafael C. Castillo, Gil Polanco, John Philip Santos, and José Angel Gutiérrez. The conference was locked down due to a massive ice storm that hit Texas on February 1, 2011, which closed major roadways, airports, and streets, and brought frequent rolling blackouts of electrical power. (Courtesy of Magdalena de la Teja.)

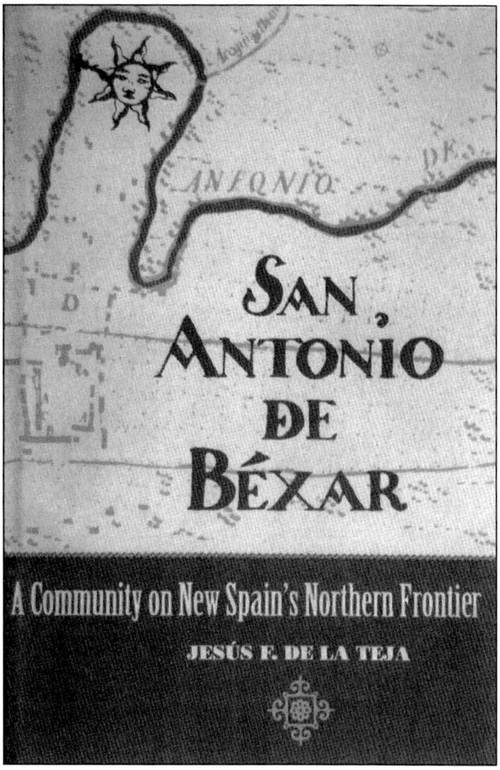

Dr. de la Teja became the first Latino to head the Texas State Historical Association and was named the state historian of Texas by Gov. Rick Perry. He is a professor of history at Texas State University, a Hispanic Serving Institution in San Marcos. (Courtesy of Magdalena de la Teja.)

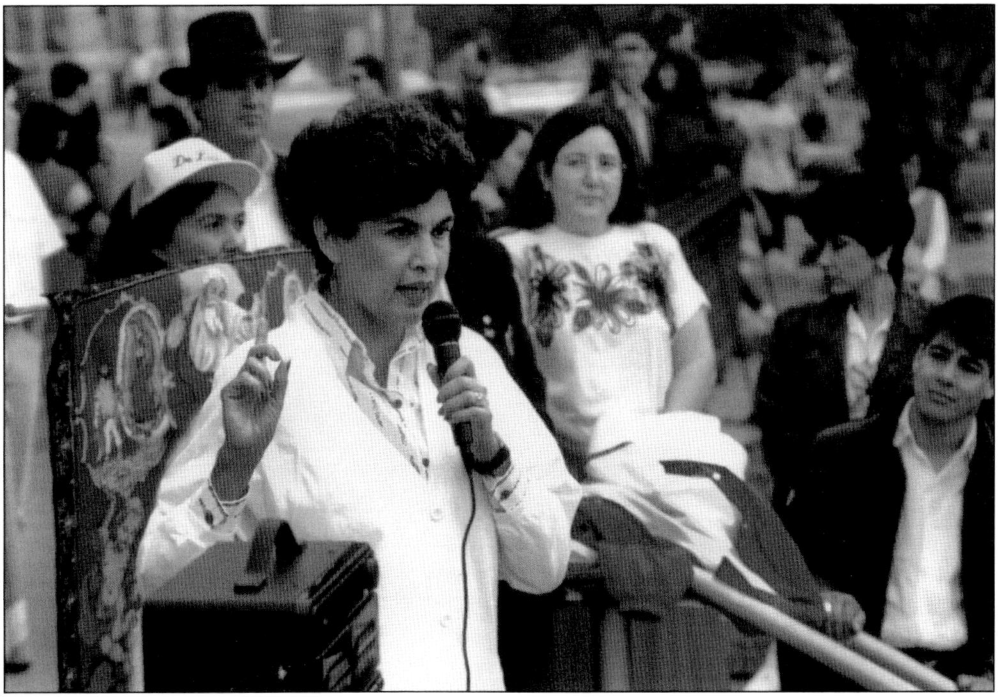

María Berriozabal was the first Chicana elected to the San Antonio City Council, in 1981, and served for 10 years. Seen at right is the cover of her autobiography, *María, Daughter of Immigrants*, published by Bryce Milligan at Wings Press. (Both courtesy of María Berriozabal.)

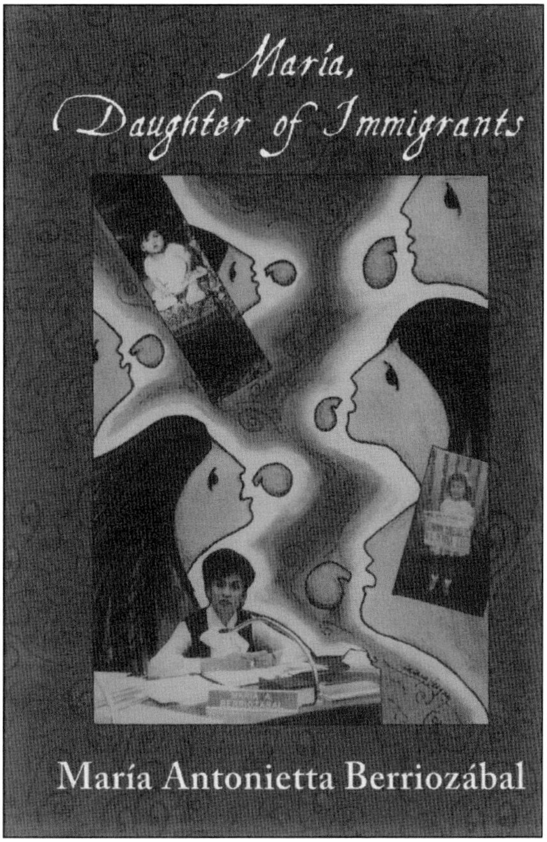

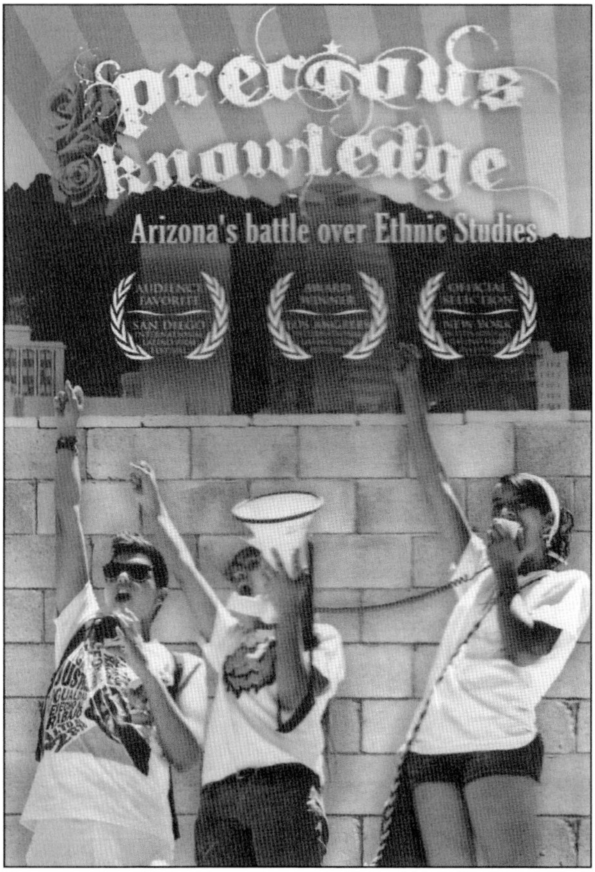

Precious Knowledge: Arizona's Battle over Ethnic Studies, a documentary about the banning of the Mexican American studies program in Tucson, Arizona, was previewed at a pre-session event before the 2013 TACHE conference. Several TACHE chapters and members screened the documentary to raise funds for the legal defense of activists in Tucson. (Courtesy of Sean Arce.)

Dr. Rogelio Sáenz, the dean of UT-San Antonio, hosted a fundraiser with TACHE members and supporters to benefit the legal defense of teachers who lost their jobs after the Tucson Unified School District was forced to terminate its Mexican American studies program. (Courtesy of Natalia Verjat Gutiérrez.)

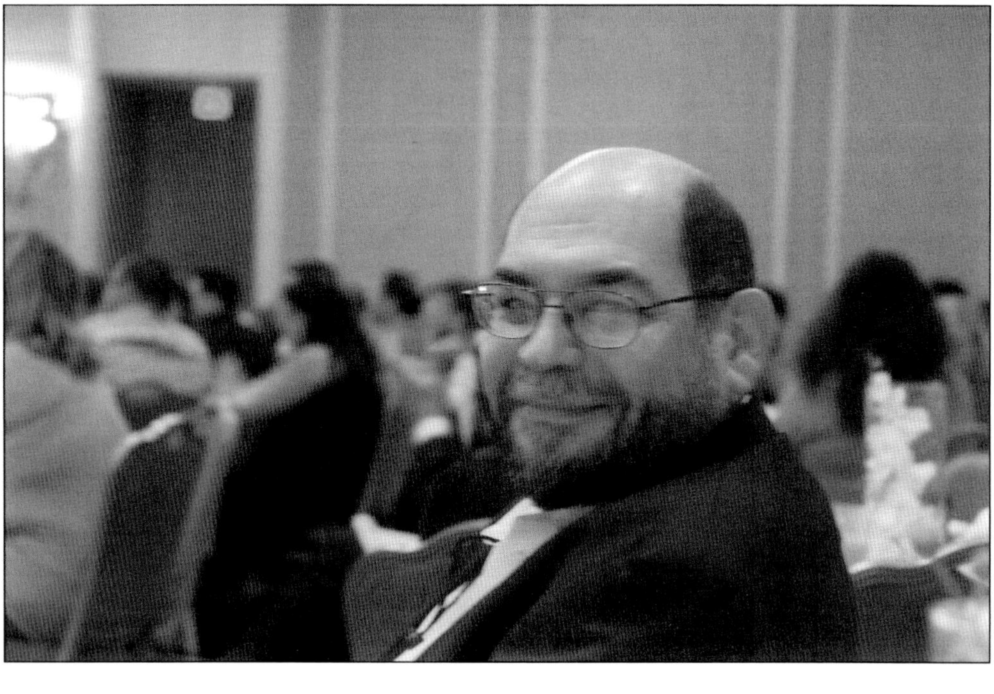

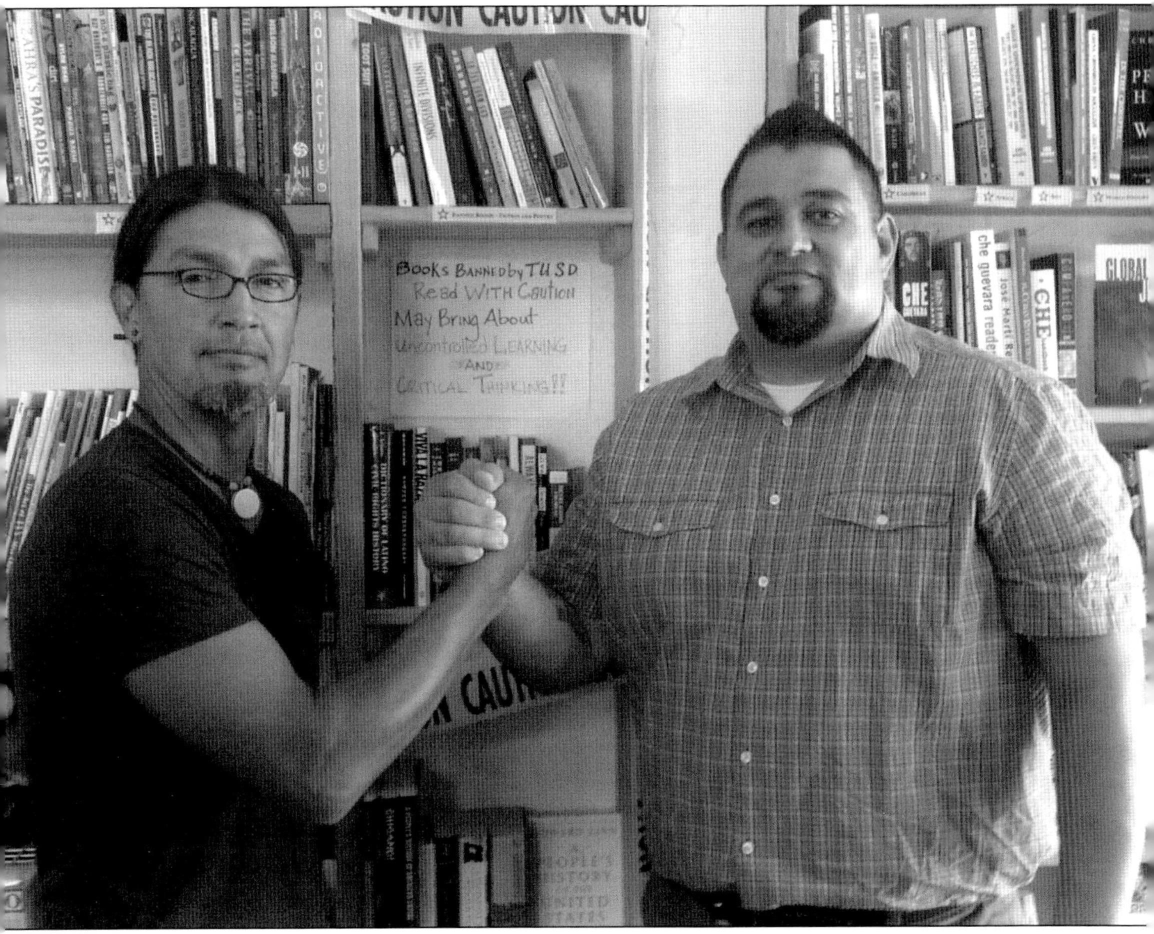

In 1998, in order to address the problem of Chicano students dropping out of high school in Tucson, Arizona, the Tucson Unified School District created the Mexican American studies program, a Chicano-centered curriculum that permitted dual-language instruction and met with great success. In 2012, however, program director Sean Arce (right), teacher José Rodríguez (left), and the program's entire staff lost their jobs after the State of Arizona banned the program. TACHE members have engaged in fundraising to help them fight the decision. (Courtesy of Sean Arce.)

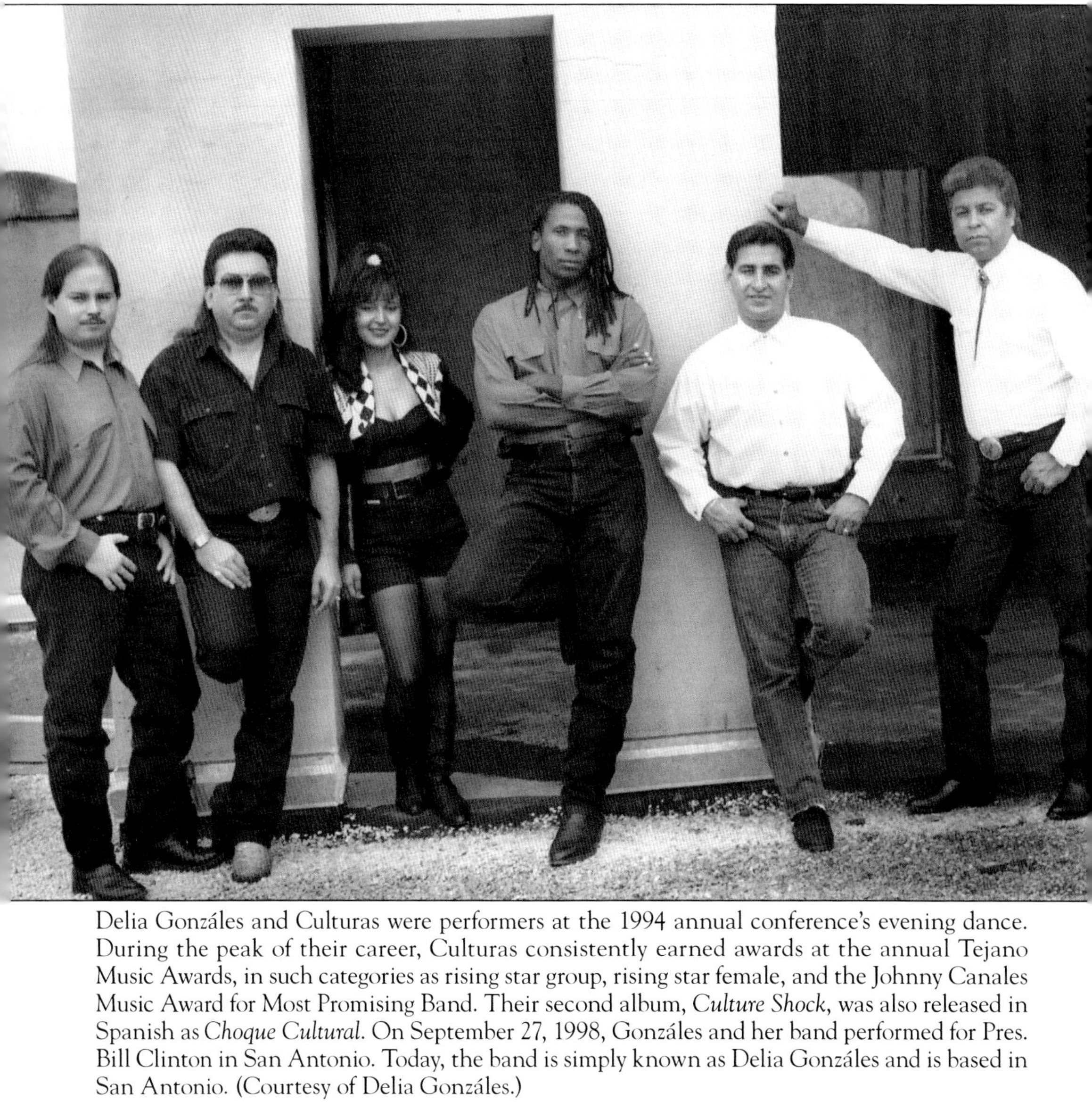

Delia Gonzáles and Culturas were performers at the 1994 annual conference's evening dance. During the peak of their career, Culturas consistently earned awards at the annual Tejano Music Awards, in such categories as rising star group, rising star female, and the Johnny Canales Music Award for Most Promising Band. Their second album, *Culture Shock*, was also released in Spanish as *Choque Cultural*. On September 27, 1998, Gonzáles and her band performed for Pres. Bill Clinton in San Antonio. Today, the band is simply known as Delia Gonzáles and is based in San Antonio. (Courtesy of Delia Gonzáles.)

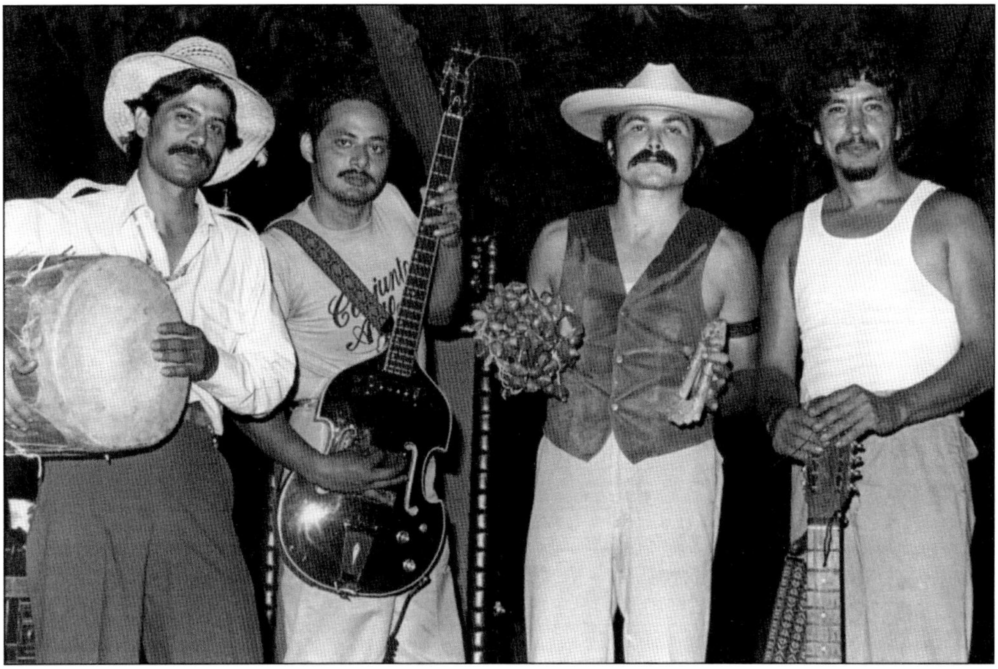

Juan Tejeda (third from left) and Conjunto Aztlán performed at the 2003 and 2013 annual TACHE conferences. The annual conference always includes musical entertainment. In some years, the entire event ends with a dance, or, as TACHE members call it, "el TACHEton," a play on words combining TACHE and *cachete*, or "cheek," because the event features TACHE members dancing cheek-to-cheek. (Courtesy of Juan Tejeda.)

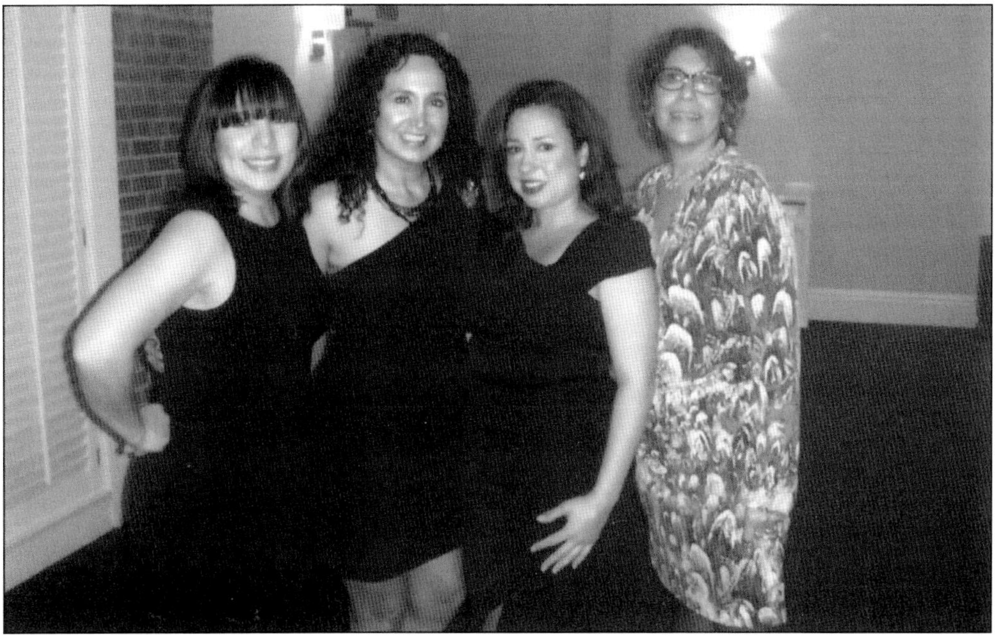

Seen here at a "TACHEton" are, from left to right, Leticia Spillane (Laredo), Ana Broadwater (Austin), Marissa Guerrero-Longoria (Laredo), and Mary Sue Galindo (Laredo). (Courtesy of Ana Broadwater.)

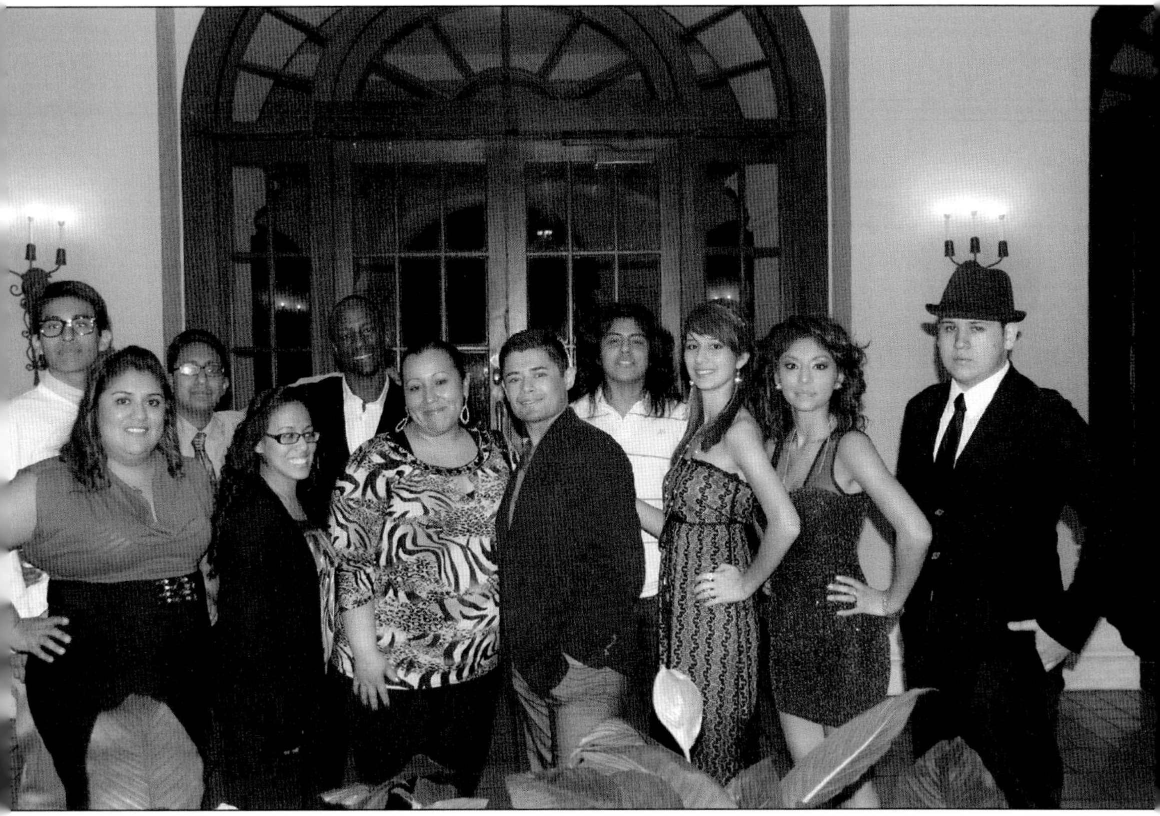

Seen here from left to right are (first row) Lucy Rojas, Nitza Gómez, Leticia Villarreal, Nelson Pacheco, Julieta Flores, Melissa Anaya, and José Almeda; (second row) Mynor Efraín-Millán, Daniel Sandoval, Shamir Iga, and Emmanuel Rincón, students of Tarrant County College. After dancing into the night, many TACHE members skip the more important meeting about finances. The last day of the conference is usually reserved for the first meeting of the newly elected board of directors and officers. At this business meeting, financial reports are made to the membership, election results of officers and regional representatives are certified, and the first quarterly board meeting is held. (Courtesy of Natalia Verjat Gutiérrez.)

Four

The President's Gallery

The dual secrets to effective leadership are solid work, practicing followership, and developing leaders from among the followers. The commitment to TACHE as president is a solid one of personal time, expense, and retreat from family obligations for a minimum of three years or more. Most presidents first begin a relationship with TACHE as members, faculty, or students, and then perhaps serve as regional representatives or statewide officers before seeking election to the presidency.

A member is first president-elect for a year before serving as president the following year, and then serves as immediate past president for another year on the board of directors and various standing committees. Five people have been TACHE president twice, beginning with Dr. Leonard Valverde, in 1975 and 1976, Dr. Jude Valdez, Félix Zamora, Gus Cedillo, and Julie Arias, in 2010 and 2014.

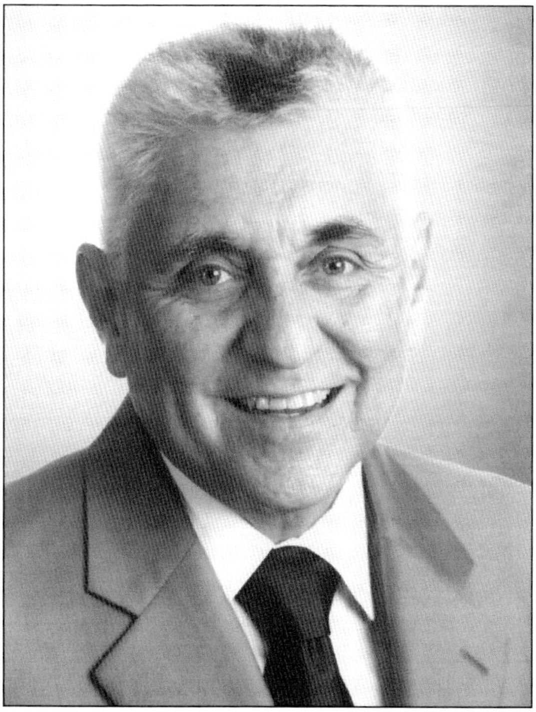

George Reyes, the 2013 TACHE president, is the dean of student services at the Pinnacle Campus of Austin Community College. Reyes has been a TACHE member for years, working up the ranks from supporter to member to regional representative to president. (Courtesy of George Reyes.)

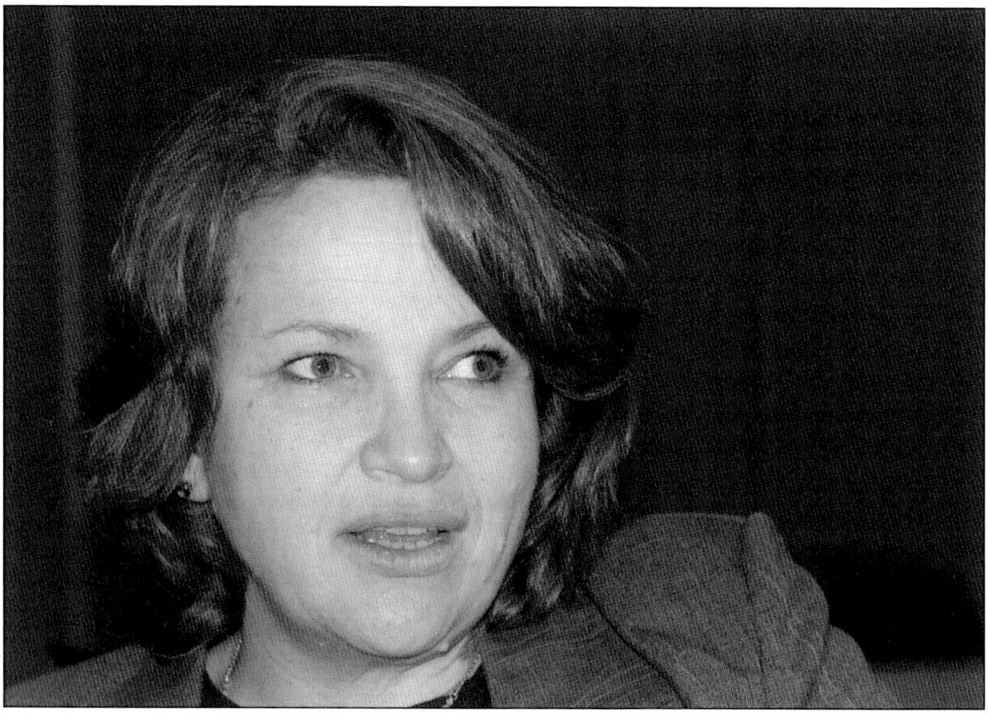

Julie Arias, the 2013 president-elect, pictured on her second time as president, is one of the five two-time presidents TACHE has had over the years. She is in constant motion and infects others with her energy. Although not of Mexican ancestry, she puts others to shame in her commitment to the advocacy of Latino interests. (Courtesy of Natalia Verjat Gutiérrez.)

Linda Rodríguez (right), the 1991 TACHE president, hands Sylvia H. Rodríguez, the TACHE president-elect, a presidential gavel plaque as a gift. This duo was the second set of Chicanas to be TACHE presidents back-to-back. (Courtesy of Sylvia Rodríguez.)

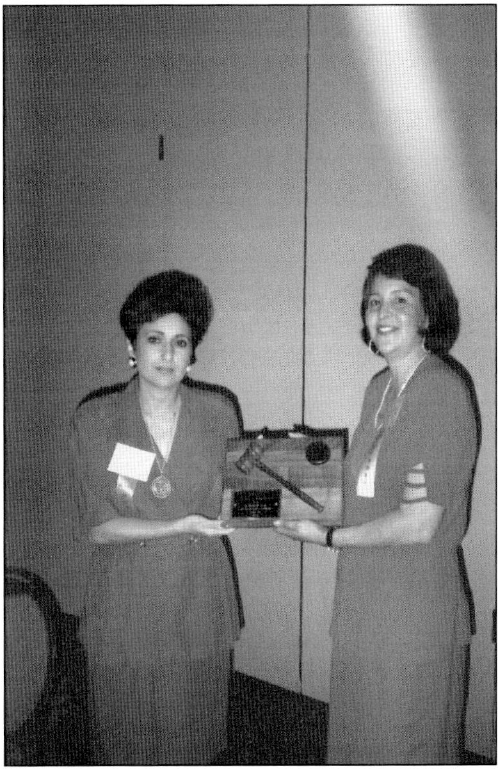

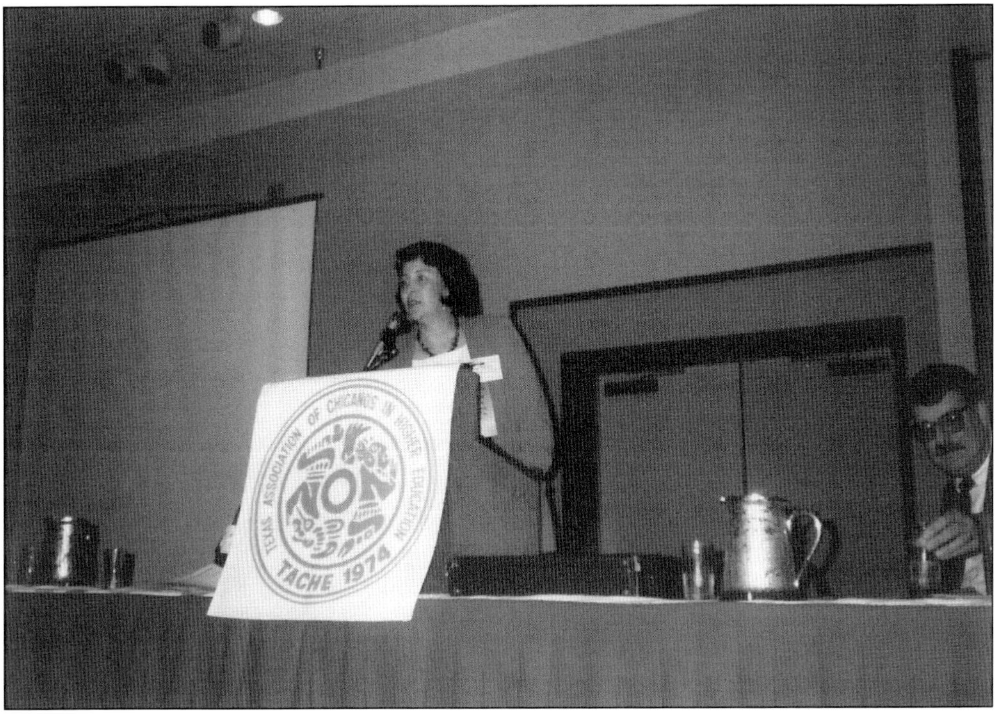

TACHE president Linda Rodríguez presides over the inaugural banquet at the 1991 annual conference. (Courtesy of Sylvia Rodríguez.)

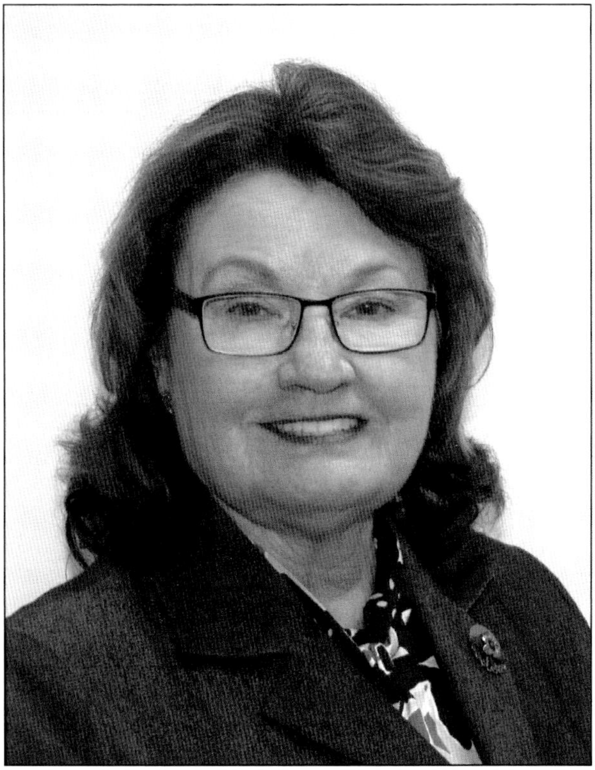

The TACHE conference of 1989 was led by TACHE president Dr. Adriana Barrera, who is currently the deputy chancellor of East Los Angeles Community College District. Her election was significant in that female leaders were voted into the presidency of TACHE for several consecutive years. Dr. Barrera was succeeded in office by Linda Rodríguez, Sylvia Rodríguez, Rosario Torres-Raínes, and, finally, R. Yvette Clark, in 1993. The first female president of TACHE was Margaret Garza of St. Mary's University, who was elected in 1979. (Courtesy of Sylvia Rodríguez.)

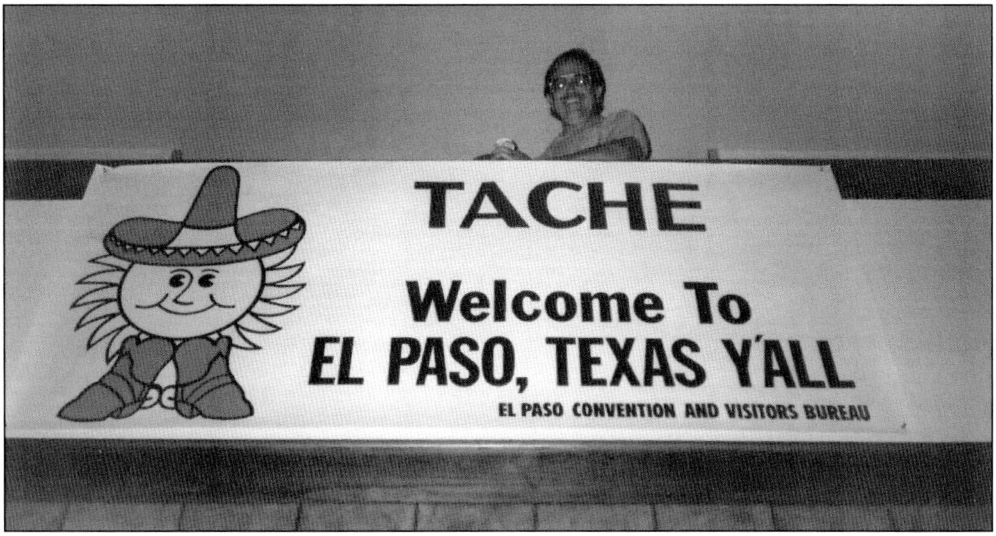

Dr. Sonny Barrera, the assistant vice president for student affairs at Southwest Texas State University in San Marcos, placed this banner for all to see. During the 1982 conference, in El Paso, several resolutions were adopted, and amendments were made to the constitution, mostly tweaking the duties of various committees and coordinators regarding dues, voting, and institutional membership. A controversial amendment was proposed from the floor. The December 1982 issue of *Noticiario* wrote, "The proposed amendment to change TACHE' name to the Texas Association of Hispanics in Higher Education died for lack of a second. I hope this issue is behind us now." (Courtesy of Jesse Rangel.)

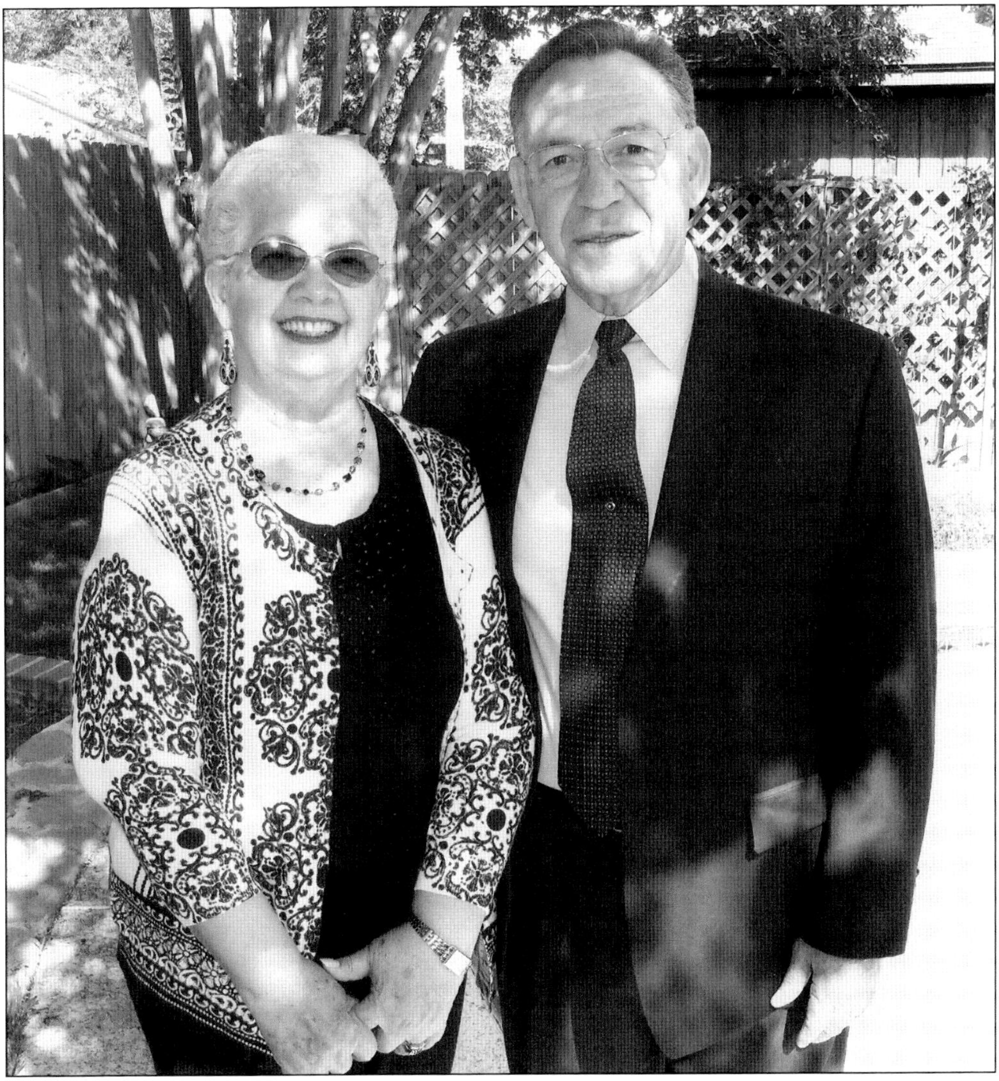

Ed Apodaca, seen here with his wife, LaVerne, was the TACHE president in 1999. On September 18, 1982, TACHE's funds were reported to be $6,730.31, and the budget was $5,700. The following year, 1983, TACHE's theme for the Houston conference was "The 1980s: Decade of the Chicano: A Three Year Report Card." As president-elect, Apodaca made the report card his cornerstone for advocacy. He presented the report card, a list of Texas public universities and community colleges graded on how well they fared in number of Chicano students enrolled and graduating, and number of Chicano faculty by rank and by percentage of the whole, among other criteria. The 2003 TACHE president Che Guzmán dropped the report card because her institution was negatively rated. In 2005, TACHE president Arturo Vega brought the report card back and made a presentation in which he said, "We were trying to be an advocacy group for Latino students and faculty, and we can't have the hard conversations because it would impact your funding?" TACHE solicits monetary support from these same colleges and universities, who act as conference sponsors and institutional members. As a past president and a member, Apodaca continued issuing his report card, the Texas Higher Education Hispanic Report, until 2010. While he was TACHE president-elect, he raised more than $40,000 for the conference. (Courtesy of Ed Apodaca.)

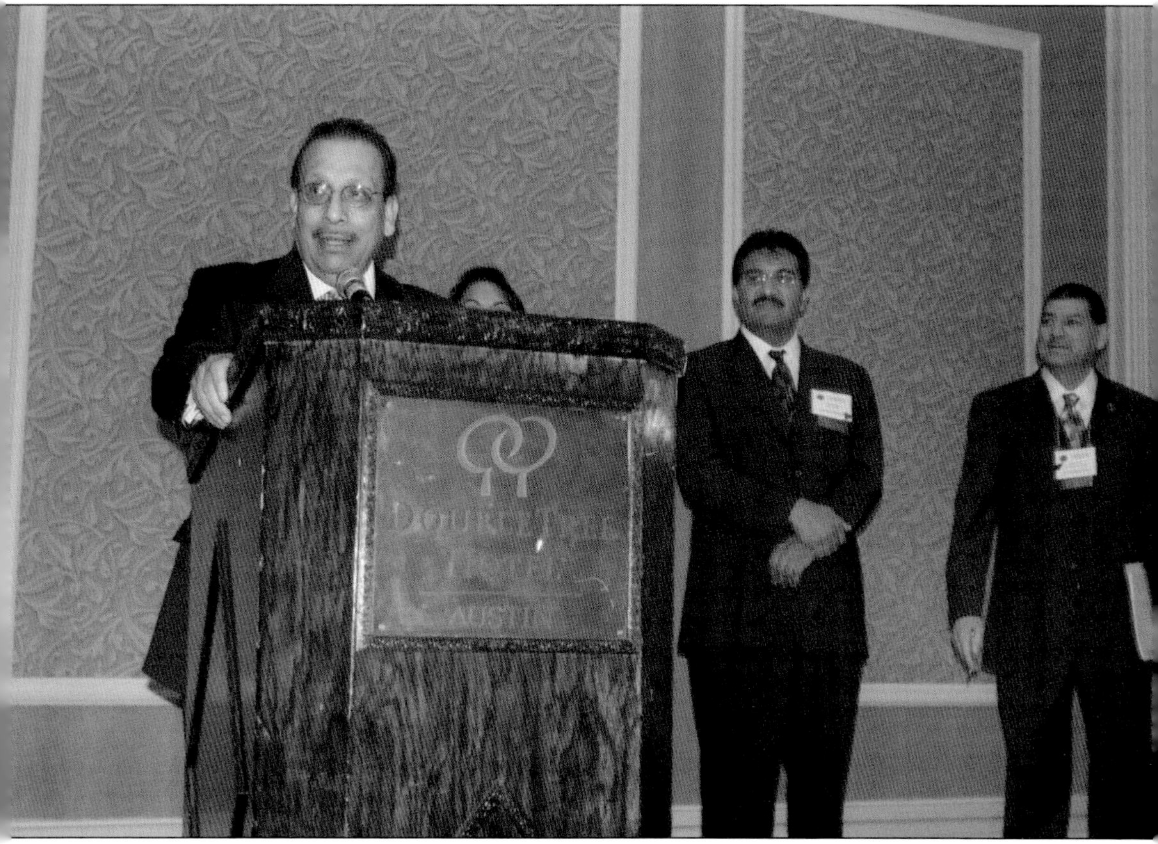

TACHE president Félix Zamora presided over the 25th annual conference, in 2001. This conference was highlighted by two remarkable events. First, TACHE held a policy forum that featured Don Brown, the commissioner of the Texas Higher Education Coordinating Board; regents of various systems; presidents of various universities, including UT-Austin's Larry F. Faulkner, Ann Stuart of Texas Woman's University, and Tito I. Guerrero III of Stephen F. Austin State University; and 28 members of the state legislature. Tony Sánchez, a regent of the University of Texas system, gave a keynote address in which he announced that he would run for governor of Texas in 2002. (Courtesy of Tito Guerrero.)

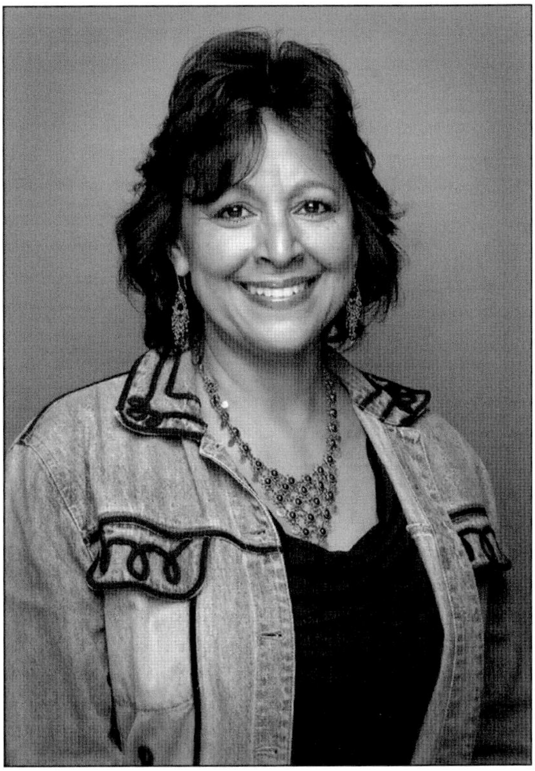

Dr. Angela Valenzuela, a professor of education in the department of curriculum and instruction at the University of Texas at Austin, held a book signing at the 2001 annual conference for her award-winning book *Subtractive Schooling: U.S. Mexican Youth and the Politics of Caring* (below). Her more recent book is *Leaving Children Behind: How "Texas-style" Accountability Fails Latino Youth*. She directs the Texas Center for Education Policy and has also directed the National Latino Education Research Agenda Project since 2009. (Courtesy of Angela Valenzuela.)

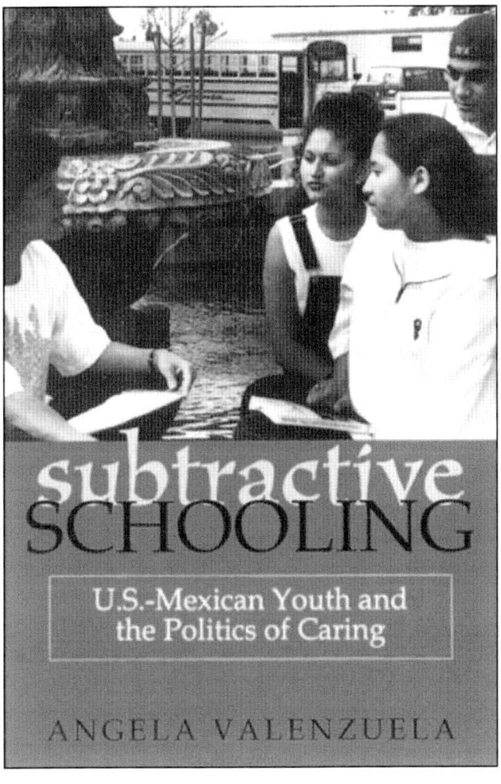

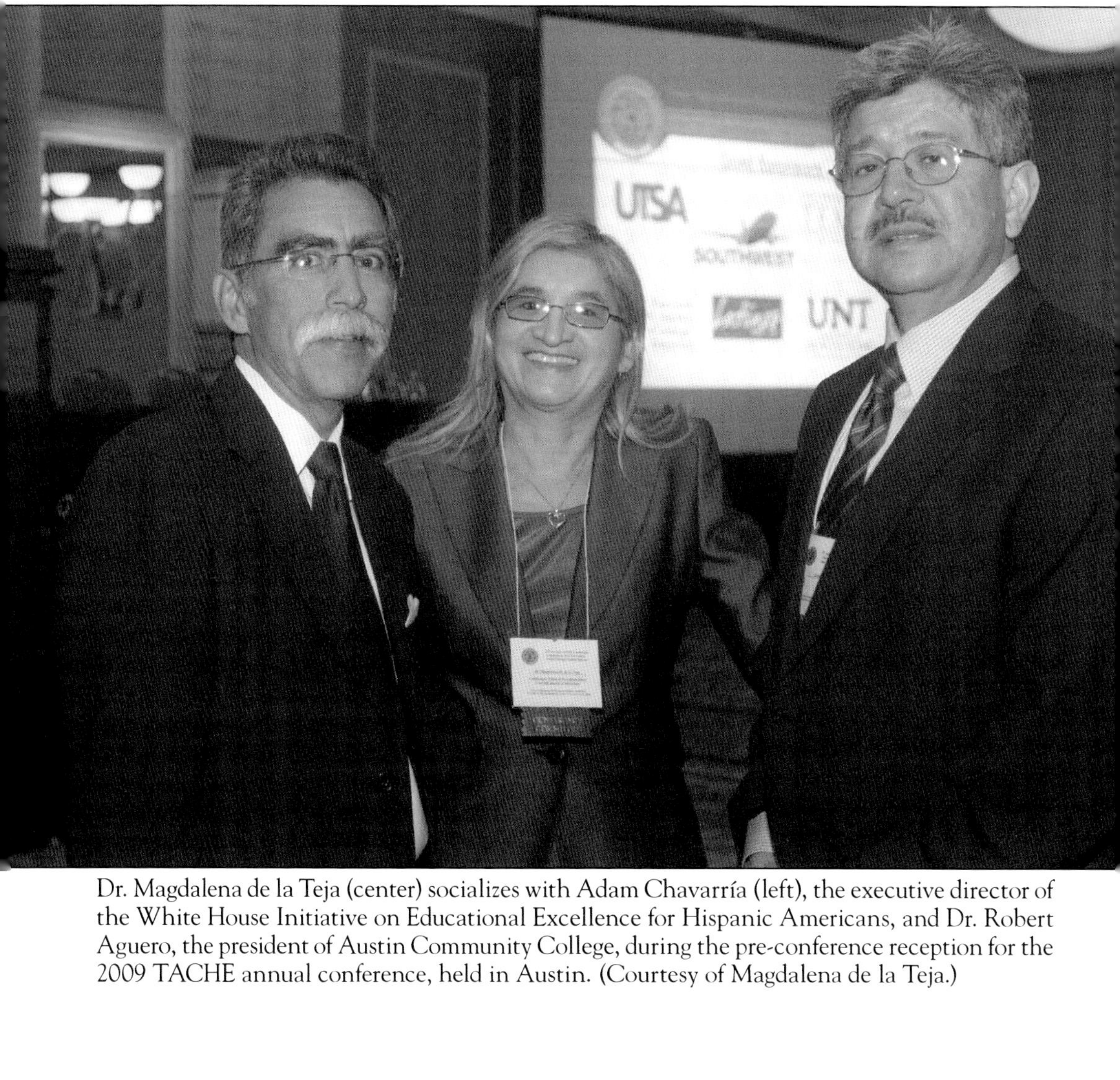

Dr. Magdalena de la Teja (center) socializes with Adam Chavarría (left), the executive director of the White House Initiative on Educational Excellence for Hispanic Americans, and Dr. Robert Aguero, the president of Austin Community College, during the pre-conference reception for the 2009 TACHE annual conference, held in Austin. (Courtesy of Magdalena de la Teja.)

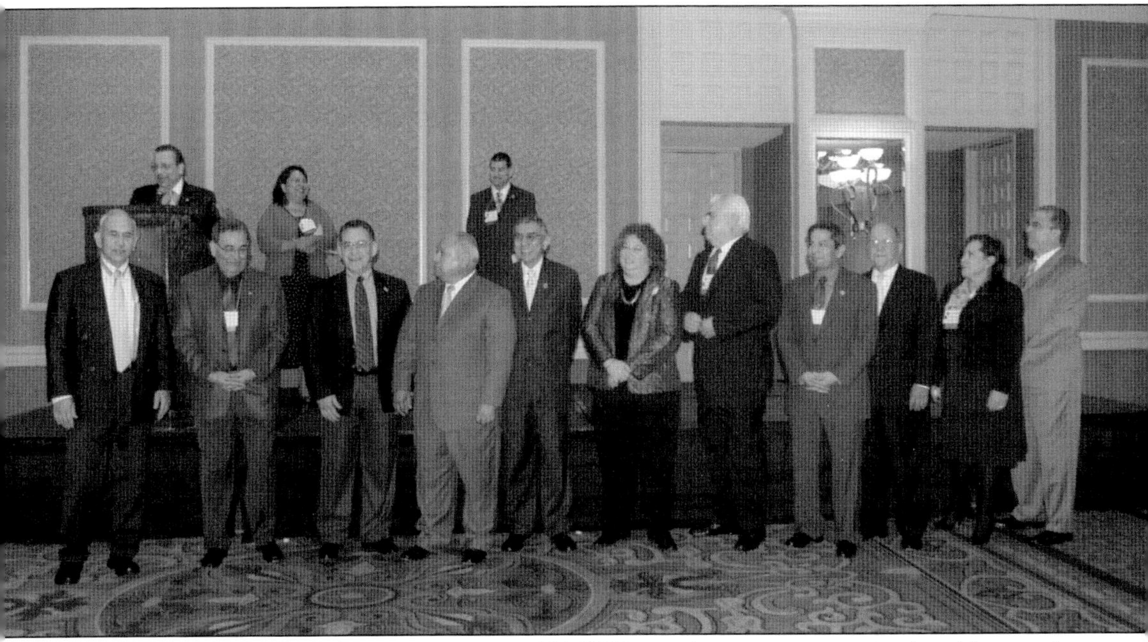

At this 2009 annual conference event, past TACHE presidents were recognized and honored at the president's reception. They are, from left to right, (first row) Dr. Max Castillo, Dr. Rudy Rodríguez, Ed Apodaca, Dr. Juan Maldonado, Dr. Jude Valdez, Yvette Clark, Dr. Ramón Dovalina, Gil Castillo, Dr. Daniel Hernández, Mary Helen Padilla, Dr. Joel Vela; (second row) Félix Zamora, event chair Linda Rodríguez, and Gus Cedillo. Each president-elect recruits volunteers to assist in the various facets of organizing the annual conference, including finding the location and hotel, fundraising, and organizing the program, presenters, awards, entertainment, food menus, and equipment needs. (Courtesy of Magdalena de la Teja.)

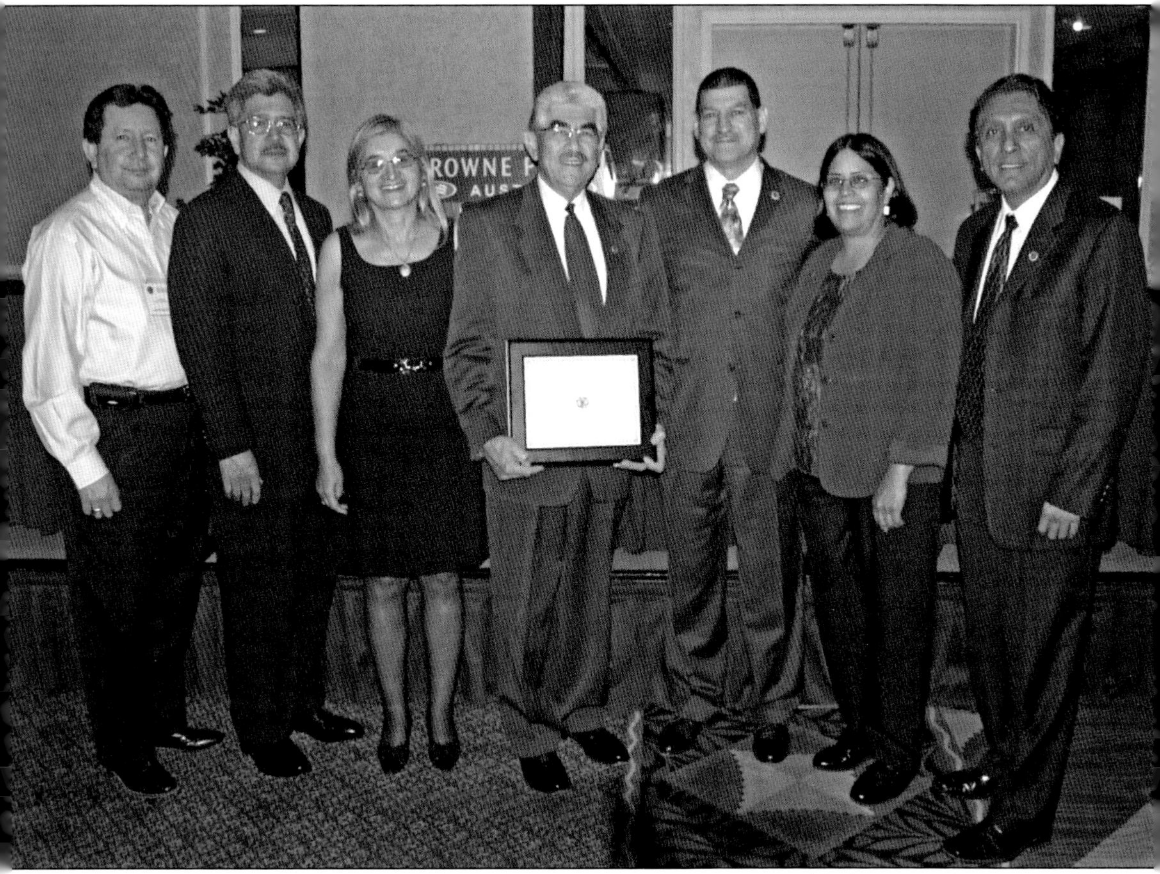

Together, TACHE president Dr. Magdalena de la Teja and Dr. Leonard de la Garza, the chancellor of the Tarrant County Community College District, each donated $5,000 to match TACHE's donation of $10,000 to form the $20,000 core of the TACHE endowment in 2010. Seen here celebrating are, from left to right, Juan García, the vice president of student development services for the Tarrant County Community College District, South Campus; Dr. Robert Aguero, the vice chancellor of the Tarrant District; Dr. de la Teja; Dr. de la Garza; Gus Cedillo; and Dr. Lily Tercero and Dr. Ricardo Coronado, associate vice chancellors of the Tarrant County Community College District. (Courtesy of Magdalena de la Teja.)

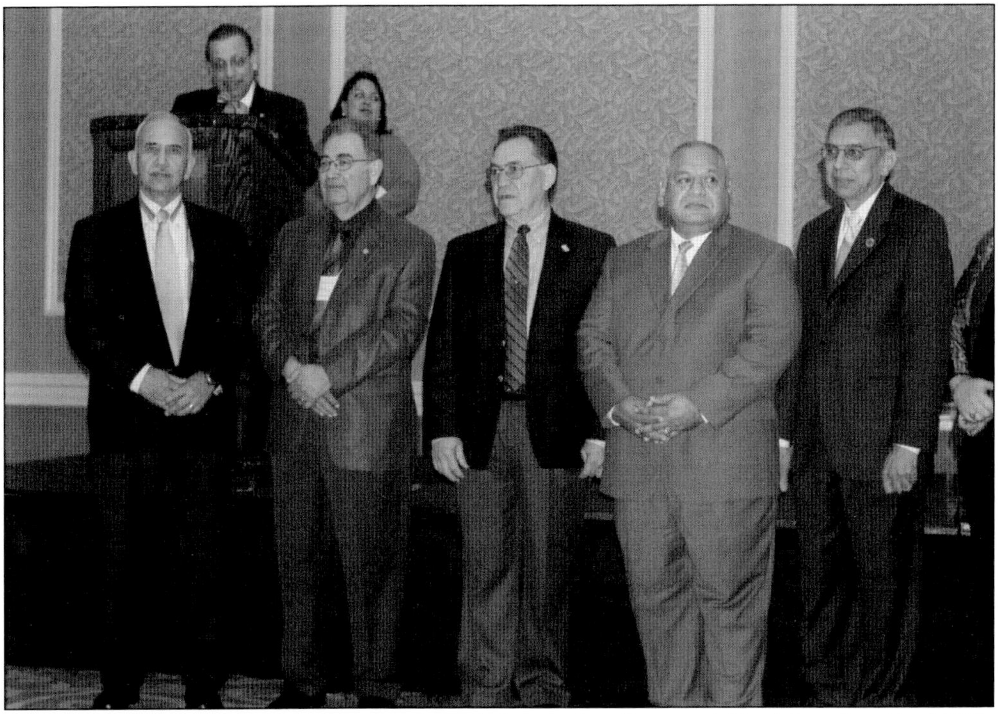

These former TACHE presidents are, from left to right, (first row) Dr. Max Castillo (1983), Dr. Rudy Rodríguez (2002), Ed Apodaca (1999), Dr. Juan Maldonado (1998), and Dr. Jude Valdez (1985, 2000); (at podium) Félix Zamora (1996, 2001). (Courtesy of Magdalena de la Teja.)

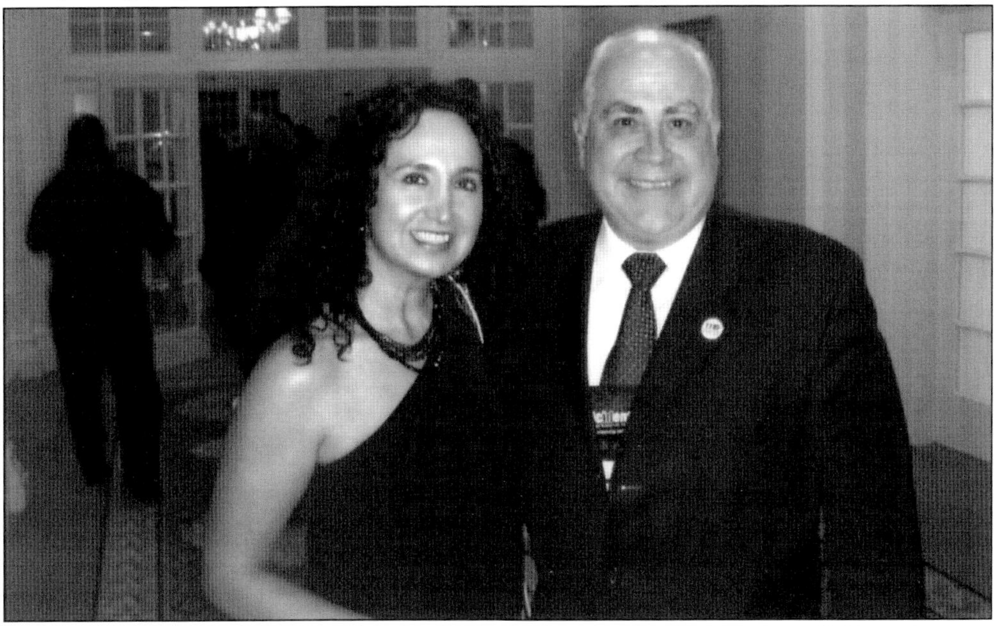

Dr. William Flores, the president of the University of Houston-Downtown since 2009, is a frequent speaker, participant, and supporter of TACHE since relocating to Texas from New Mexico. Ana Broadwater has been a member of Austin TACHE for years and is an annual volunteer at the state conference, ready to take on any tasks. (Courtesy of Ana Broadwater.)

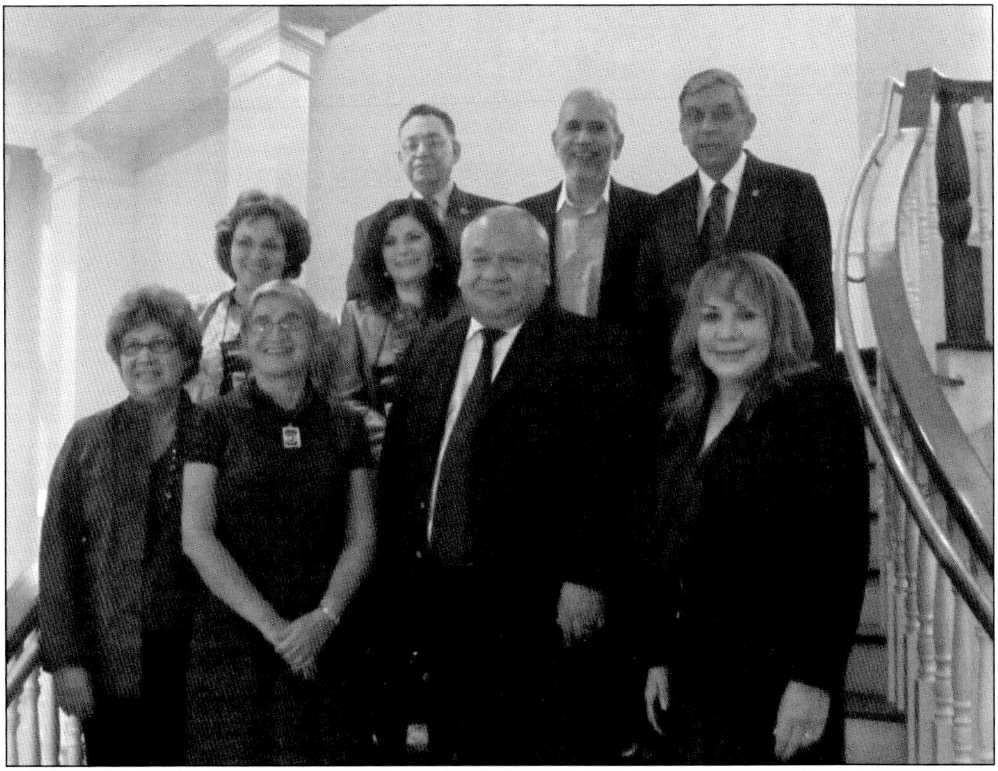

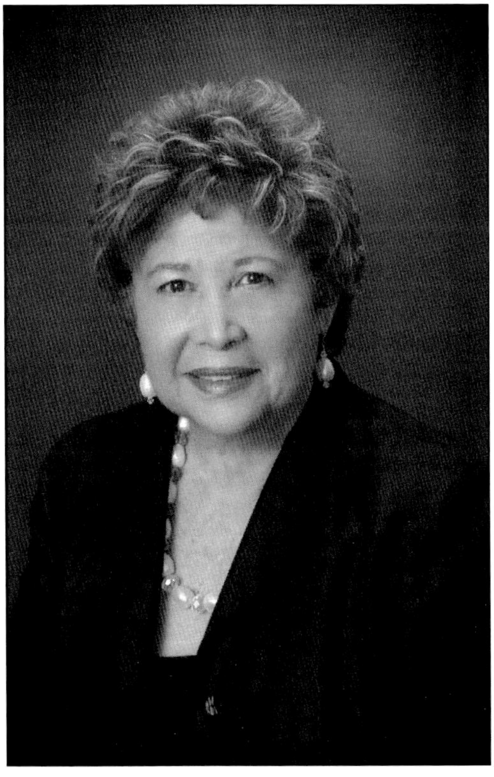

Former TACHE presidents are seen here at the 37th annual TACHE conference, held in Galveston. They are (first row) Linda Contreras Bullock, 2012; Magdalena de la Teja, 2008; Juan Maldonado, 1997–1998; Rosario Martínez Castillo, 2006; (second row) Julie Arias, 2010 and 2014; and Criselda Leal, 2011; (third row) Ed Apodaca, 1998; Max Castillo, 1982; and Jude Valdez, 1984 and 1999. (Courtesy of Natalia Verjat Gutiérrez.)

Linda Contreras Bullock of the University of Houston–Clear Lake was the TACHE president-elect in 2012 and held the annual conference at the Tremont House in Galveston, the first time it was held in that city. As president in 2013, she was instrumental in making major revisions, tweaking operations, and drafting procedures to ensure that the organization was run efficiently. (Courtesy of Linda Contreras Bullock.)

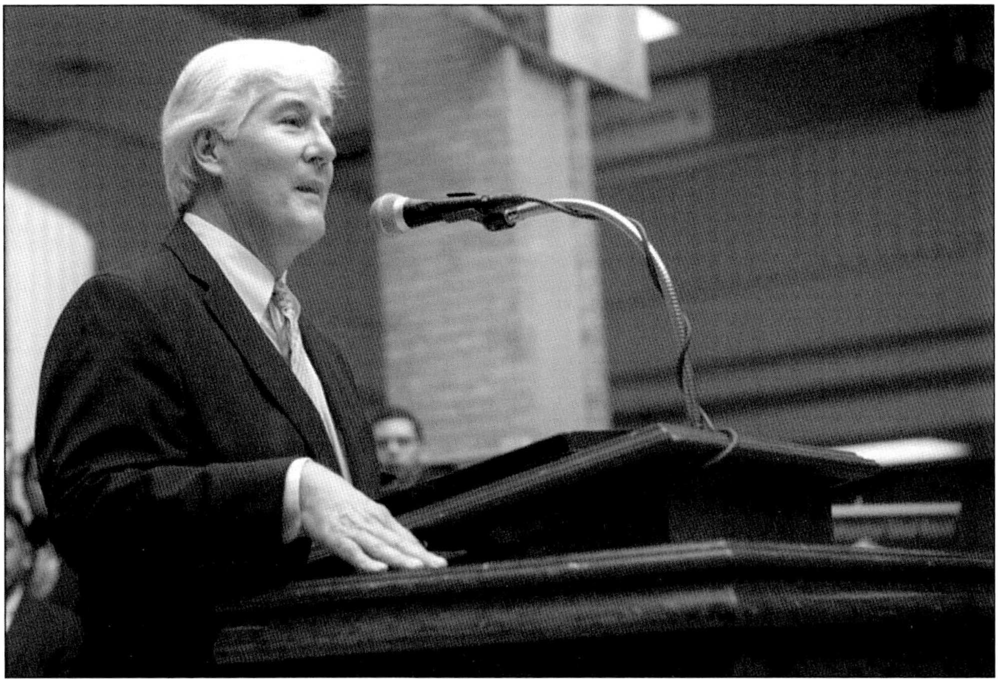

Seen here is Dr. Raymund Paredes, the Texas commissioner of higher education. Early in his tenure as commissioner, he convened a task force of educators that was heavily represented by TACHE members from across the state, called the Closing the Gaps for Latino Students Task Force. (Courtesy of Magdalena de la Teja.)

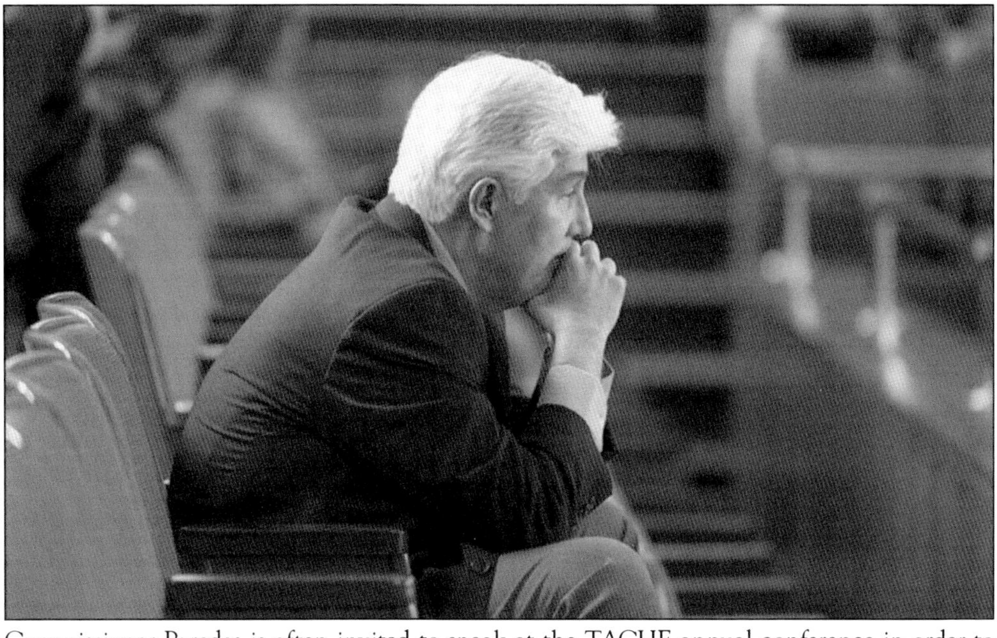

Commissioner Paredes is often invited to speak at the TACHE annual conference in order to bring the membership up to date on the state of higher education. Equally as often, his message is not well received, given the austerity measures imposed by the legislature on public education, and higher education in particular. (Courtesy of Magdalena de la Teja.)

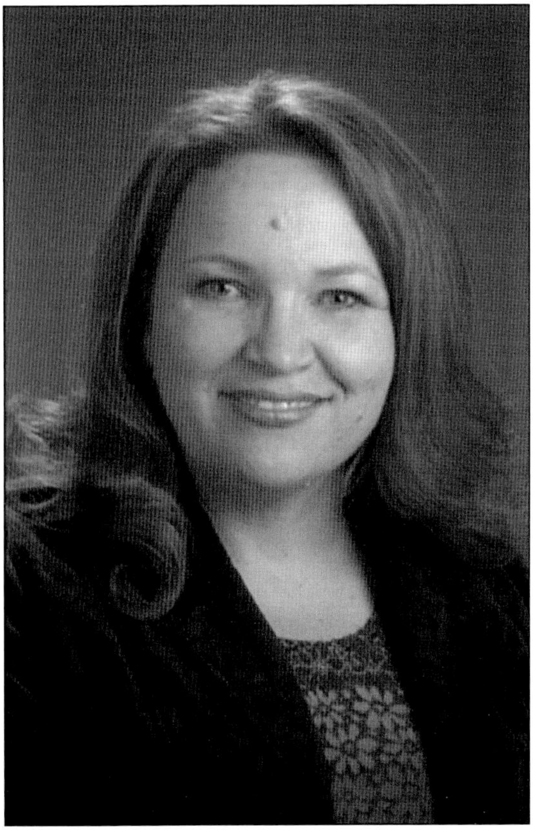

Julie Arias, the TACHE president in 2010 and now again in 2014, is a former ESL teacher in the Amarillo public school system who is now the executive director of university outreach at West Texas A&M University. She is also a licensed professional counselor. (Courtesy of María Guerrero.)

As TACHE's executive administrator, María Guerrero does a full-time job for a part-time salary and is always busy at work. Julie Arias, during her first presidency in 2010, was instrumental in obtaining major support from her institution, West Texas A&M University, in Canyon. She set up the first TACHE office there and recruited Guerrero as the first paid staff member. (Courtesy of María Guerrero.)

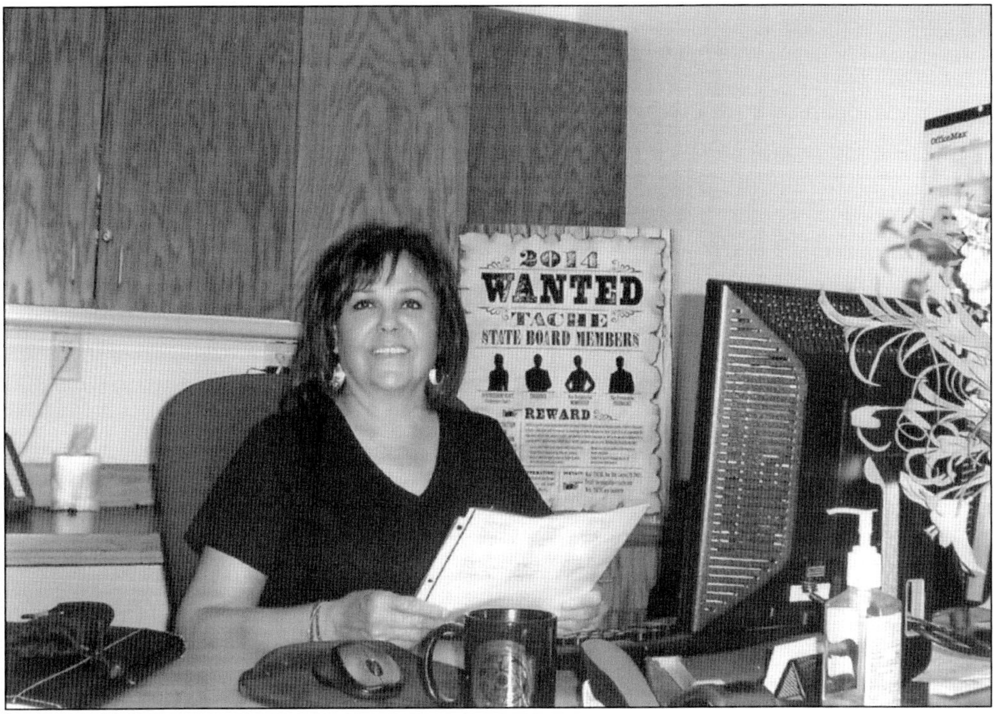

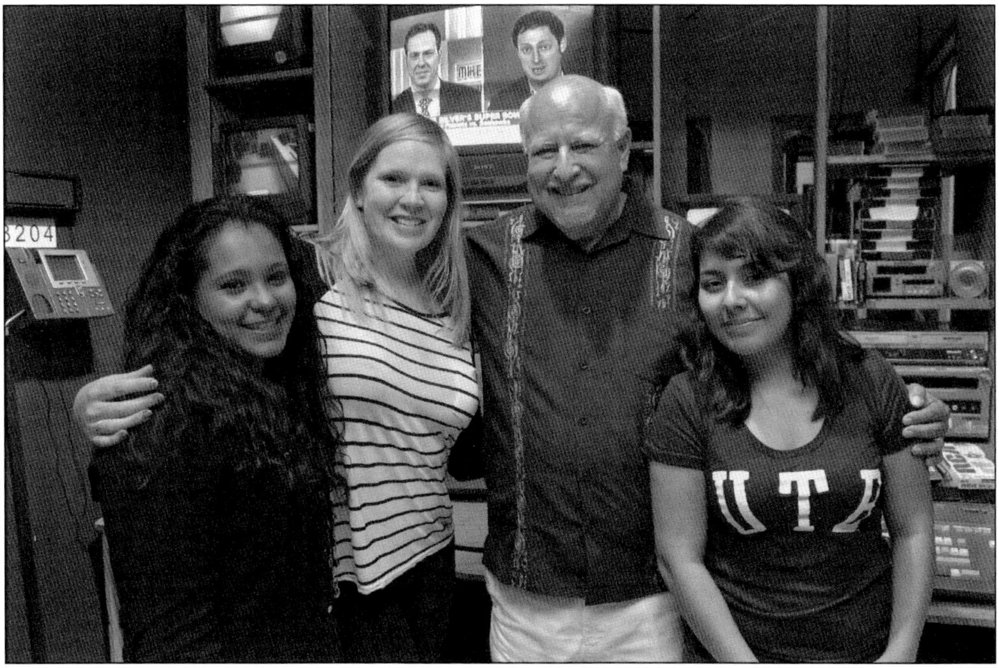

Dr. Manuel Medrano, a history professor at the University of Texas at Brownsville, represents TACHE's south Texas region. The Houston Endowed Chair for Civic Engagement, Dr. Medrano was also honored with the University of Texas Board of Regents Outstanding Teacher Award in 2009. (Courtesy of Manuel Medrano.)

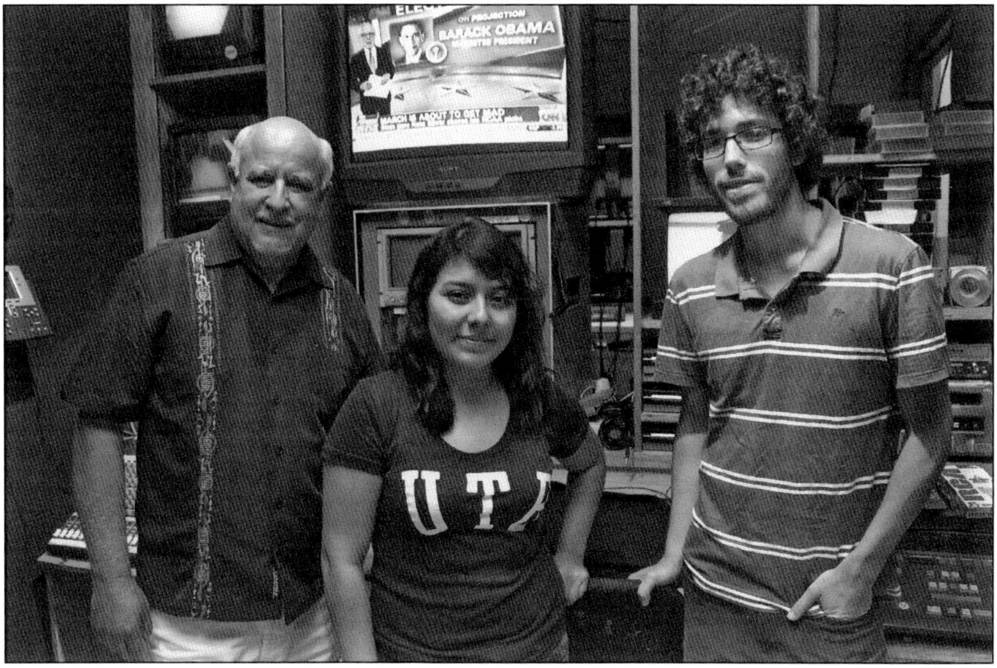

Dr. Medrano is also the creator and producer of Los Del Valle, an oral history project on public figures in southern Texas. He presented his work at the 2010 TACHE annual conference. Dr. Medrano is seen here with UTEP students. (Courtesy of Manuel Medrano.)

014 Julie Arias
013 George Reyes
012 Linda Contreras-Bullock
011 Criselda Leal
010 Julie Arias
009 Gustavo F. Cedillo
008 Magdalena H. de la Teja
007 Gustavo F. Cedillo
006 Rosario Martinez Castillo
005 Arturo Vega
004 Elías Villarreal
003 Ana "Cha" Guzmán
002 Rudy Rodríguez
001 Rudy Rodríquez

2000 Félix Zamora
1999 Jude Valdez
1998 Ed Apodaca
1997 Juan Maldonado
1996 Daniel Hernández
1995 Félix Zamora
1994 Gil Castillo
1993 R. Yvette Clark
1992 Rosario Torres Raines
1991 Sylvia H. Rodriguez
1990 Linda Rodriguez
1989 Adriana Barrera
1988 Ramón Dovalina
1987 Joel Vela

1986 Mary Helen Padilla
1985 Sylvia Ramos
1984 Jude Valdez
1983 Baltazar Acevedo, J
1982 Max Castillo
1981 Frank Longoria
1980 Neptalí García
1979 Margaret Garza
1978 Ernesto Ramírez
1977 Michael Sáenz
1976 Leonard Valverde
1975 Leonard Valverde

This is a list of TACHE presidents through the years. (Courtesy of Dr. Rudy Rodríguez.)

Five

The Six Regions and Chapters

TACHE has been organized into six regional areas since it was founded. Members from each region elect their regional representatives during the annual conference. Serving as a regional representative provides good training for future TACHE presidents and state officers. Regional representatives are also members of the board of directors for the organization.

Today, the regional geography of the state is causing major problems for TACHE. In 1974, when the organization was founded, there were very few Chicano faculty and few Chicano students, so the few chapters and members could meet either on their campuses or at the annual conference. By 2000, the faculty and student ranks had increased, as had the number of TACHE chapters. In 2013, it is quite a task to drive from one end of the Panhandle to the other for regional meetings, and, similarly, it is laborious to contend with traffic to attend meetings in Houston, the center of the Gulf Coast region.

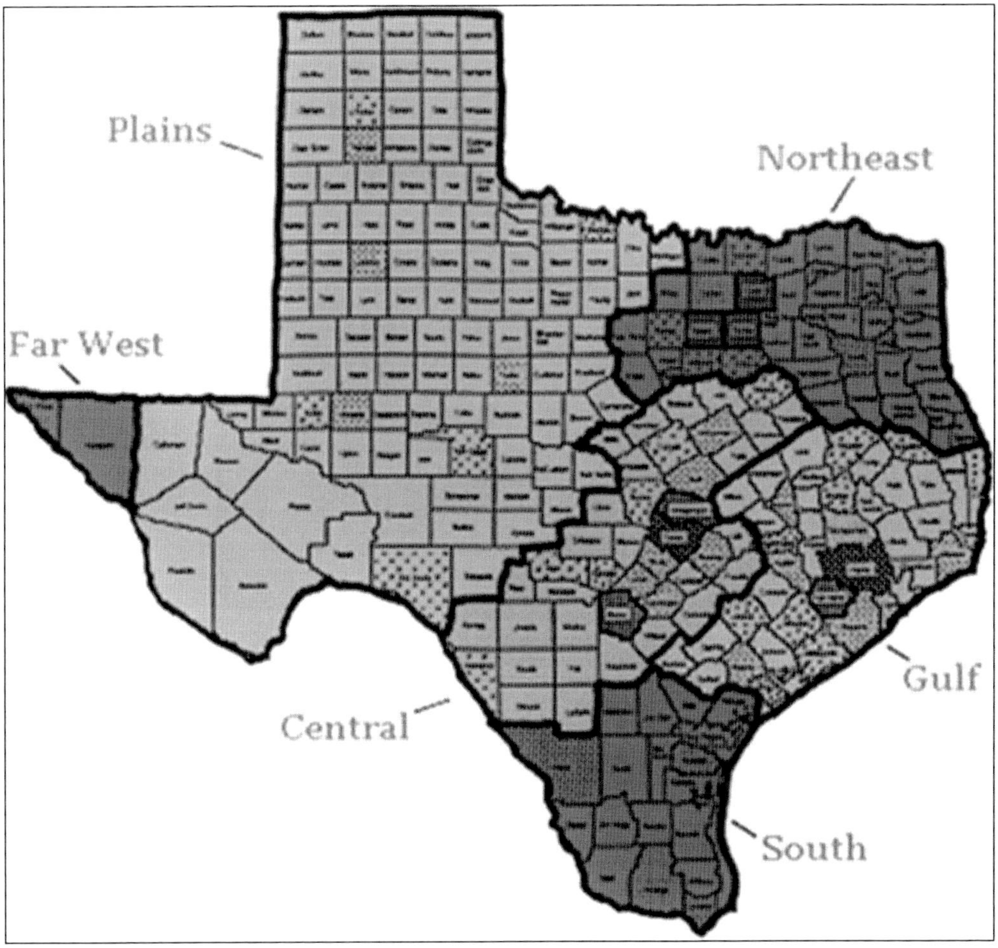

This map shows TACHE's six geographical regions.

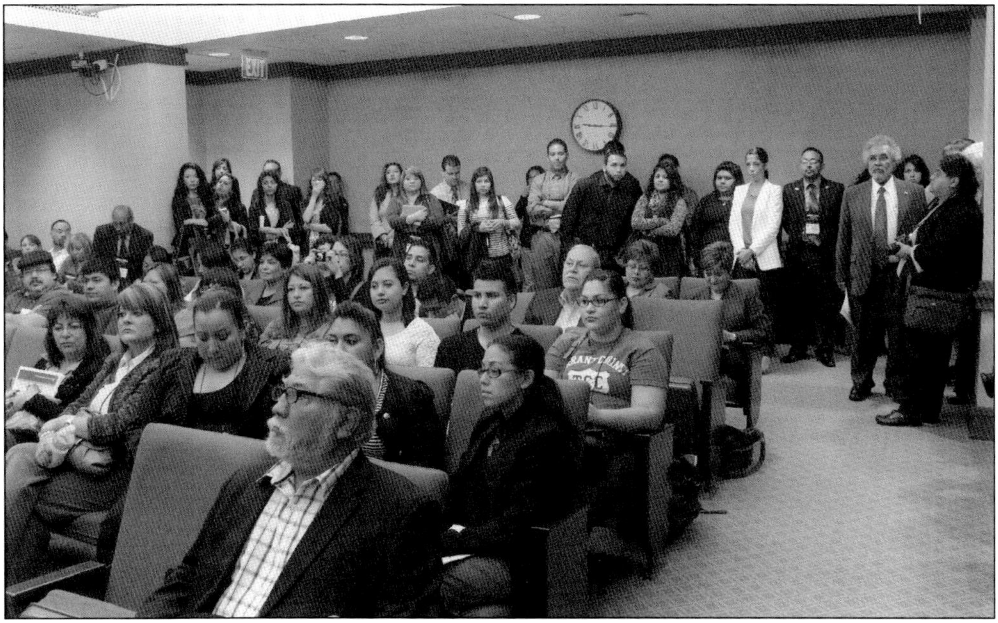

Dr. Reynaldo Garay (sitting, foreground), the dean of Houston Community College-Southeast, served as TACHE's Gulf Coast regional representative in 2000–2001. Serving with him as regional representatives during that term were Dr. María D. Salinas (South), Armando Díaz (Central), Gloria B. Bahamón (Northeast), Julio Llanas (Plains), and David Porras Jr. (Far West). Dr. Garay is still active with TACHE today. (Courtesy of Natalia Verjat Gutiérrez.)

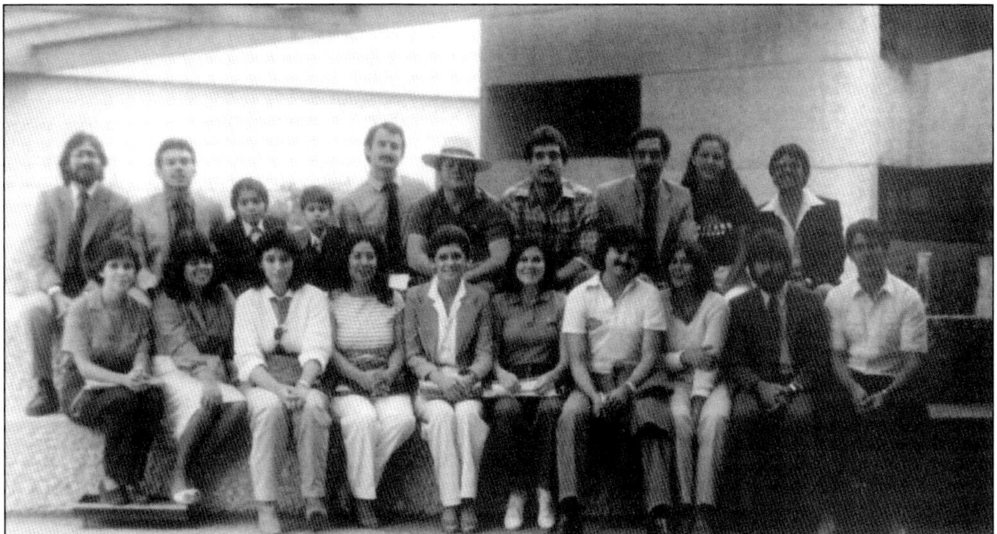

The University of Houston's Mexican American studies program was started in 1972. Dr. Tatcho Mindiola has been its director since succeeding Dr. Margarita B. Melville. Both have been TACHE members for years. Dr. Melville was among the early members, in 1978, while Dr. Mindiola is a frequent presenter at TACHE conferences. His program also contributes annually to the cost of the conference. Dr. Mindiola (second row, third from right) is seen here with students in the Becas Para Aztlán Intensive Study Mexico summer program at the Colegio De México in 1978. (Courtesy of Tatcho Mindiola.)

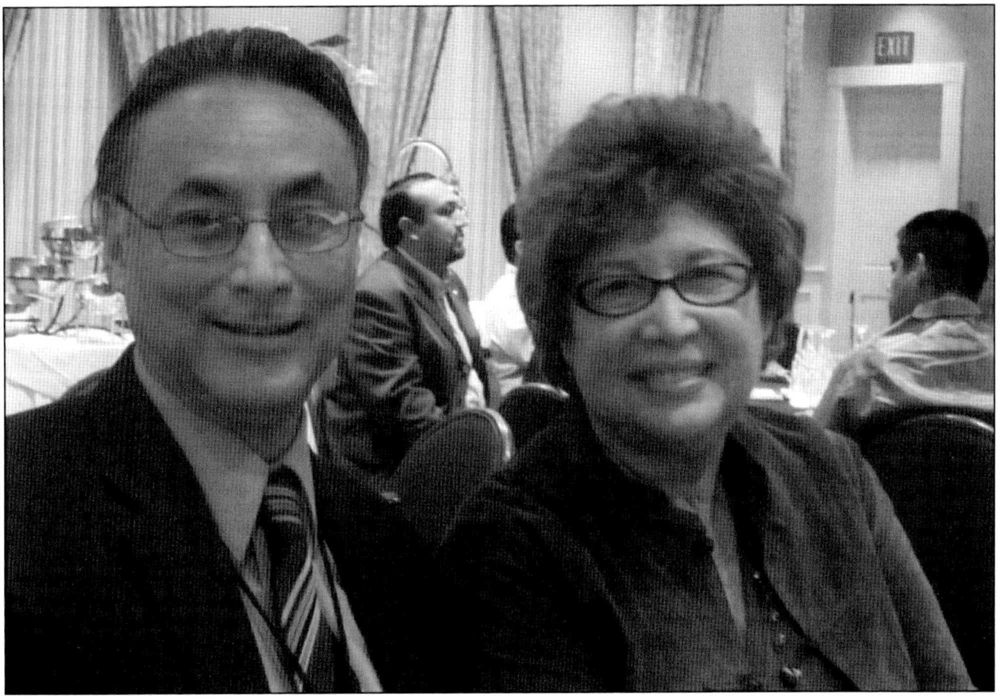

Lorenzo Cano is the associate director of the Mexican American studies program at the University of Houston and has been a TACHE member for many years. He has served as a Gulf Coast regional representative and attends the annual conference regularly. In 2013, he is once again the alternate representative for the area. Linda Contreras Bullock, a past TACHE president and Houston chapter member, is on the right. (Courtesy of Natalia Verjat Gutiérrez.)

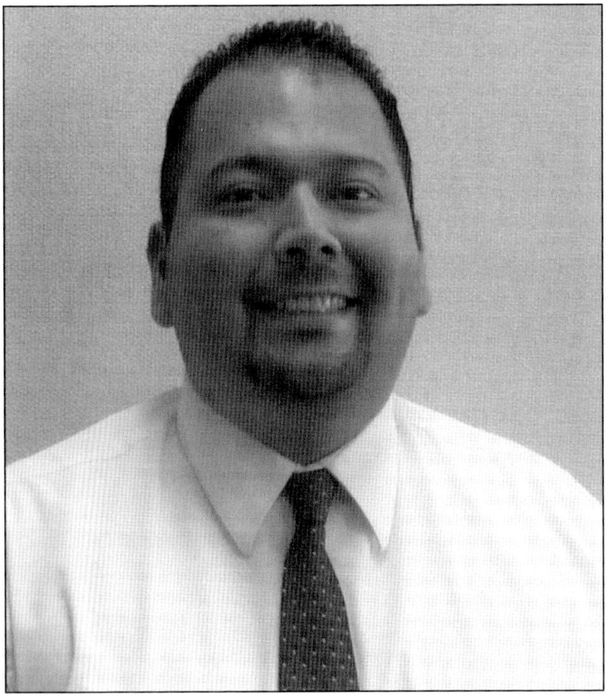

Saúl Zarco of San Jacinto College (SJC) is the current Gulf Coast regional representative. An educational planner, he began his TACHE membership in 2010 while a recruiter at Palo Alto College in San Antonio. He is a cosponsor of the student TACHE chapter at SJC with Dina Castillo, a professor of government. Zarco has begun the Latino Leadership Initiative at SJC, modeled after Harvard University's Latino Leadership Initiative, to increase Chicano and Latino student enrollment and graduation rates. (Courtesy of Saúl Zarco.)

The Del Mar TACHE chapter participates in the César Chávez Marcha, which involves teaching, mentoring, fundraising, and, of course, marching in honor of civil rights legend César Chávez. Seen here holding the TACHE banner are, from left to right, Guadalupe Valdez III, Blanca Ordner, Andrea Montalvo-Hamid, and Dr. Gilda E. Ramírez, who pushes future TACHE member Iliana Naíma Hamid in the stroller. (Courtesy of Gilda E. Ramírez.)

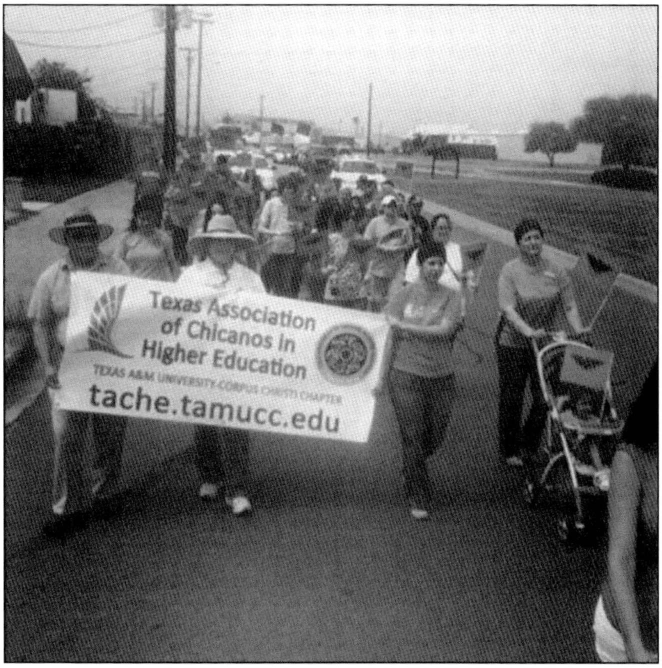

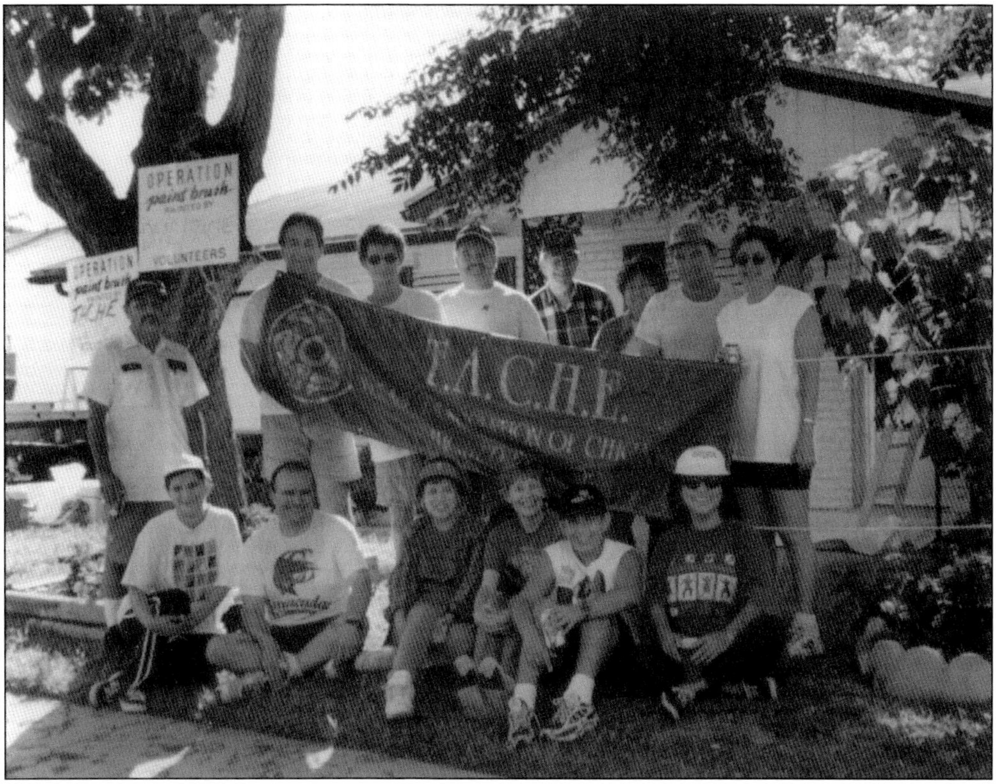

In 1988, TACHE chapter members from Del Mar College formed a painting crew to help residents paint their houses in Corpus Christi. They called the program Operation Paintbrush. This chapter is among the oldest groups formed and is still going strong today. (Courtesy of Gilda E. Ramírez.)

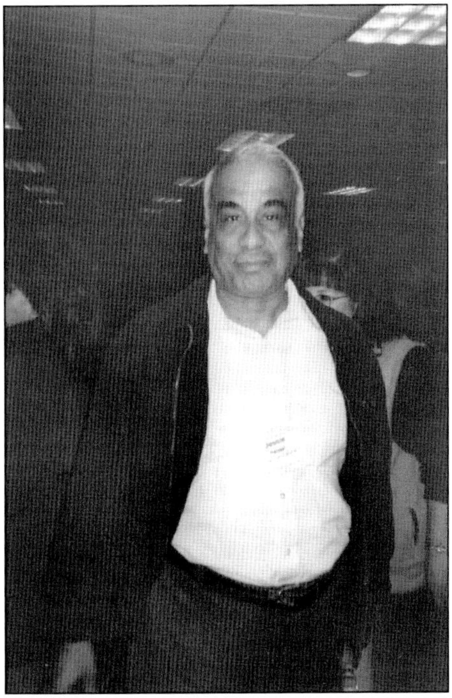

Seen here is Jesse Rangel, the Panhandle regional representative from 1975. The first regional representatives elected, in San Antonio in 1975, were Dr. José Juárez (South); Jesse Rangel (Panhandle); Oscar Valadez (Northeast); Margaret Garza (Central); Fidel De León (Far West); and Enrique Medrano (Gulf Area). In 1978, the regional representatives, also elected in San Antonio, were Derly Guajardo (South), Manuel L. Flores (Central), Dr. Margarita B. Melville (Gulf), Edward Sandoval (Northeast), Julio T. Llanas (Panhandle), and Dr. Saúl Sánchez (Far West). (Courtesy of José Angel Gutiérrez.)

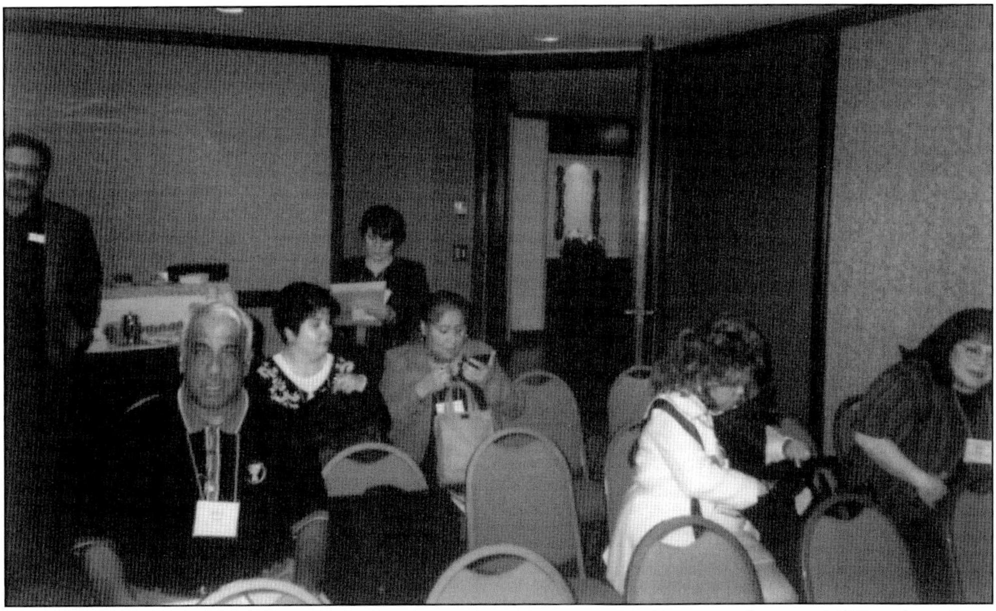

After 20 years of service to TACHE as an organizing committee member in 1974, a founding member, and a regional representative since 1975, Jesse Rangel (sitting, left foreground) was again elected the Panhandle area representative when it was redesignated as the Plains region. Alternate representatives were also elected, but they did not have voting privileges at board meetings unless the representative could not attend. In 1994, the regional representatives were Velma D. Menchaca and alternate Augustine Garza (Central); Luís Chaparro (Far West); Daniel Hernández (Gulf); Félix Zamora and alternate Syl Flores (Northeast); Julio Llanas and alternate Jesse Rangel (Plains); and Santiago Villanueva (South). (Courtesy of José Angel Gutiérrez.)

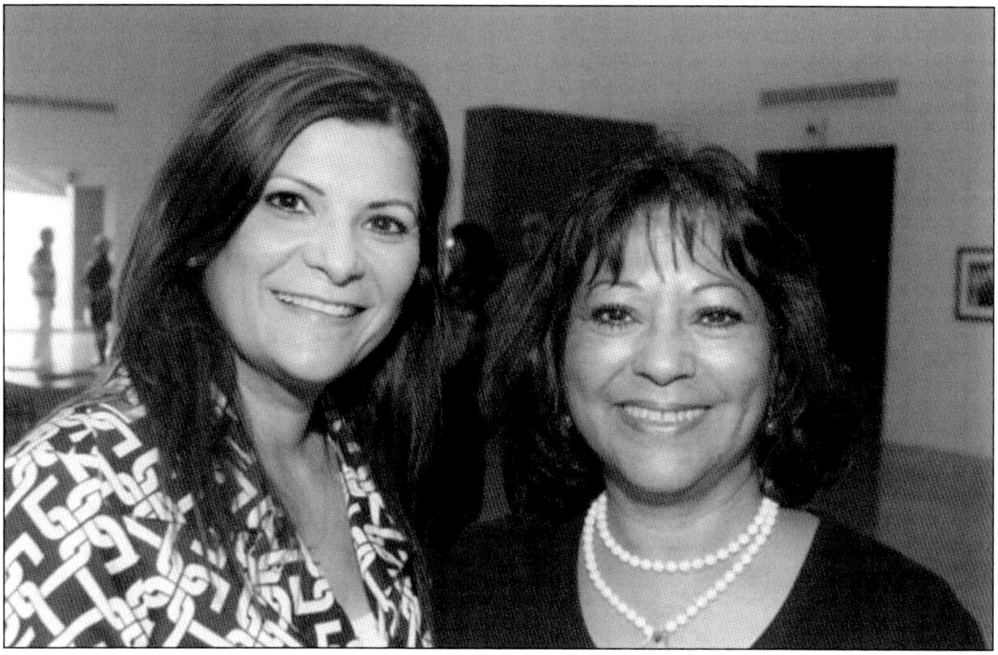

Dr. Criselda Leal (left), the 2011 TACHE president, is seen here with Dr. María Salinas of the Del Mar chapter. Dr. Leal, from Corpus Christi, rose through the TACHE ranks from the Del Mar chapter. The Del Mar chapter is very active and full of creative fundraising ideas, including dances, walks, and barbecue cookouts. (Courtesy of María Salinas.)

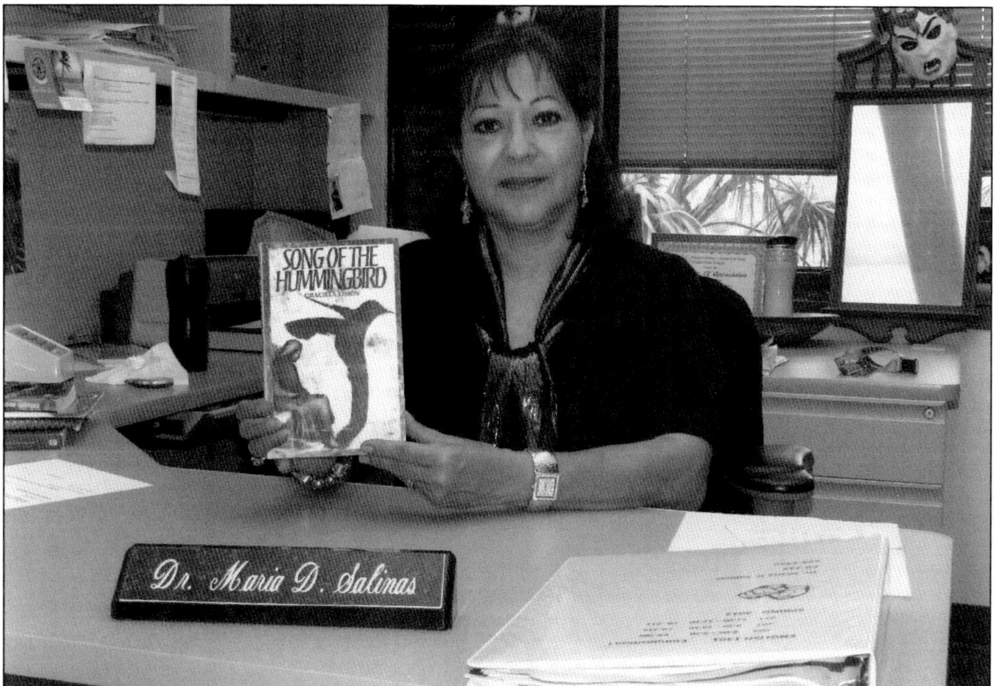

English professor Dr. María D. Salinas shows off her favorite book for the spring semester in 2011. (Courtesy of María Salinas.)

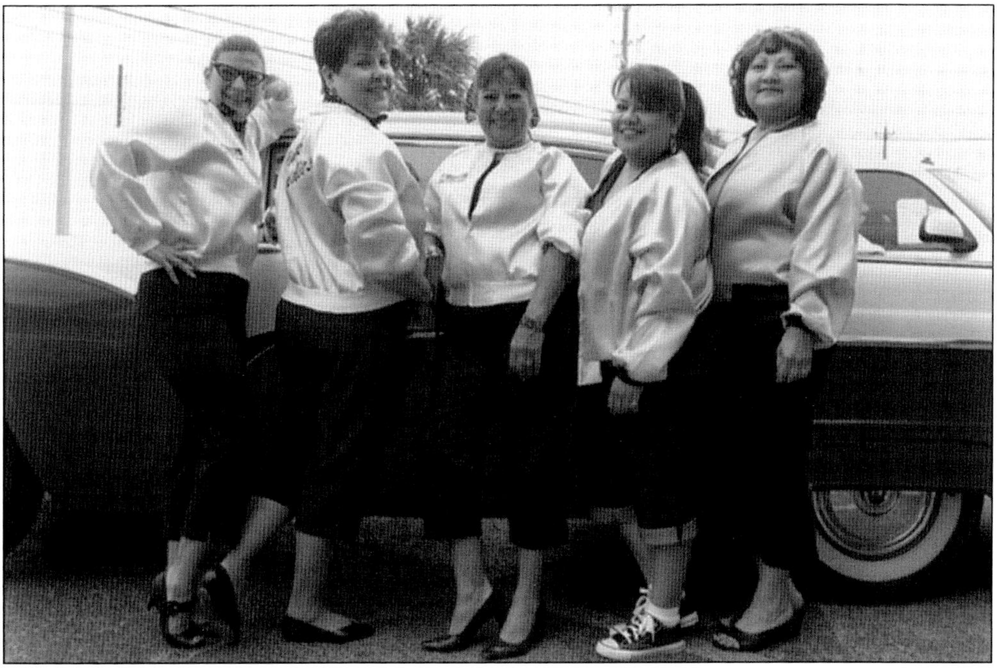

From left to right, TACHE members Dr. Criselda Leal, Dr. Eva Muñiz, Dr. María Salinas, Anna Tischler, and Verónica Gutiérrez are ready for the 1950s Rock and Roll fundraising dance. All are TACHE members from Del Mar College. Dr. Salinas and Dr. Leal, the 2011 TACHE president, assisted the authors in taking inventory of the TACHE archive holdings at the University of Texas at Austin's Benson Library in 2011. (Courtesy of María Salinas.)

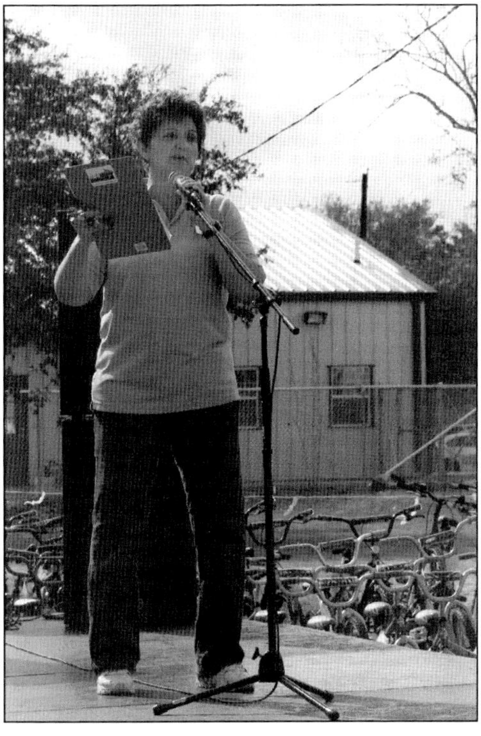

Dr. Gilda E. Ramírez was a presenter at TACHE's 36th annual conference, held in San Antonio in 2010. The 2013 regional representative for south Texas, Dr. Ramírez is the director of the Antonio E. García Arts and Education Center at Texas A&M University Corpus Christi. (Courtesy of Gilda E. Ramírez.)

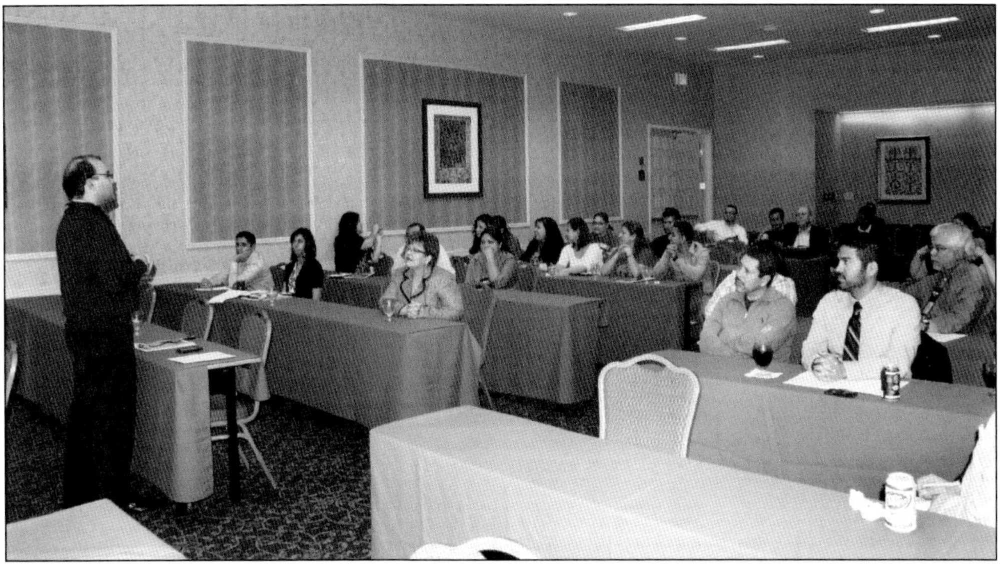

Luís Franco conducts an election during a regional caucus. At the 2013 annual conference, the largest chapter delegation present was from the Austin Community College District. The second-largest delegation came from Tarrant County Community College District campuses, in the northeast region, and the third-largest delegation came from Tyler Junior College, also in the northeast region. The northeast was the largest of all regions represented, with 59 members, with attendees also from the Dallas Community College District and the University of Texas at Arlington. (Courtesy of Natalia Verjat Gutiérrez.)

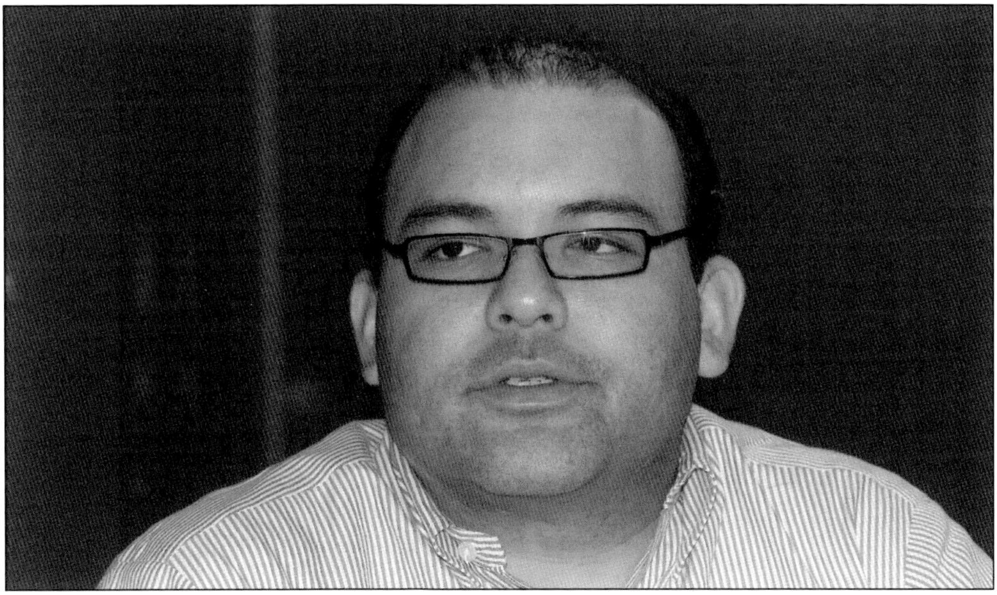

Luís Franco joined TACHE in 2007 and was elected the vice president of the northeast chapter in 2009. The following year, he served as a committee member for the annual conference, and, in 2011, he was elected regional representative for the northeast. In 2013, he was elected as secretary to the board of directors, a statewide office. He is the director for Hispanic outreach and student programs at Texas A&M University-Commerce and has a goal to make it a Hispanic Serving Institution. (Courtesy of Natalia Verjat Gutiérrez.)

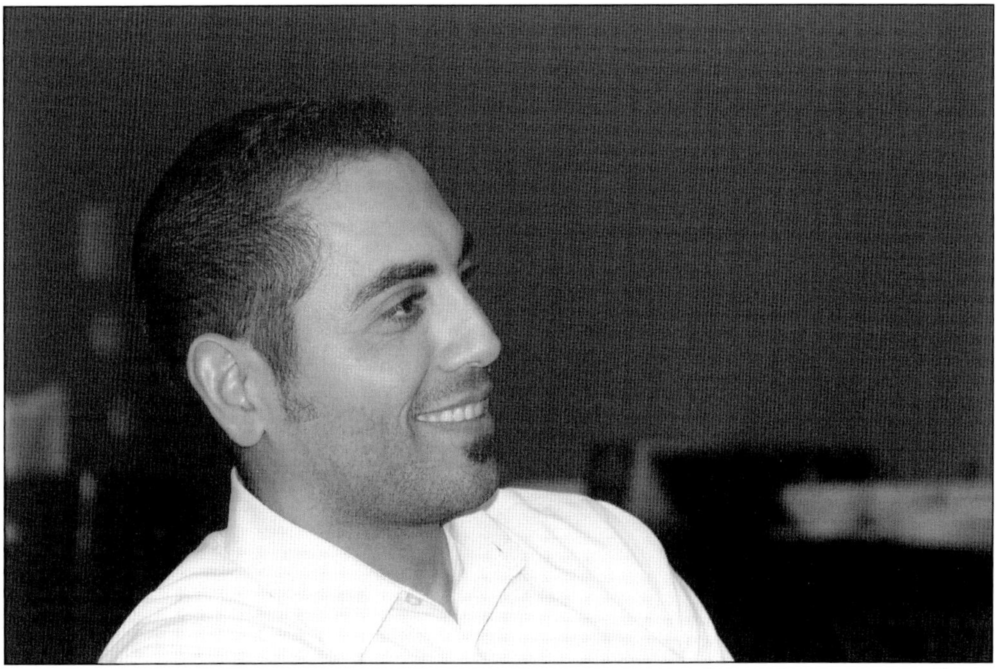

Mauricio Rodríguez is an English and Chicano studies instructor at El Paso Community College's Valle Verde campus. He is the founding member of the Chicano studies program for the district and serves as the district coordinator of the new program being implemented across all campuses. In 2013, at TACHE's 38th annual conference, he was the recipient of the Distinguished Community College Faculty Award and was elected as the far west's regional representative. He also serves on the board of directors. (Courtesy of Natalia Verjat Gutiérrez.)

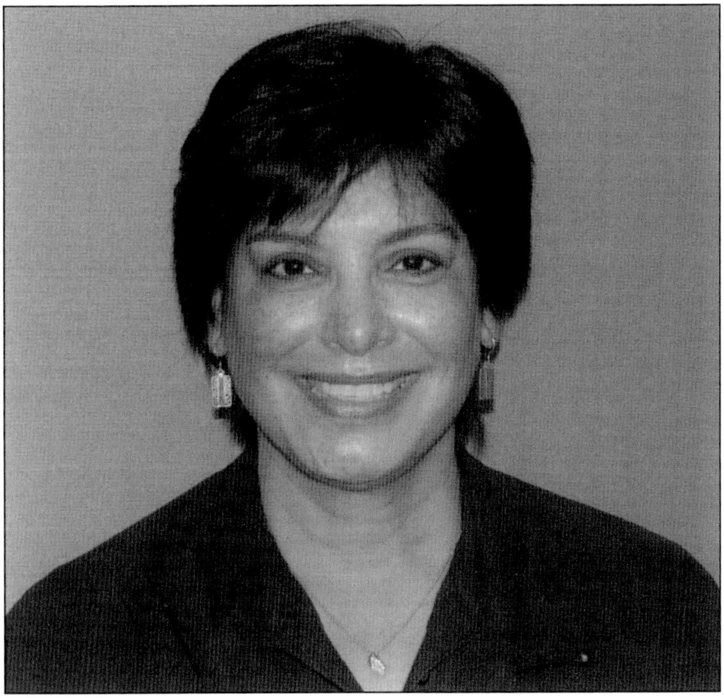

A TACHE member from the Gulf Coast region, Becky Gustamante is the dean of business at Lone Star College-Montgomery. In 2011, Dr. Gustamante was the regional representative of the Gulf area. She was elected vice president for membership in 2013. (Courtesy of Natalia Verjat Gutiérrez.)

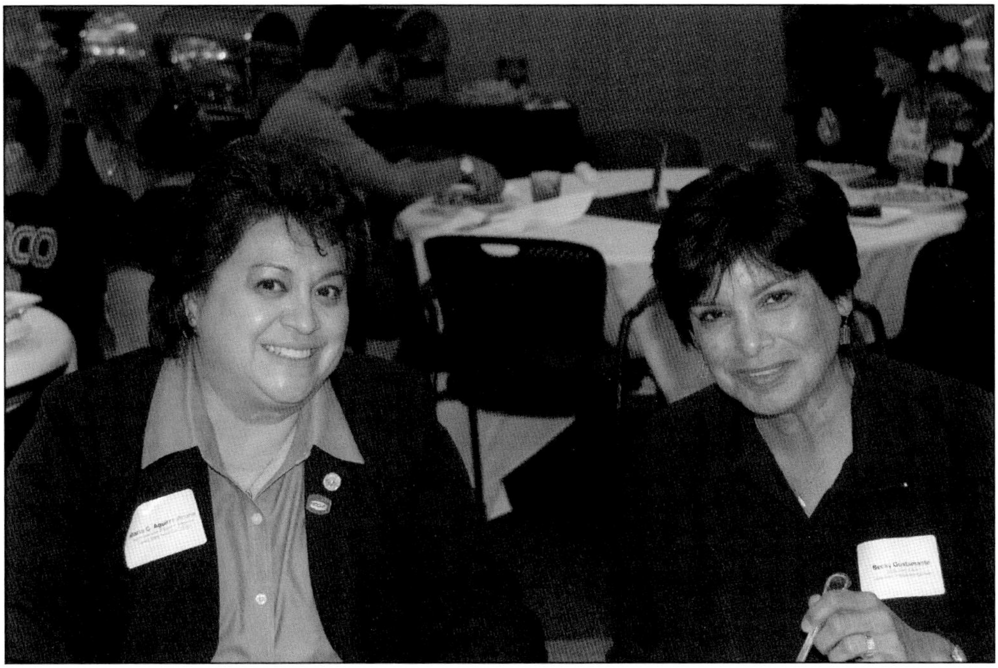

María Aguirre-Acuña (left) is TACHE's vice president for communications in 2013. She is from Texas State Technical College West Texas, in Sweetwater. Becky Gustamante is on the right. (Courtesy of Natalia Verjat Gutiérrez.)

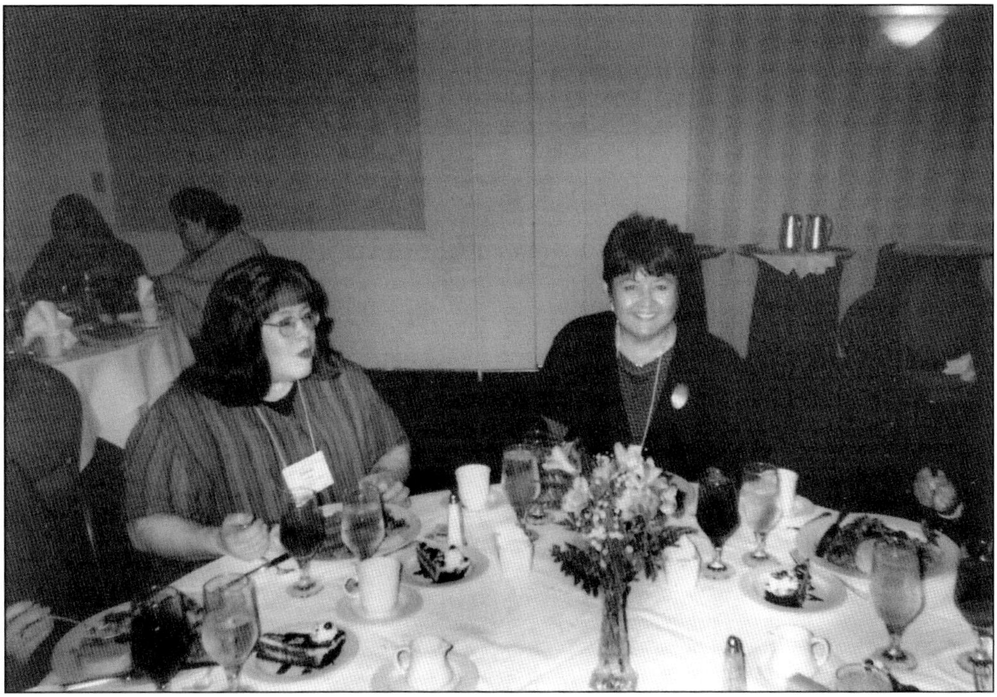

Diana Flores (left) was the northeast's regional representative in the 1990s. She was the first Chicana elected to the Dallas County Community College District's board of trustees and is currently on her third term in office. (Courtesy of José Angel Gutiérrez.)

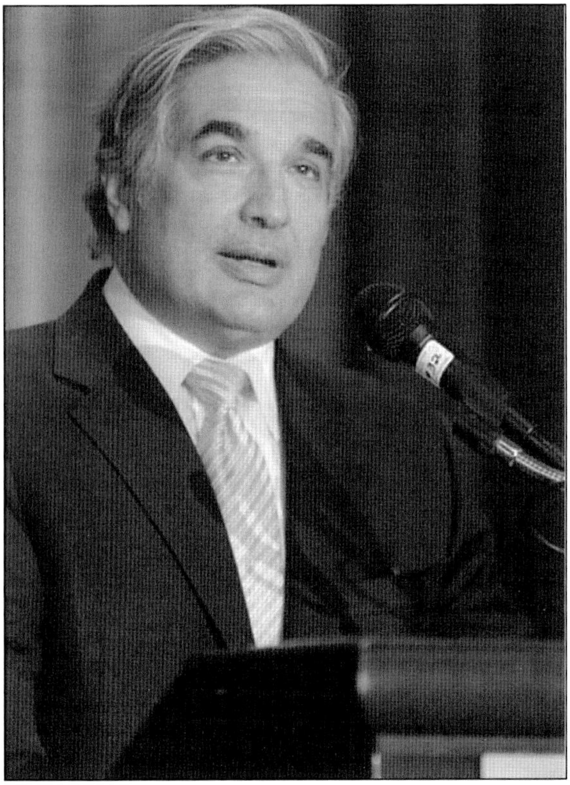

Francisco Cigarroa is the chancellor of the University of Texas system, one of seven systems of public higher education in the state. The UT system began in 1883. TACHE accesses leaders at every campus in order to promote its agenda and seek support for its programs. The older and larger system is Texas A&M, which began in 1876 and also has multiple campuses across the state. (Courtesy of Rudy Robles.)

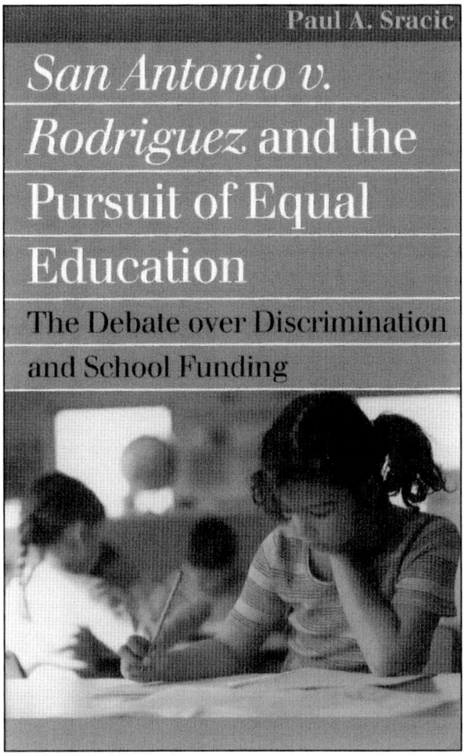

In 1968, Demetrio Rodríguez sued his daughter's (Patricia) school district over the unequal financing of public education. The lower Texas courts decided in his favor, ruling that school funding in Texas was unequal and unconstitutional, but the US Supreme Court reversed the decision in 1973. Its opinion held that education in the United States is not a fundamental right protected under the constitution; it is a state matter. This issue has been litigated for the past 40 years to no avail. The courts find discrimination in funding, but the legislature continues to distribute funds unequally.

Six

The Future of TACHE

In 2012, there were 56 Hispanic Serving Institutions (HSIs) in Texas, most of which were community colleges along the border counties with Mexico. As the decade goes on, 45 more institutions of higher education are getting closer to reaching the 25-percent threshold of Hispanic students they need to qualify as HSIs. Hispanic students are predominantly enrolled in community colleges, and many find it difficult to make the transfer to senior college, but the numbers are getting better with each year, despite the grim statistics that 12 students per hour leave school before obtaining a high school diploma and that 103,140 students are lost per year from public high schools in Texas. Hispanic students had the highest attrition rate of all students in 2012, at 35 percent.

In 2011, Latinos became the second-largest racial/ethnic group, after whites, in postsecondary education. Access, however, does not guarantee success. Only 20 percent of Latinos had an associate's degree or higher, compared to 36 percent of all adults in the United States with such an education. Over half of all Latinos in college in America are enrolled in Hispanic Serving Institutions, while the rest are often in the smallest minority at their respective institutions. TACHE's mission is to improve the educational opportunities of Hispanics in postsecondary education for both faculty and students. TACHE student chapters are few, but they are growing across the state. The annual conference offers a student track, with sessions and training for students. The students graduating from high school and enrolling in the colleges and universities across the state and the country are the future of TACHE.

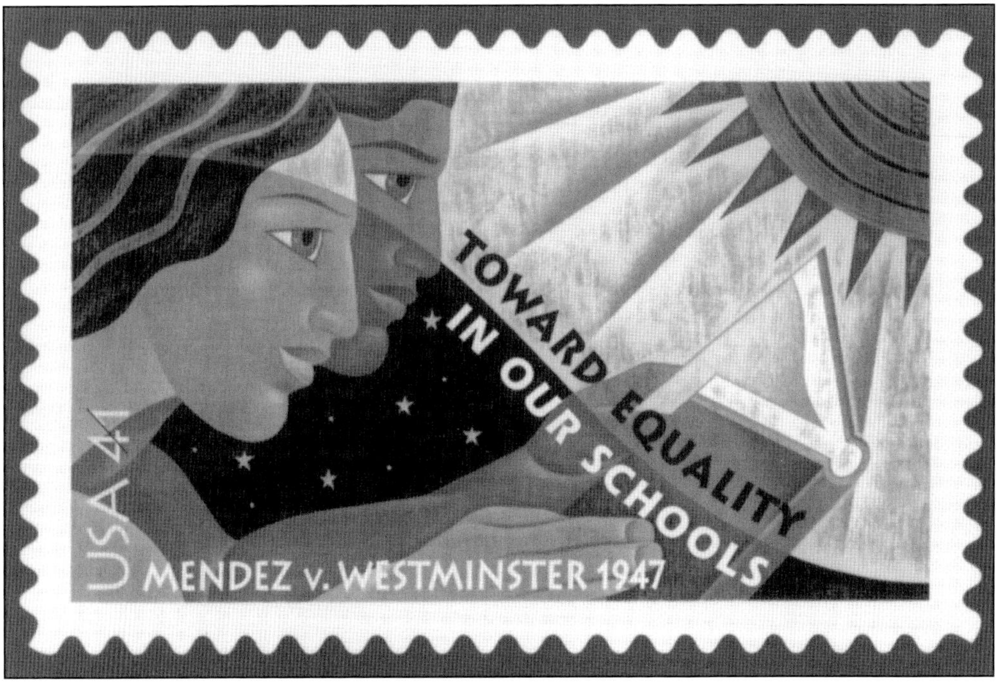

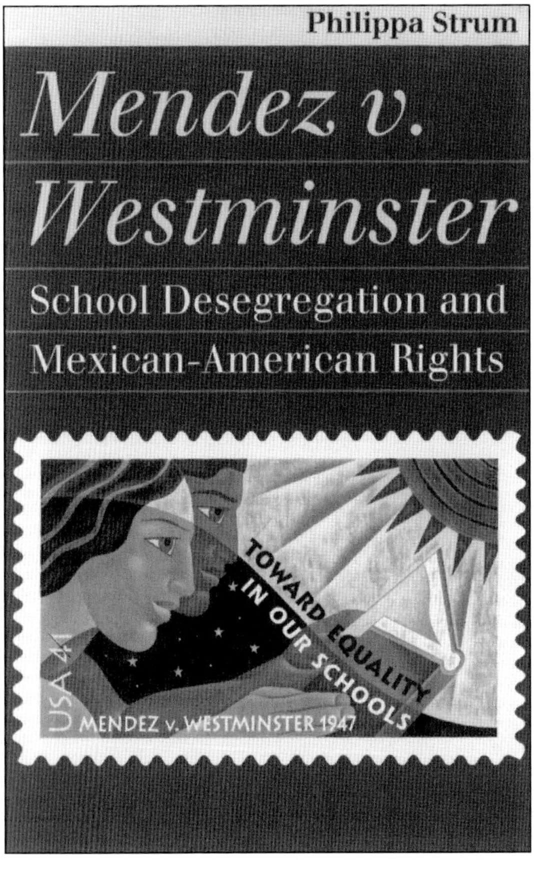

The stamp above is in honor of the Méndez family, who first filed in federal court seeking to end school segregation of Mexican-ancestry children in California in 1946. The case was eventually settled by the 9th Circuit court of appeals. Segregation ended somewhat in California at that time, but it continued in Texas. On February 15, 2011, Pres. Barack Obama conferred the Medal of Freedom on Sylvia Méndez, the child in the suit. (Above, courtesy of US Postal Service.)

State representative Roberto R. Alonzo presents TACHE president-elect Dr. Magdalena de la Teja with a Texas flag and a certificate of authenticity that it was flown over the capitol. (Courtesy of Javier Olguín.)

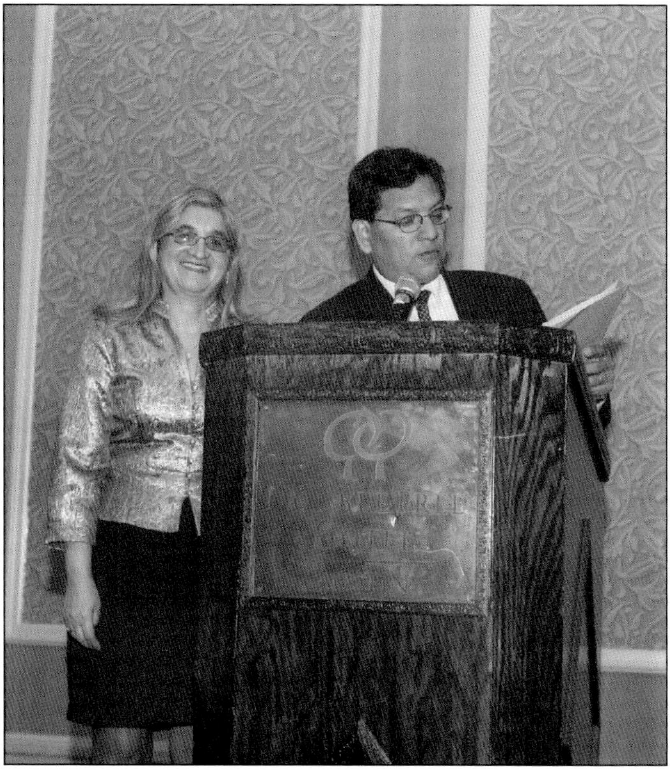

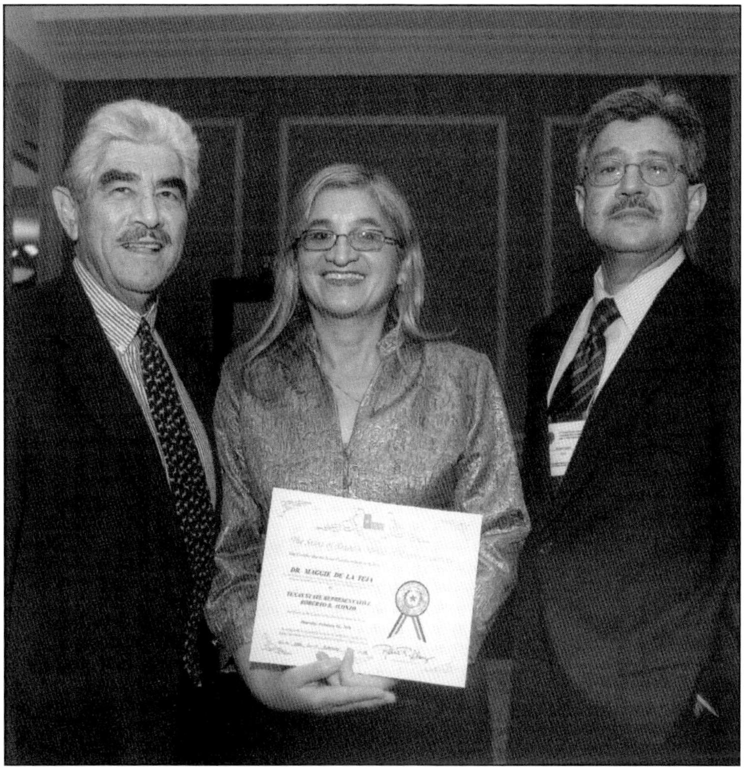

Dr. de la Teja poses with her certificate, along with Dr. Leonardo de la Garza (left), the chancellor of Tarrant County Community College District, and Dr. Roberto Aguero, then the vice chancellor for learning support services for the Tarrant District. (Courtesy of Javier Olguín.)

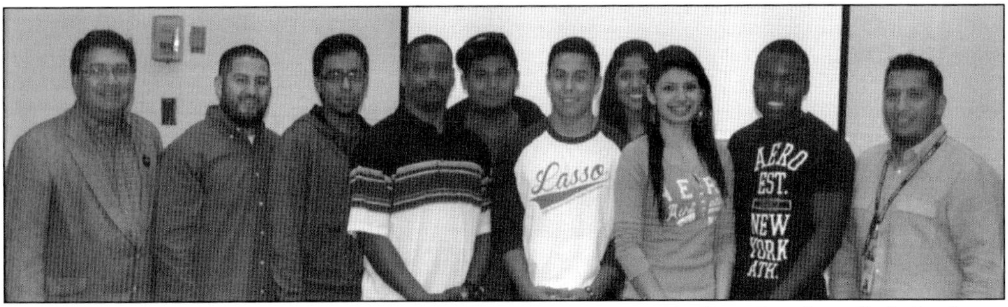

The TACHE student chapter at Tarrant County Community College South, called the Latin American Spanish Speaking Organization (LASSO), is mentored and advised by TACHE member and history professor Armando Villarreal, Johnathan Pérez, and Ramón Mireles. Seen here from left to right are Villarreal, Pérez, Carlos Avalos (vice president), Wallace Aries, Pedro Macillas, Ray Herrera (president), Amanda Villegas (in back), Griselle Avina (secretary), Marcellus Williams (treasurer), and Mireles. (Courtesy of Armando Villarreal.)

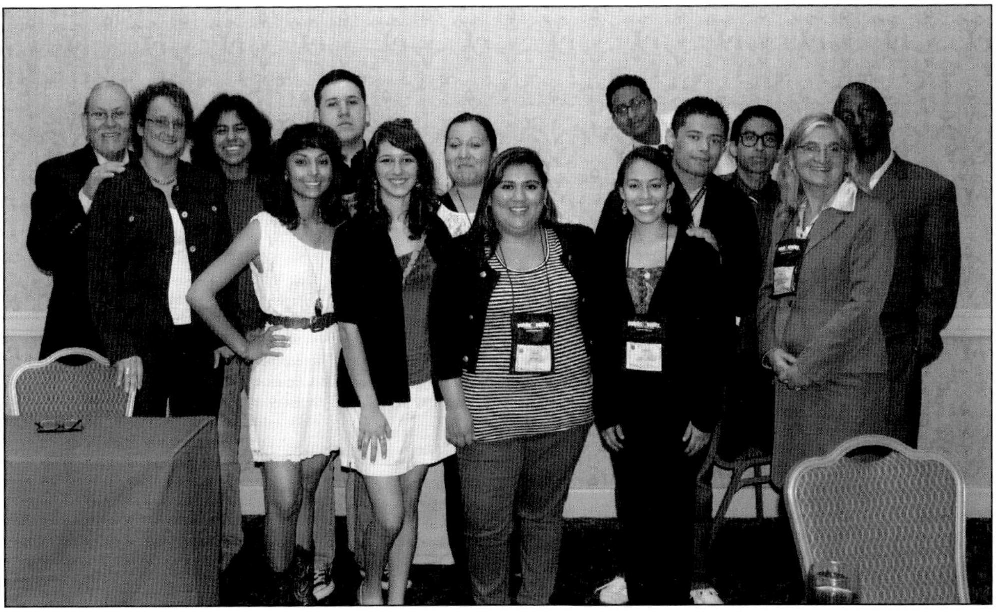

OLAS is the acronym for the Organization for Latin American Students at Tarrant County Community College Northeast. This student affiliate of TACHE attends the annual conference with assistance from its advisor, Spanish instructor Natalia Verjat Gutiérrez, also a TACHE chapter president-elect in 2013. Seen here from left to right are (first row) Melissa Anaya, Julieta Flores, Lucy Rojas (president), Nitza Gómez, and Dr. Magdalena de la Teja; (second row) Natalia Verjat Gutiérrez, Leticia Villarreal, and Nelson Pacheco; (third row) José Angel Gutiérrez (TACHE northeast regional representative), Emmanuel Rincón, José Almeda, Daniel Sandoval, Mynor Efrín-Milián, and Shamir Iga. (Courtesy of Natalia Verjat Gutiérrez.)

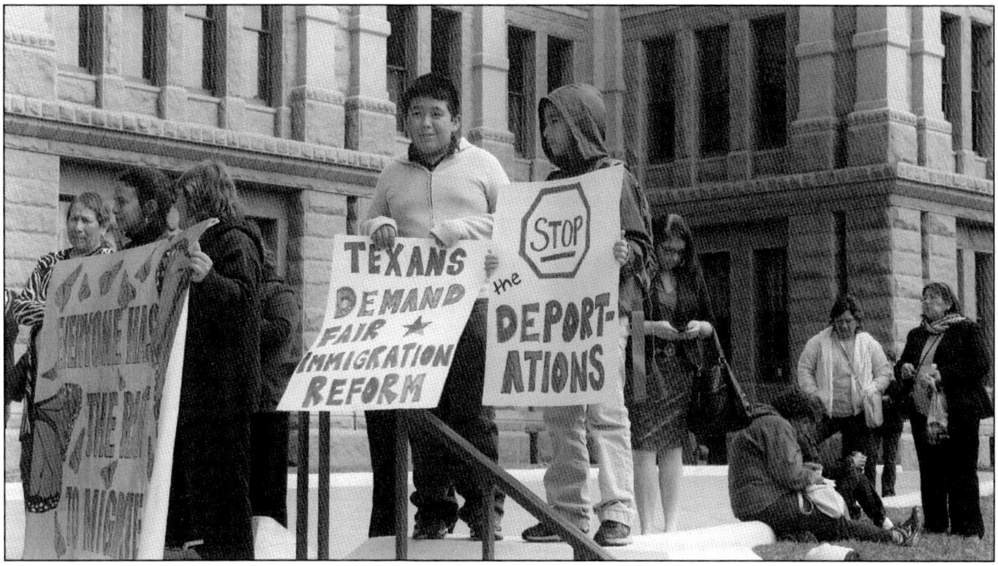

Pictured are TACHE members and others protesting at the Texas capitol in February 2013. Since the late 1990s, TACHE members have been pressing for passage of the DREAM Act. Diana Flores, a trustee on the Dallas Community College District board and a TACHE member, first initiated the proposal to have noncitizen students pay in-state tuition. State representative Rick Noriega took the issue and made it a state law. Rep. Luis Gutiérrez (D–Illinois) then introduced the measure in Congress, where it has repeatedly failed to pass. (Courtesy of Natalia Verjat Gutiérrez.)

Tayrn Ozuna received her graduate degree from the University of Texas at Austin in May 2013 and is now a member of the faculty. In 2009, she was part of a team of seven graduate students that presented with Dr. Víctor Sáenz at the 34th annual TACHE conference. In 2012, she received a TACHE fellowship of $2,000 that enabled her to complete her dissertation and earn a doctoral degree. (Courtesy of Javier Olguín.)

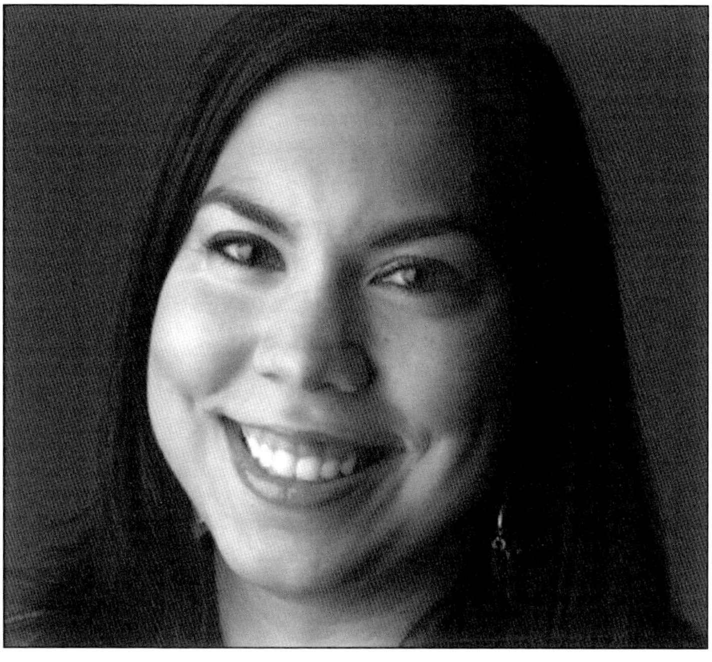

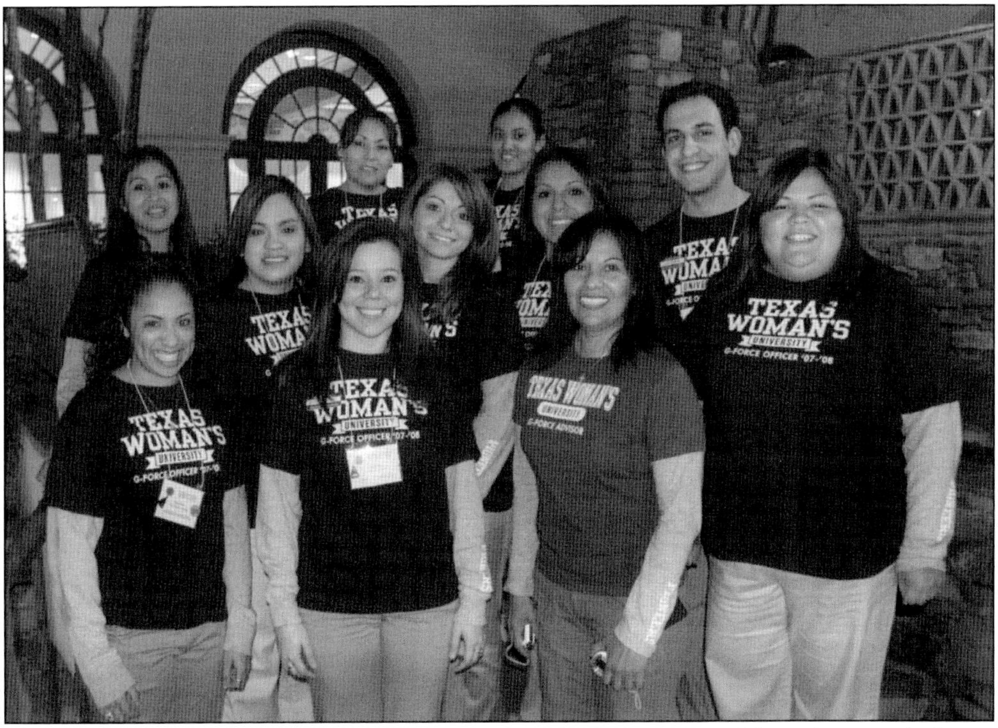

This group of students from Texas Woman's University, in Denton, posed for a photograph during the 2008 annual convention. (Courtesy of Javier Olguín.)

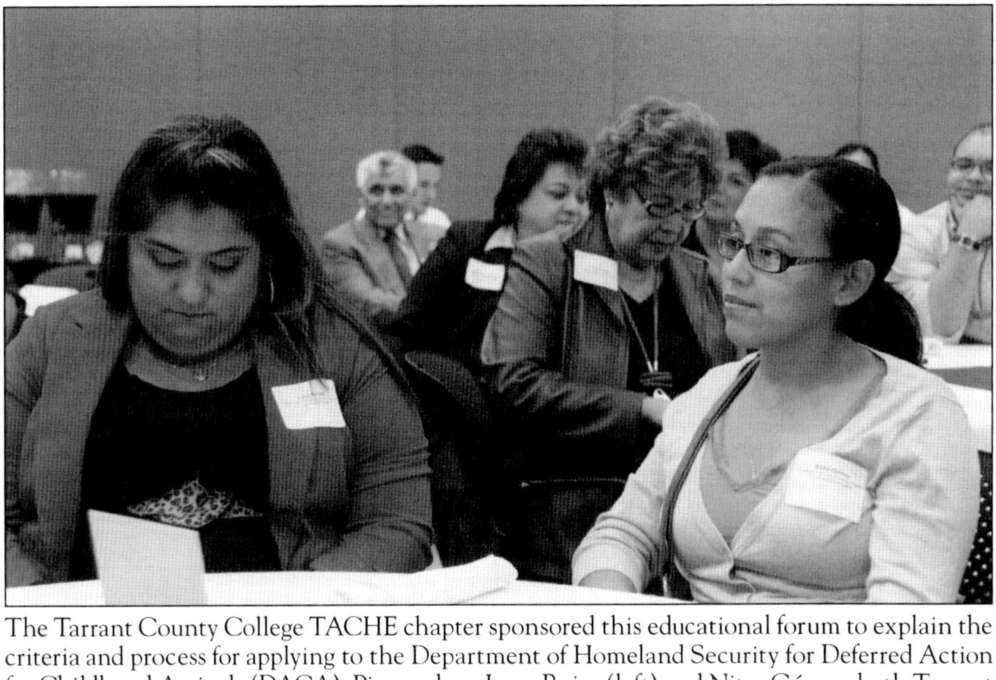

The Tarrant County College TACHE chapter sponsored this educational forum to explain the criteria and process for applying to the Department of Homeland Security for Deferred Action for Childhood Arrivals (DACA). Pictured are Lucy Rojar (left) and Nitza Gómez, both Tarrant County College Northeast Campus students and members of OLAS-TACHE. (Courtesy of Natalia Verjat Gutiérrez.)

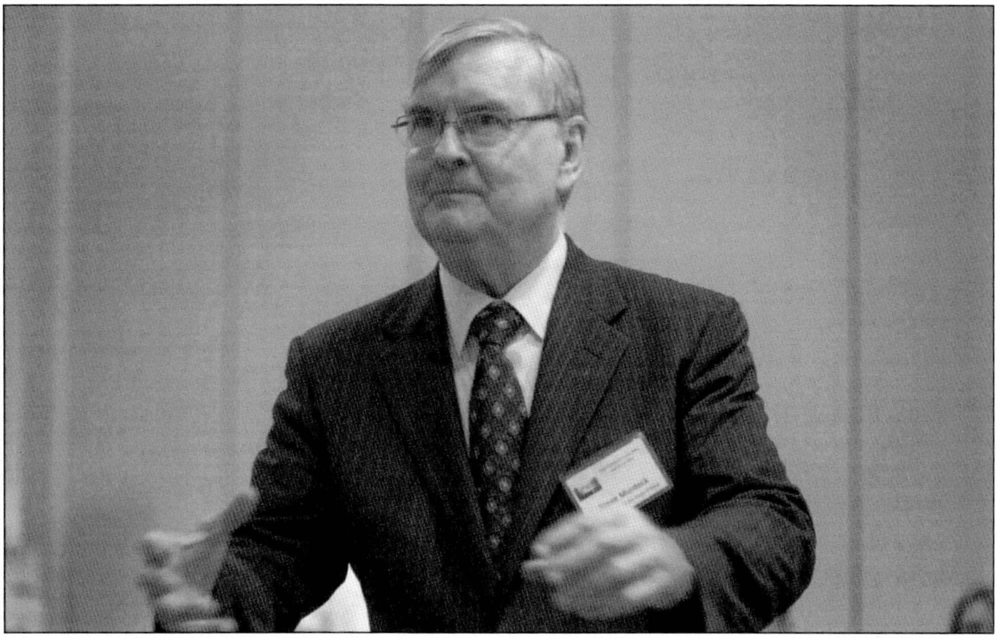

Dr. Steve H. Murdock presented "Demographic Shifts: Implications for Latino Education and the Future of Texas," at the 34th annual conference. Among the points he made was that Chicano and other Latino students were not only the majority of students in the public schools in 2010 but also that they will be at the doors of community colleges and universities in record numbers by 2020. (Courtesy of Steve Murdock.)

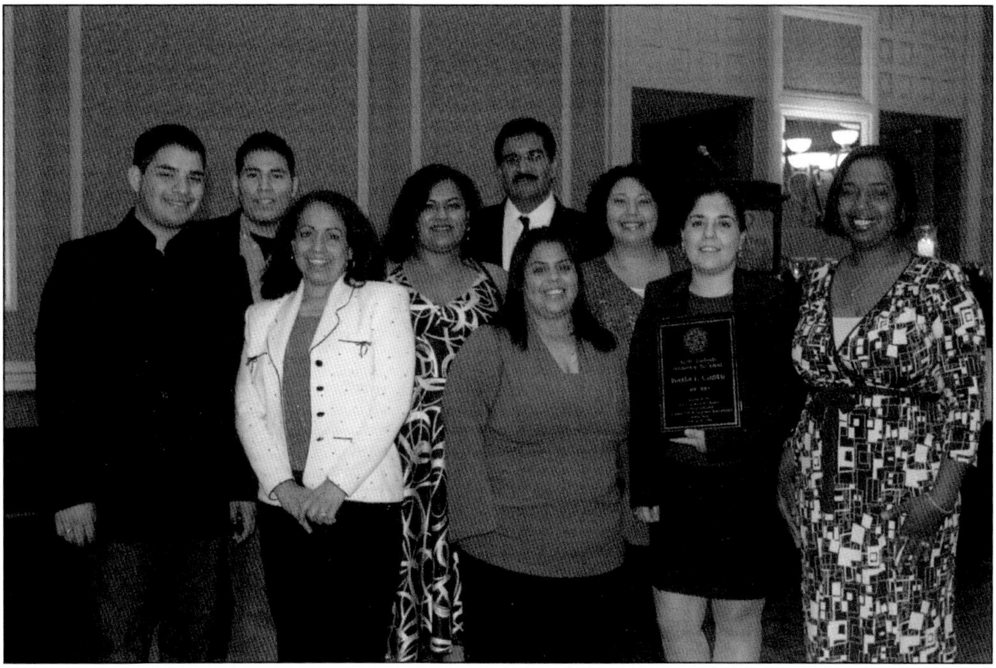

Fellowship winner Karla Cantú (first row, second from right) poses for a photograph with fellow students from the San Antonio TACHE chapter and chapter president Dr. Daniel Rodríguez (center, background). (Courtesy of Javier Olguín.)

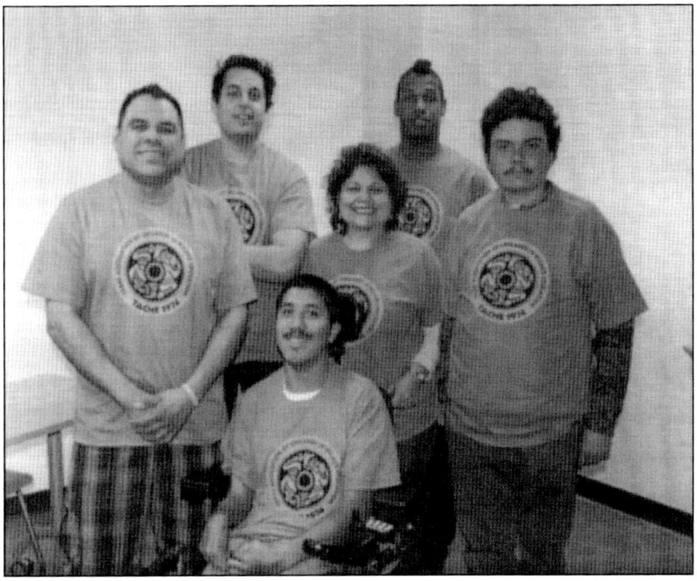

Sara Samano (center) is an advisor and leader of the TACHE student chapter Students with DisAbilities at San Antonio College. The group posed for this photograph at a TACHE state board of directors meeting in San Antonio. They are, clockwise from front center, Josué Estrada, Telesforo Mandujano, Jacob Alvarez, Mariano Bula, Juan P. Luján, and Samano. (Courtesy of Sara Samano.)

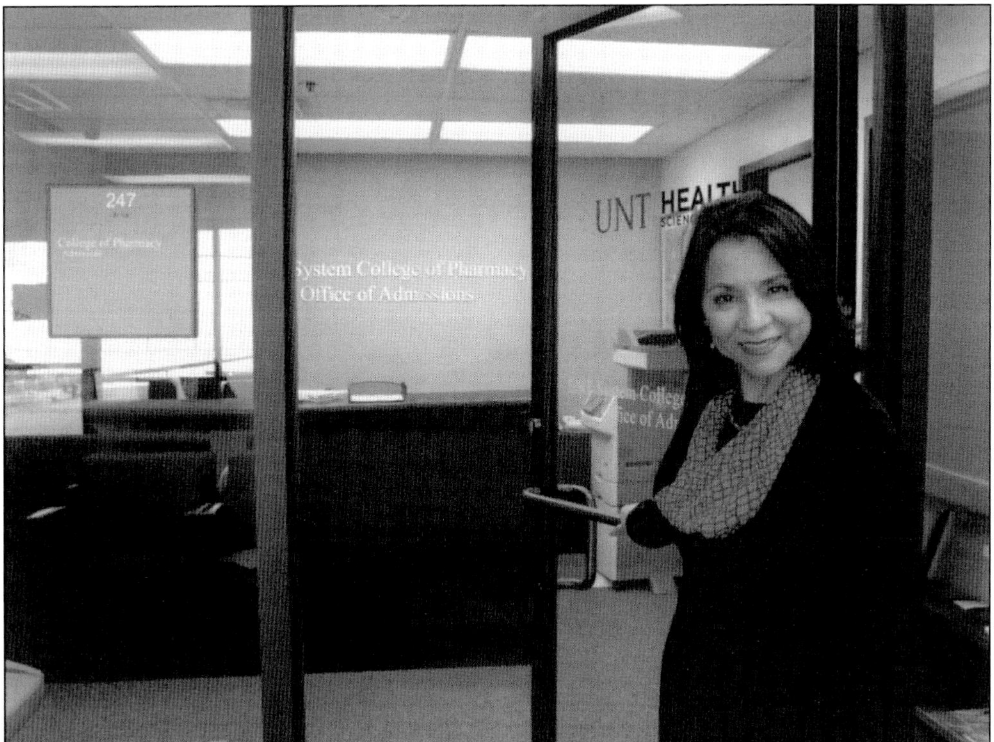

Dr. Antonia Kilpatrick, who is also an attorney, was the TACHE regional representative for the northeast region from 2009 to 2011. She is now the officer in charge of admissions for the University of North Texas System College of Pharmacy. (Courtesy of Antonia Kilpatrick.)

Lorenzo Cano presented at the 2006 annual conference on the Academic Achievers Program within the University of Houston's Mexican American studies program. (Courtesy of Natalia Verjat Gutiérrez.)

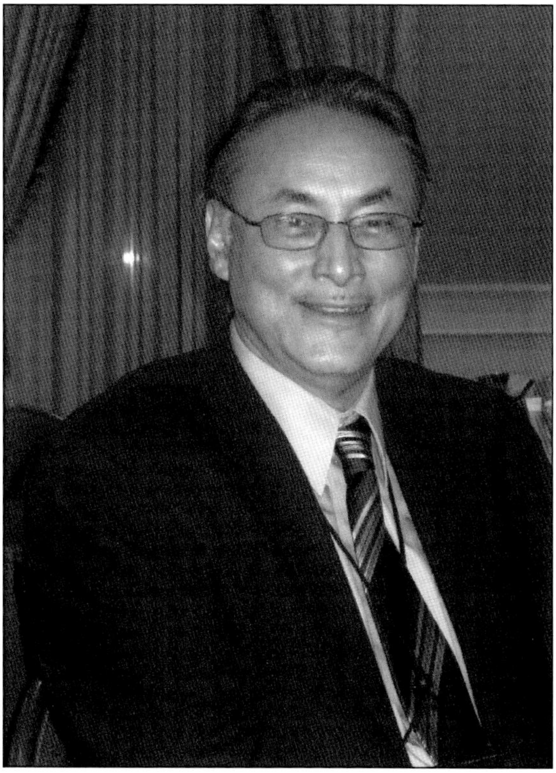

TACHE student members, faculty, and staff from various campuses of the Tarrant County Community College District pose for a photograph at Hotel Galvez, built in 1911 and named after Bernardo de Galvez, the Spanish colonial governor who first chartered the Texas Gulf Coast and for whom the city of Galveston was named. (Courtesy of Natalia Verjat Gutiérrez.)

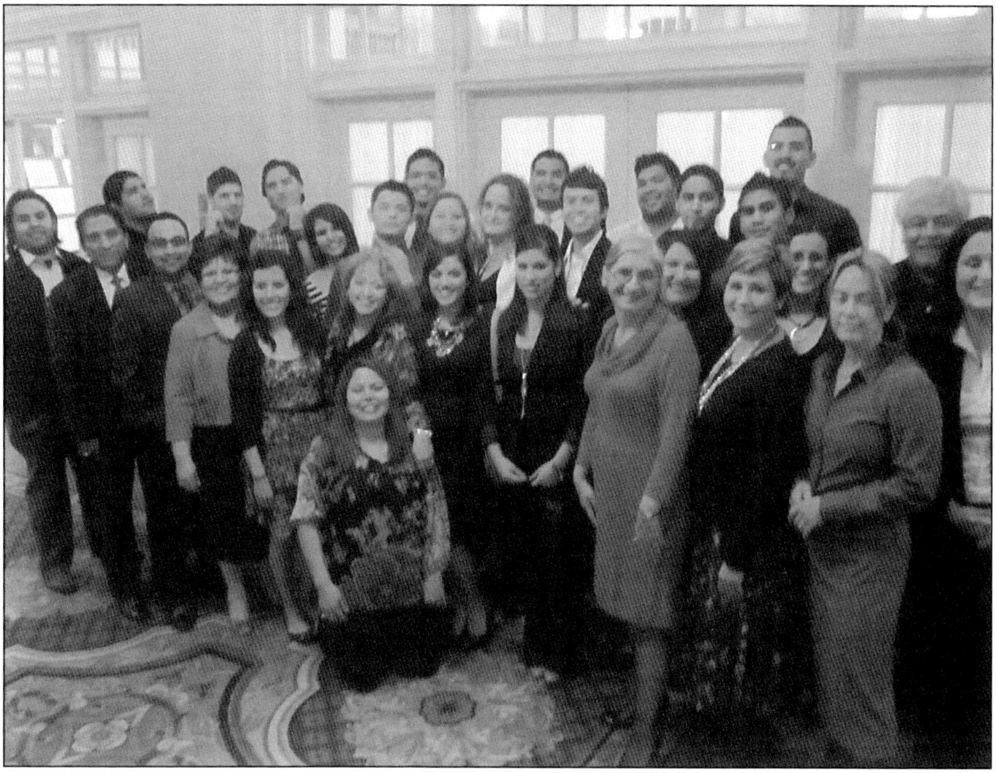

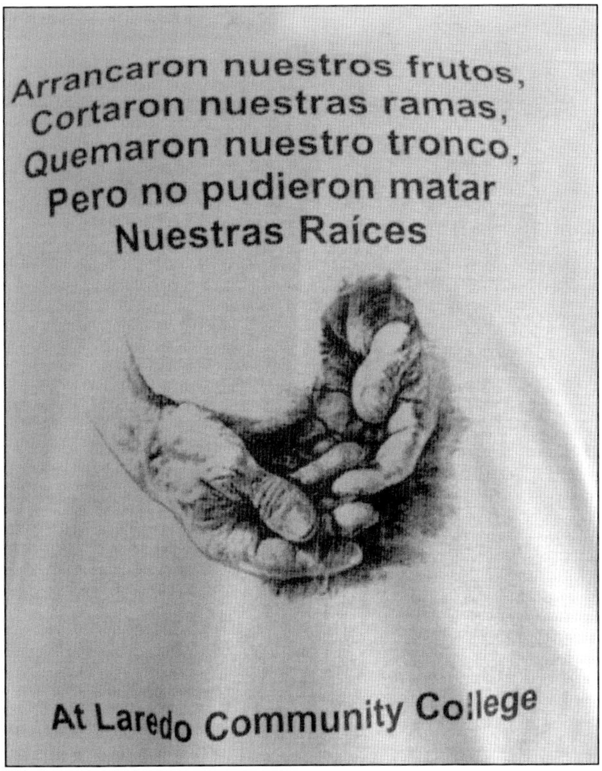

Border-area students face competing loyalties stemming from the duality of their geography. Are they Chicano, Mexican, Mexican American, Hispanic, Latino, or something else? The "Chicano" in TACHE's name has been a contested issue occasionally through the years, as it was during the fourth annual conference in 1978. At every instance, the membership votes to keep it. TACHE member and Laredo chapter advisor René Montemayor is proud of the words on this tee shirt, which they sell for fundraising. The front has the TACHE logo and the words, "Nuestras Raíces." (Courtesy of Natalia Verjat Gutiérrez.)

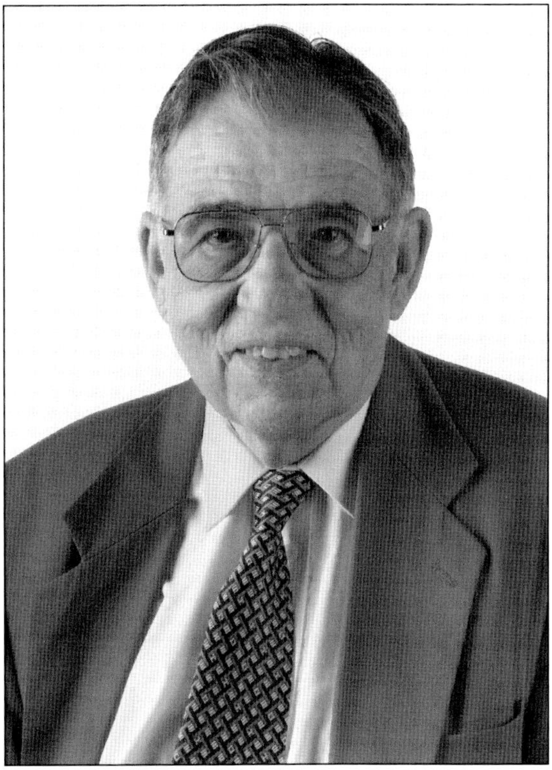

Dr. Manuel "Manny" Berriozabal is a San Antonio native and a longtime TACHE member. In 1961, he was the first Chicano awarded a doctorate in mathematics from the University of California, Los Angeles. After holding several academic positions across the country, he returned home to be a faculty member at the University of Texas at San Antonio. In 1979, he conceptualized and began the Prefreshman Engineering Program (PREP). This highly acclaimed program has gone national and has earned Dr. Berriozabal many much-deserved awards. It has done great things for Chicano and Latino students in math. (Courtesy of María Berriozabal.)

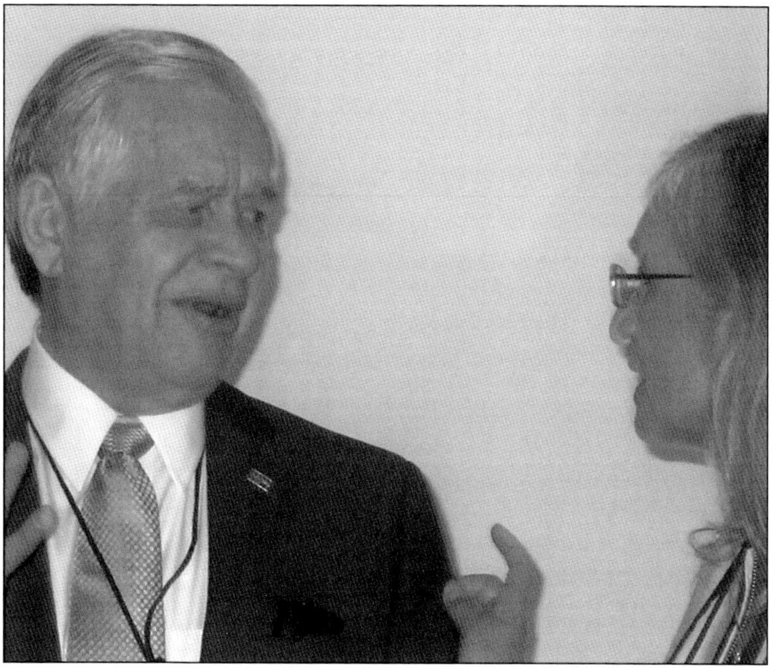

Jaime Chahín, the dean of the College of Applied Arts at Texas State University, and Dr. Magdalena de la Teja discuss her presentation at the annual event held at Tarrant County College-Northeast, *Abrazando al Exito*. (Courtesy of Magdalena de la Teja.)

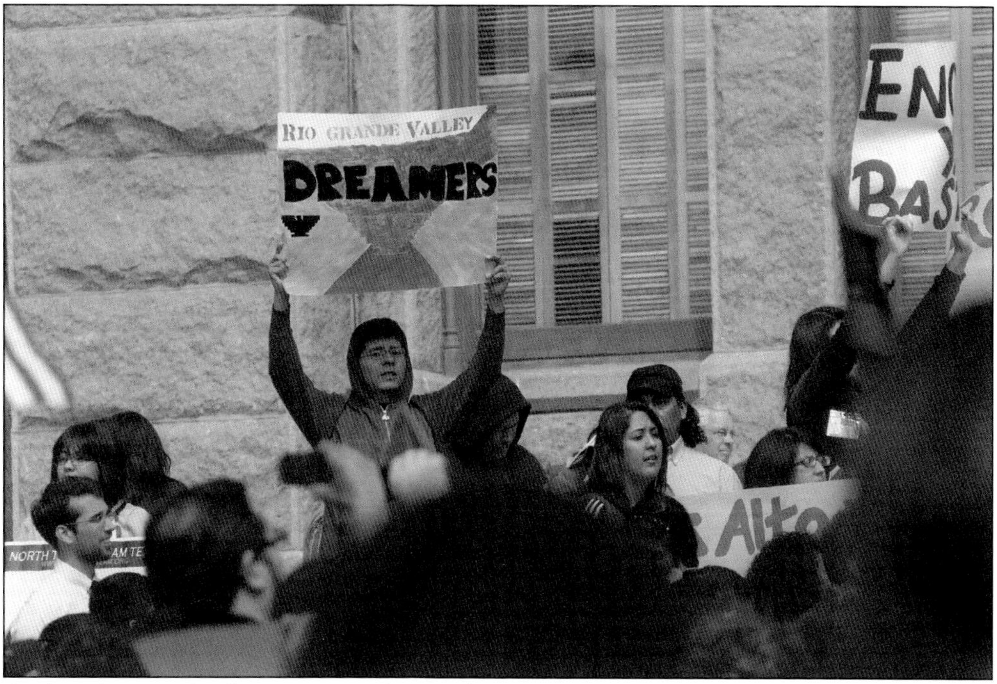

As this photograph of TACHE members and others protesting at the Texas capitol in February 2013 shows, immigration reform remains a politicized and polarized issue today. Despite promises of reform by Presidents George W. Bush and Barack Obama, immigration policy has remained roughly the same. President Obama has deported more Mexican immigrants than any other president in history, according to Politifact.com. (Courtesy of Natalia Verjat Gutiérrez)

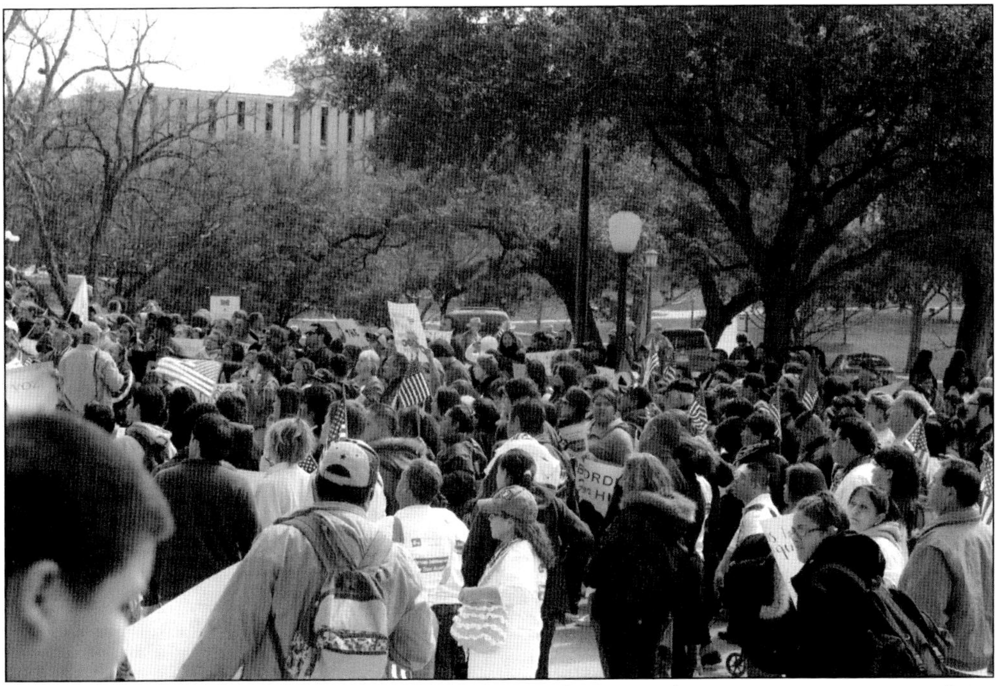

In 2013, "Ahora Marchamos, Mañana Votamos" was the saying for many immigrants marching for immigration reform in Austin, as seen here, and in many cities across the country. Since 2006, marches for immigration reform have seen strong participation. (Courtesy of Natalia Verjat Gutiérrez.)

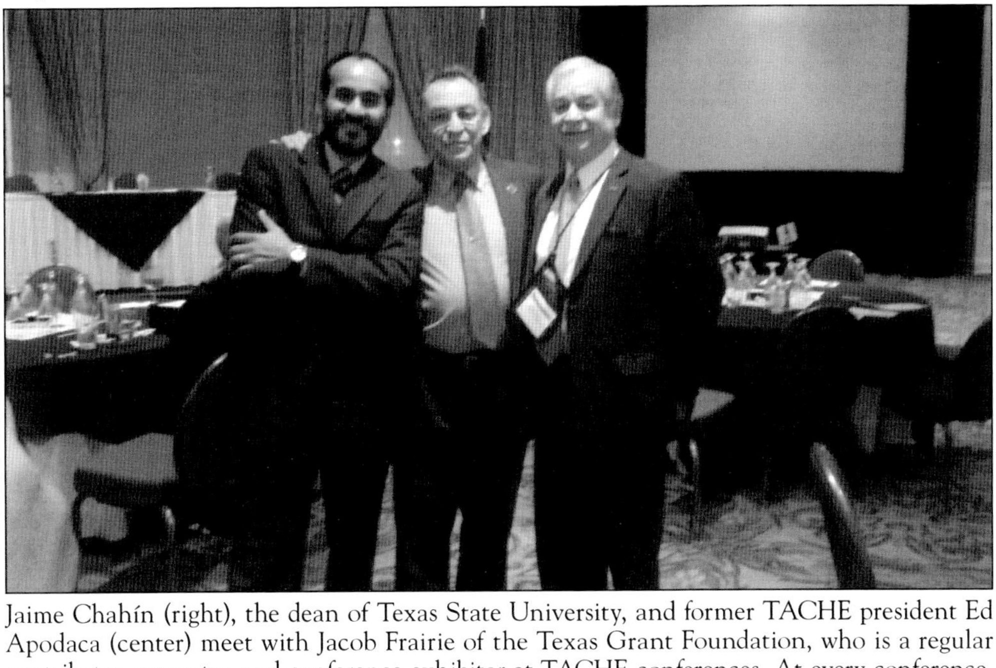

Jaime Chahín (right), the dean of Texas State University, and former TACHE president Ed Apodaca (center) meet with Jacob Frairie of the Texas Grant Foundation, who is a regular contributor, presenter, and conference exhibitor at TACHE conferences. At every conference, both in the program and in the hallways, TACHE posts the names of sponsors and encourages the membership to personally thank them. (Courtesy of Ed Apodaca.)

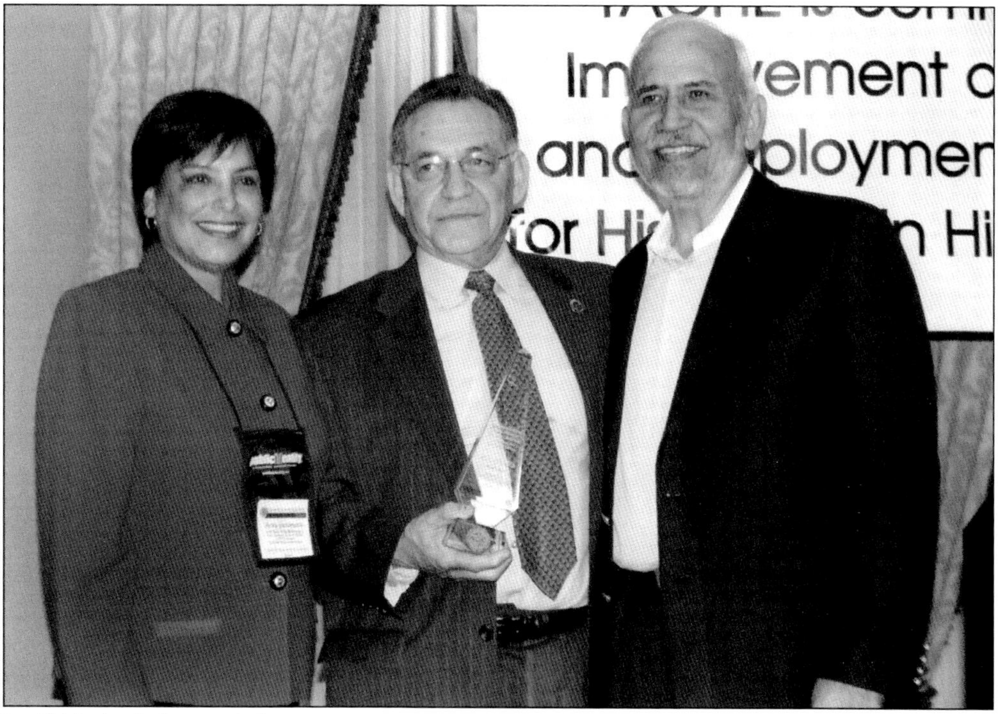

In 2012, the Lifetime Achievement Award went to Ed Apodaca (center), who had recently retired as vice president for student services and enrollment management at the University of Houston-Downtown. Presenting the award are Becky Gustamante (left) and 1994 TACHE president Dr. Max Castillo. At the same conference, Héctor Menchaca of Tarrant County College–Trinity River and Dr. James Salazar of Galveston College both received the Distinguished Community College Faculty Award. (Courtesy of Ed Apodaca.)

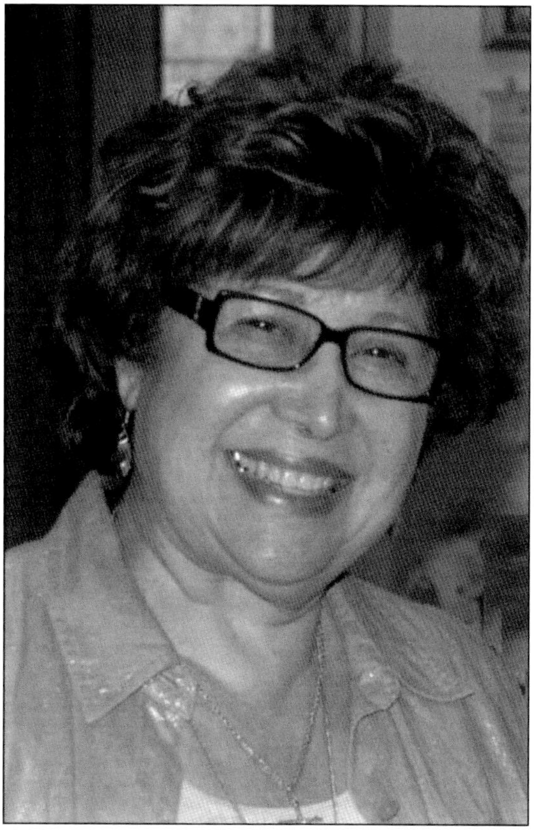

TACHE president Linda Contreras Bullock announced that the four graduate fellowships awarded at the 37th annual conference went to Cynthia Denise Alvarado of Texas A&M-Kingsville, Fernando Fuentes Jr. of Texas A&M–Commerce, and Manuel González and Cecilia López of UT–Austin. (Courtesy of Linda Contreras Bullock.)

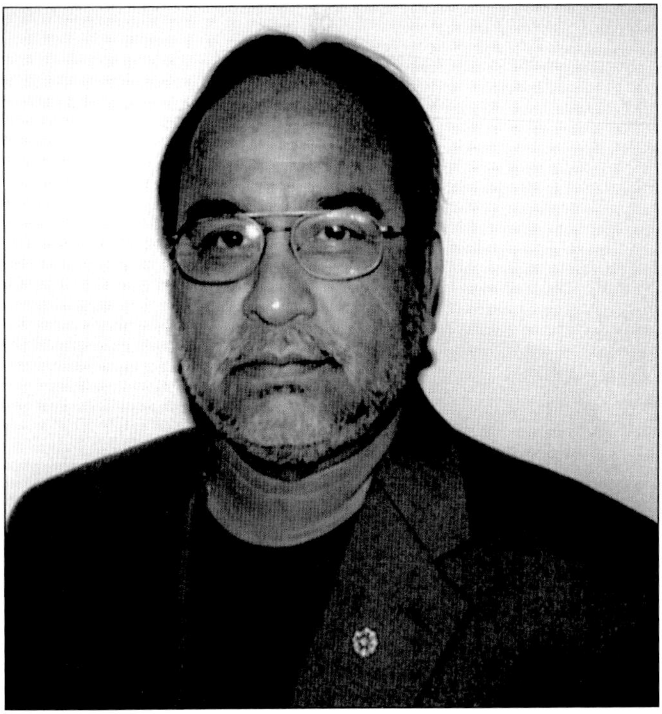

Doroteo Franco is an adjunct professor at El Paso Community College. In 2010, as TACHE's vice president for technology, he helped upgrade the TACHE website. (Courtesy of Javier Olguín.)

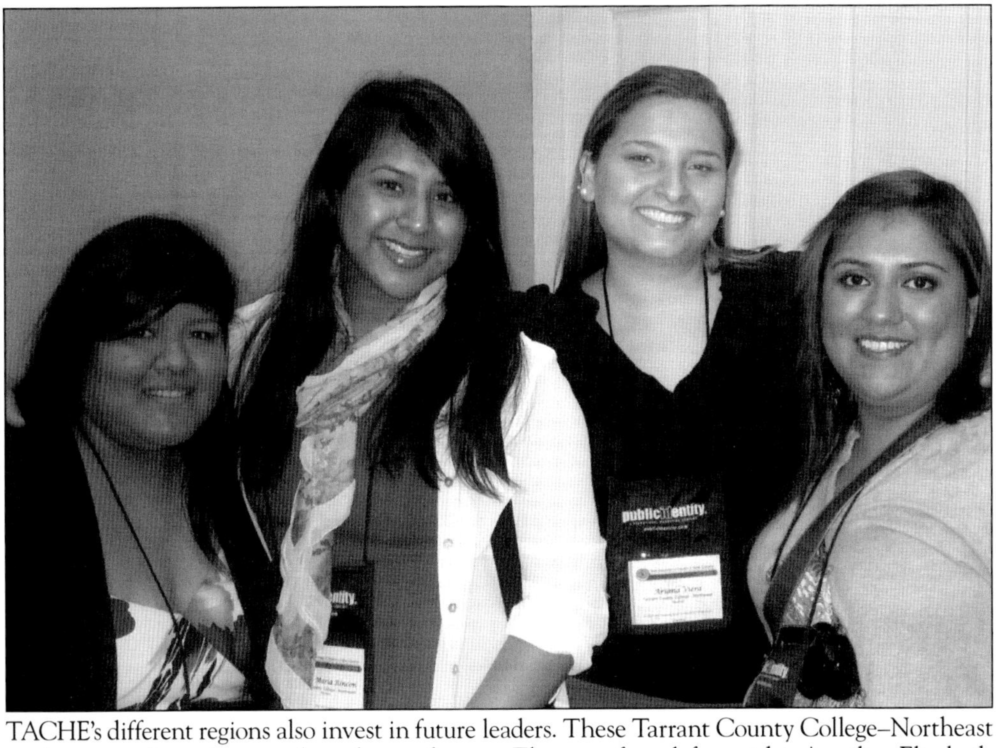

TACHE's different regions also invest in future leaders. These Tarrant County College–Northeast students pose for a photograph at the conference. They are, from left to right, Angélica Elisabeth Uriostegui, Rosie Rincón, Adriana Vieira, and Lucy Rojas. (Courtesy of Natalia Verjat Gutiérrez.)

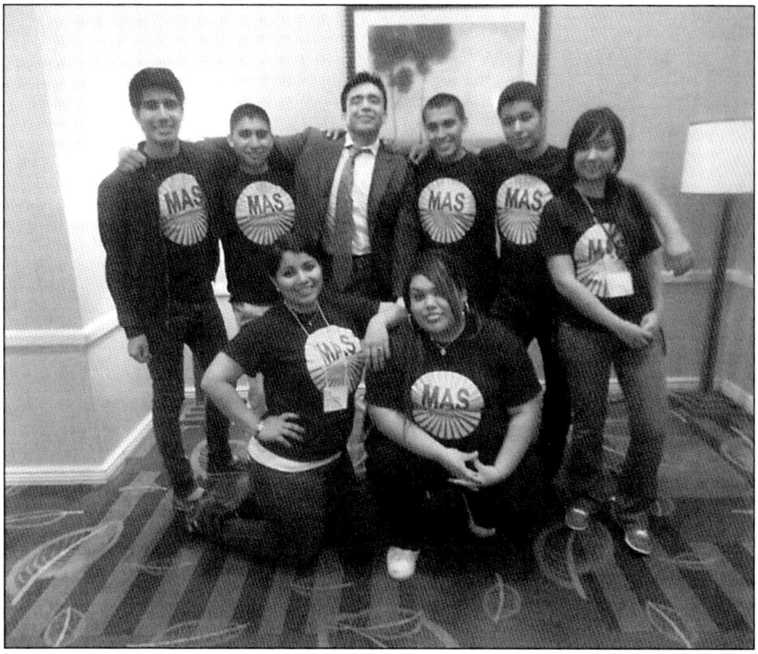

Tony Díaz (second row, third from left), the Libro Traficante organizer and leader, posed for this photograph with students from the University of Texas-Pan American. Díaz took to the road to smuggle books back into Arizona after the Tucson Mexican American studies program was banned. (Courtesy of Zeke Pérez.)

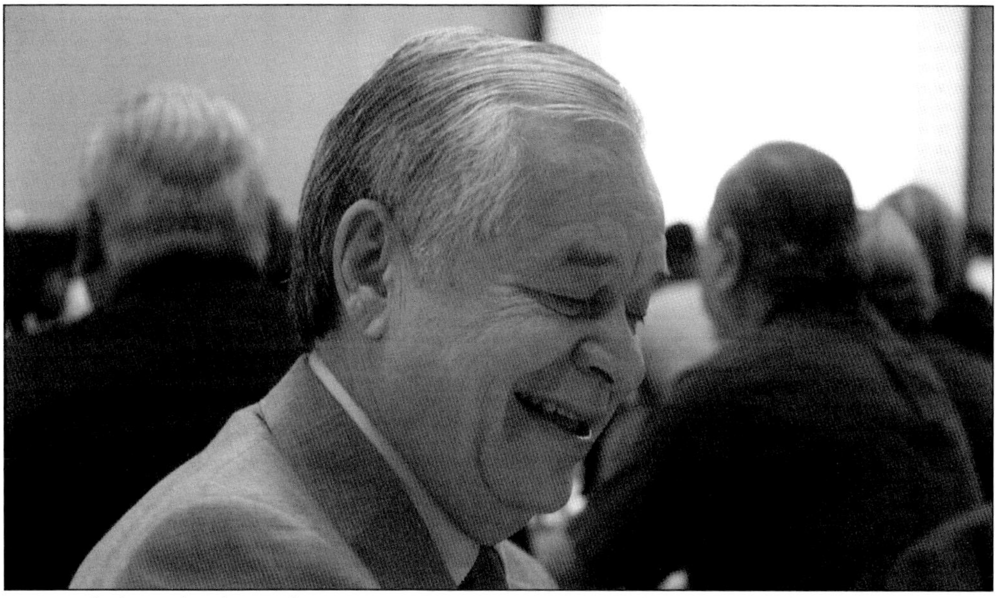

Jaime Chahín, the dean of Texas State University, is seen here. He recalls that, until 1986, there were only two four-year postsecondary institutions along the Texas-Mexico border and in southern Texas. Texas A&I University (now Texas A&M University–Kingsville) and Sul Ross State College, in Alpine, were the only two four-year colleges in the region, which many Chicano students transferred to after going to community college. After litigation, in 1986, the University of Texas and Texas A&M systems established campuses along the larger borderlands cities, followed by the University of Texas at San Antonio in 1997. Whereas in the past, Chicano students found it difficult to cover the cost of education, housing, and transportation, given the distance from their homes, the challenge today is just to afford the more expensive education costs, even if there is a nearby institution. (Courtesy of Natalia Verjat Gutiérrez.)

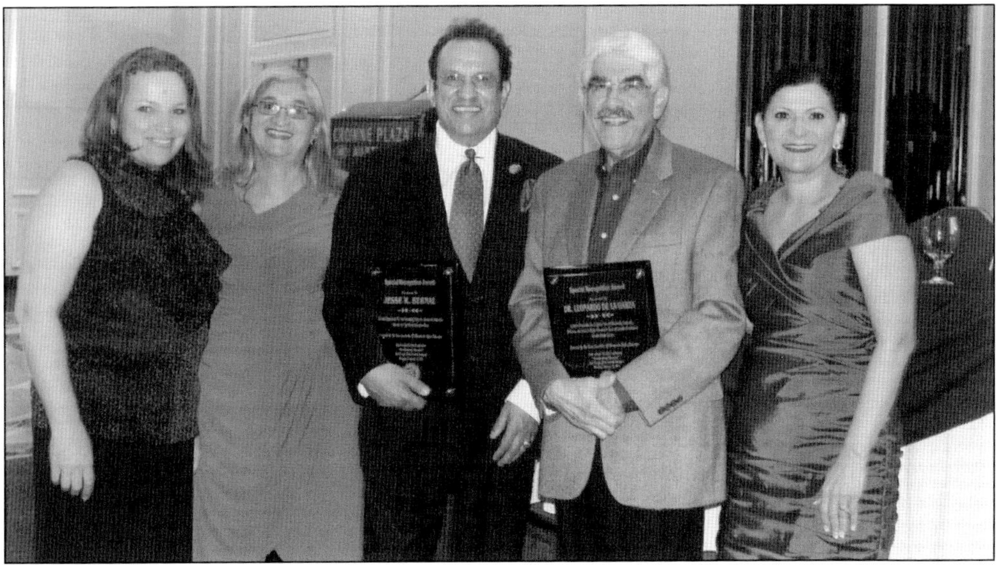

In 2010, awards were given to legislative staffer Jesse Bernal (center) and Dr. Leonardo de la Garza (second from right). Posing with them for this photograph are Julie Aria (far left), Dr. Magdalena de la Teja (second from left) and TACHE president Criselda Leal (far right). The number of Chicano members has increased in both chambers of the state legislature. Sylvia García is the newest first-term senator from Houston, while longtime senator Carlos Truán of Corpus Christi eventually became the dean of the Texas senate. Both chambers have organized caucuses to support and advocate specific initiatives to further the goals and mission of TACHE. In 1993 and 1994, TACHE presented the Meritorious Service Award to both the Senate Hispanic caucus and the House Mexican American caucus. (Courtesy of María Aguirre-Acuña.)

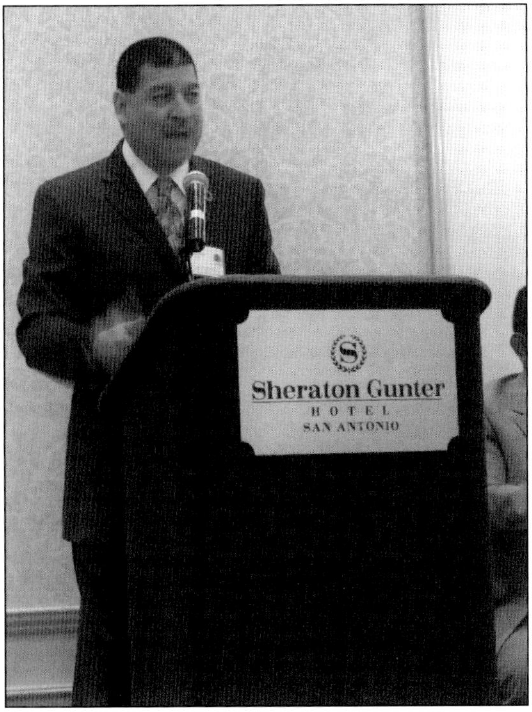

TACHE past president Gus Cedillo announces the graduate students who were awarded fellowships at the 34th annual conference, in 2009. They were Alyssa G. Cavazos (Texas Christian University), Emily Calderón Galdeano (UT-Pan American), Javier Cavazos Jr. (UT-Pan American), and Jared Vanderpool (UT-Austin). The only faculty award presented that year went to Dr. Antonio Juárez of UTEP. (Courtesy of Natalia Verjat Gutiérrez.)

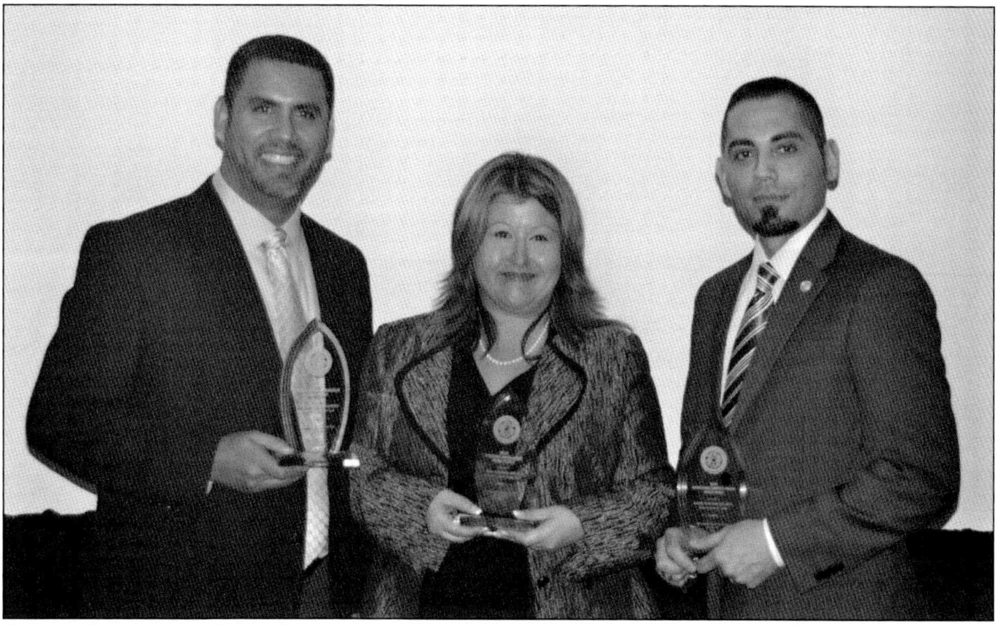

At the 38th annual conference, TACHE awarded the community college Distinguished Faculty Award to Mauricio Rodríguez (right) of the Valle Verde campus of El Paso Community College and Norseman M. Hernández (left) of Lone Star College-Montgomery. The university Distinguished Faculty Award went to Dr. María Hinojosa of Texas A&M-Commerce. (Courtesy of Natalia Verjat Gutiérrez.)

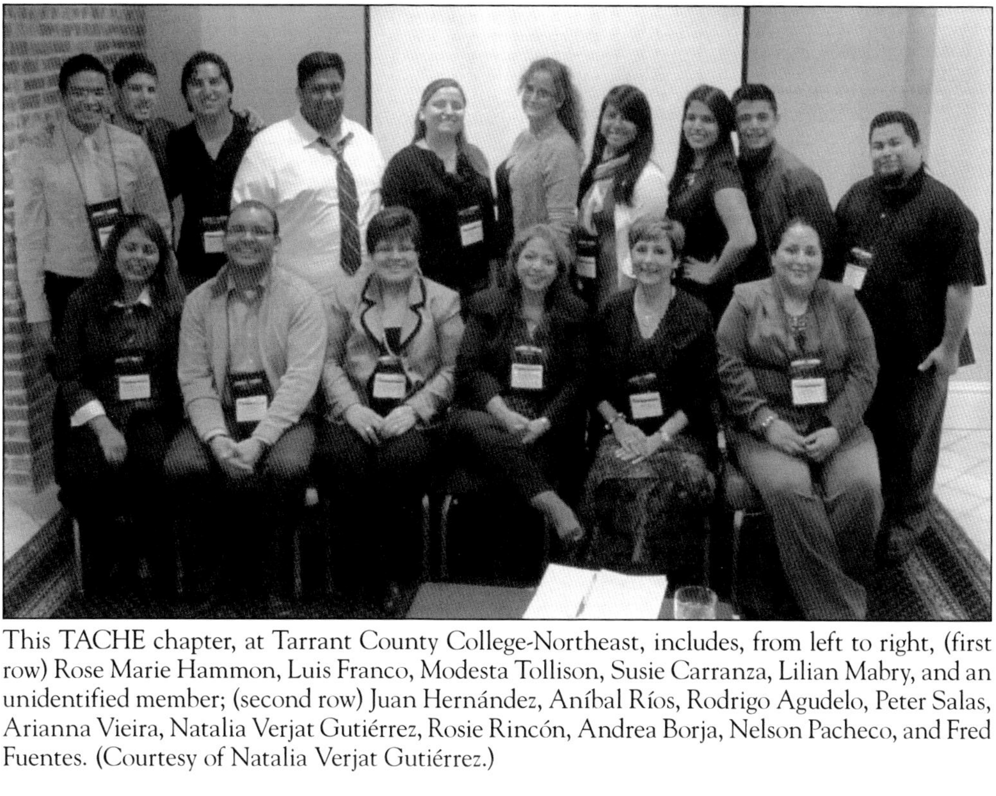

This TACHE chapter, at Tarrant County College-Northeast, includes, from left to right, (first row) Rose Marie Hammon, Luis Franco, Modesta Tollison, Susie Carranza, Lilian Mabry, and an unidentified member; (second row) Juan Hernández, Aníbal Ríos, Rodrigo Agudelo, Peter Salas, Arianna Vieira, Natalia Verjat Gutiérrez, Rosie Rincón, Andrea Borja, Nelson Pacheco, and Fred Fuentes. (Courtesy of Natalia Verjat Gutiérrez.)

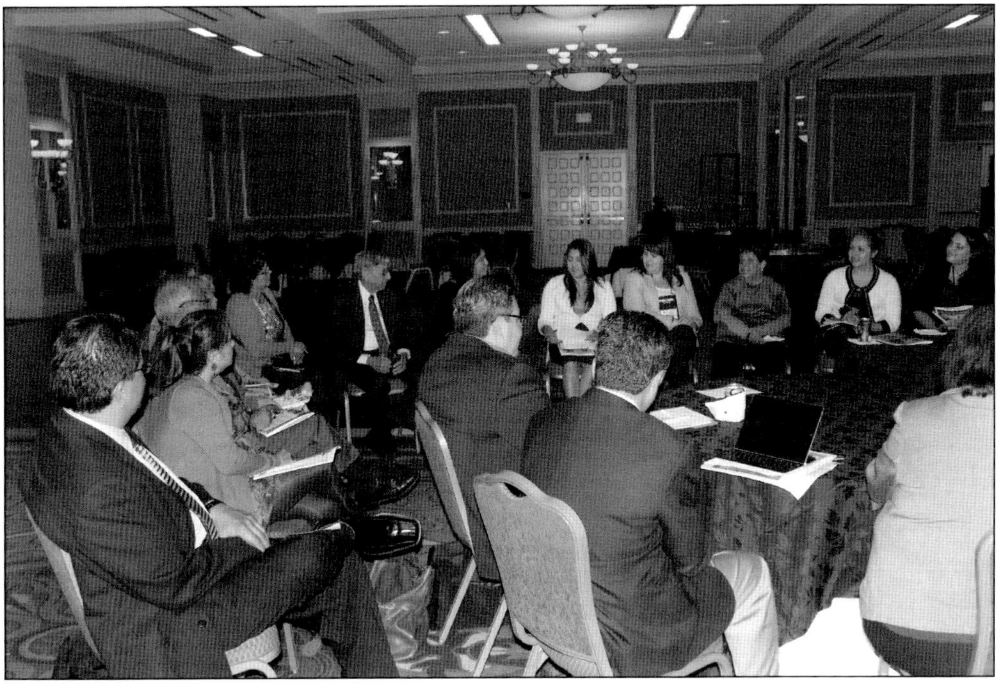

At the 34th annual conference, in 2009, the only faculty award presented that year went to Dr. Antonio Juárez of UTEP. (Courtesy of Javier Olguín.)

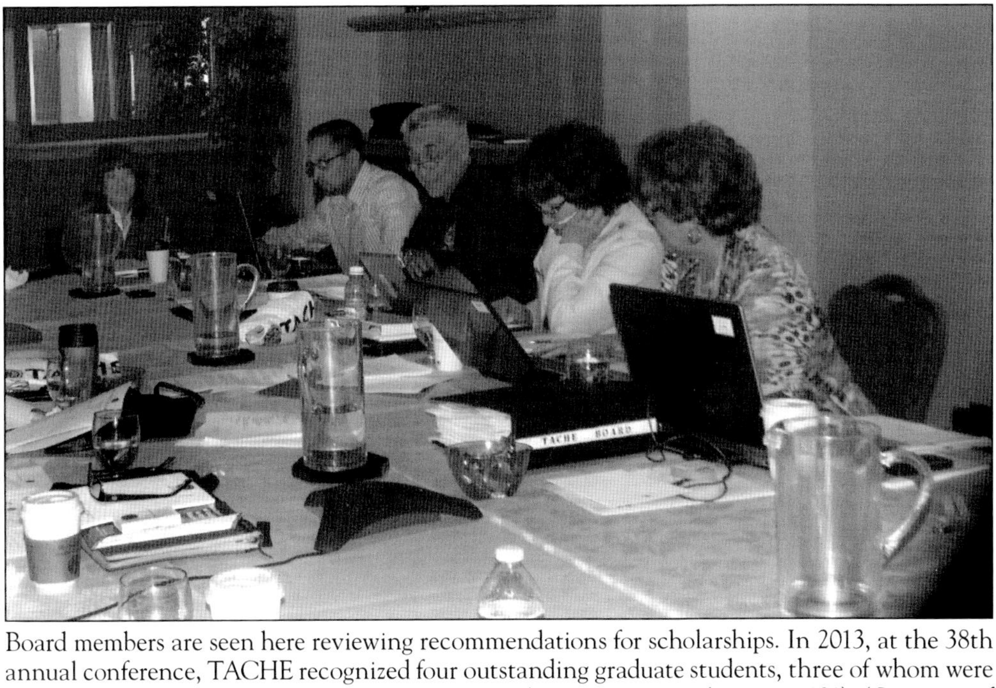

Board members are seen here reviewing recommendations for scholarships. In 2013, at the 38th annual conference, TACHE recognized four outstanding graduate students, three of whom were pursuing doctoral degrees and one who was completing a master's (see page 121). (Courtesy of María Aguirre-Acuña.)

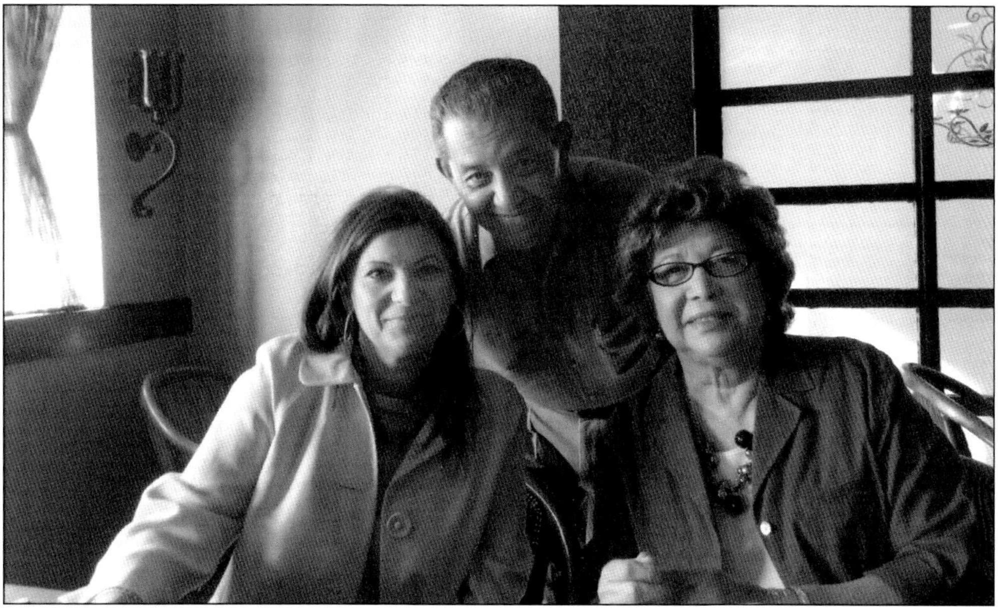

State officers (from left to right) Griselda Leal, David Porrás, and Linda Contreras Bullock pose for a photograph while conferring over the list of possible TACHE fellowship recipients. The 2011 recipients were Graciela Castillo, the oldest child in an immigrant family: Esther López, the ninth child of twelve children of an immigrant family; Ivonne Torres, the first in her family to graduate from college; and María Melissa Manzano-Alemán, who was pursuing a doctoral degree at UT-Austin. (Courtesy of María Aguirre-Acuña.)

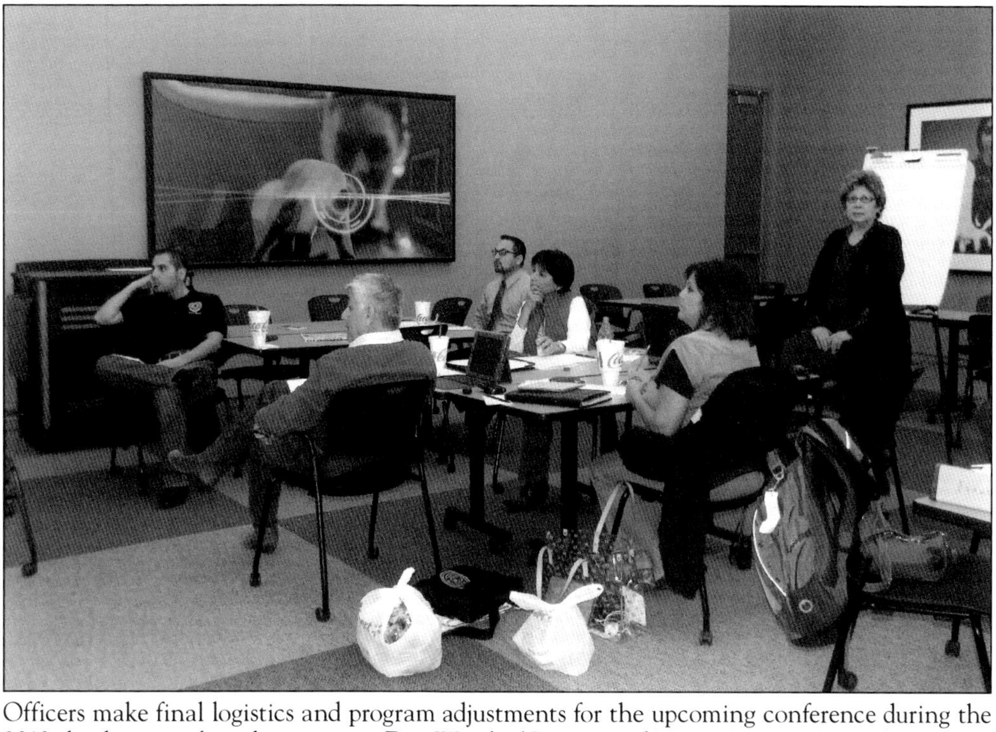

Officers make final logistics and program adjustments for the upcoming conference during the 2012 third-quarter board meeting in Fort Worth. (Courtesy of María Aguirre-Acuña.)

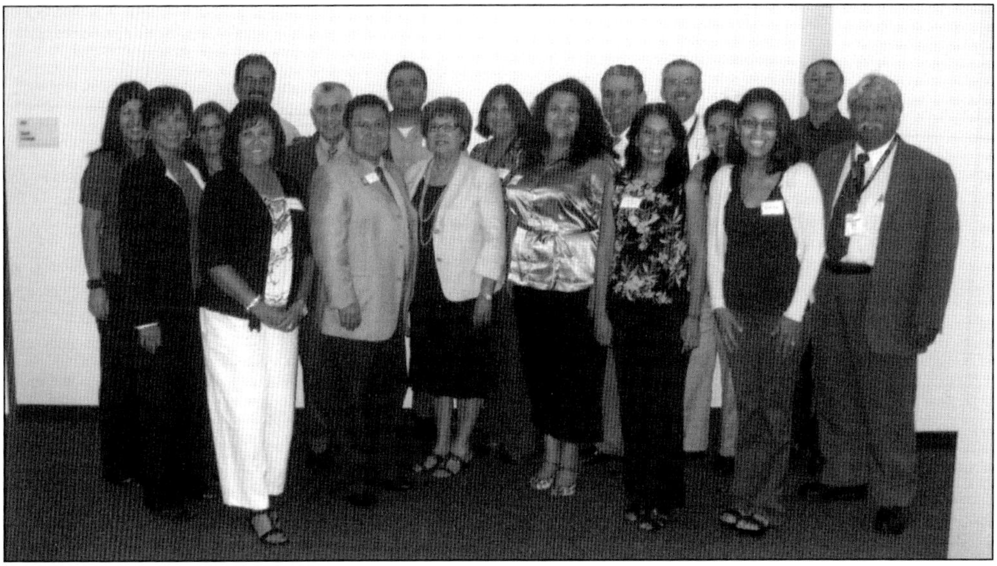

Dr. Reynaldo Garay (first row, far right), the dean of Houston Community College-Southeast, poses with TACHE members on the eve of the 37th annual conference, in Galveston. Dr. Garay and Luciano "Lucky" Salinas initiated the HEROES program, a mentoring program using five workshops in support of academic success for male Latino students, in 2002. At the 2012 conference, Dr. Garay made a presentation about how successful the program has been. (Courtesy of Luciano Salinas.)

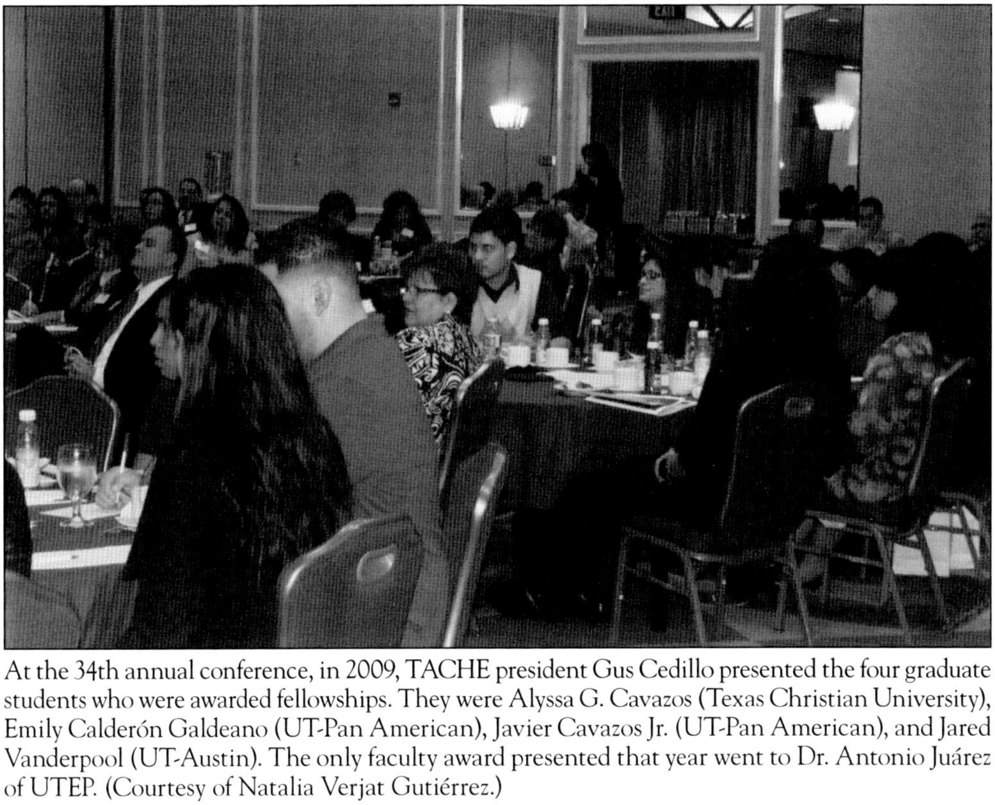

At the 34th annual conference, in 2009, TACHE president Gus Cedillo presented the four graduate students who were awarded fellowships. They were Alyssa G. Cavazos (Texas Christian University), Emily Calderón Galdeano (UT-Pan American), Javier Cavazos Jr. (UT-Pan American), and Jared Vanderpool (UT-Austin). The only faculty award presented that year went to Dr. Antonio Juárez of UTEP. (Courtesy of Natalia Verjat Gutiérrez.)

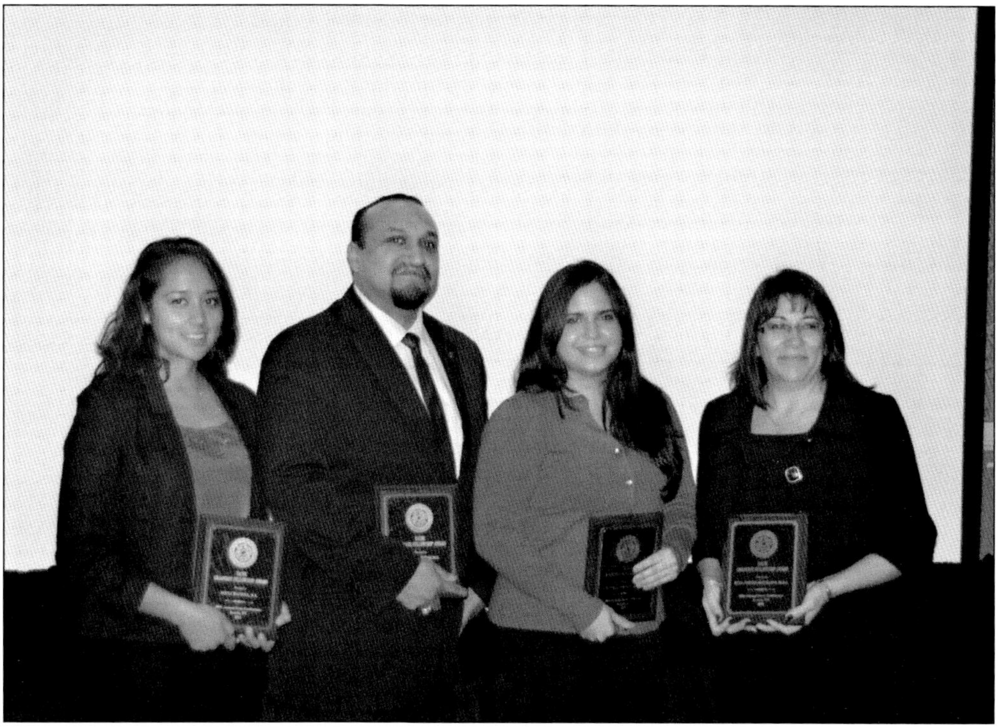

The 2013 graduate fellowships were awarded to, from left to right, Sofía Bahena (Harvard), David Barrientos (Texas Tech), Verónica Pecero (UT-Austin), and Elsa Diego-Medrano (West Texas A&M). The fellowship recipients took home $8,000. (Courtesy of Javier Olguín)

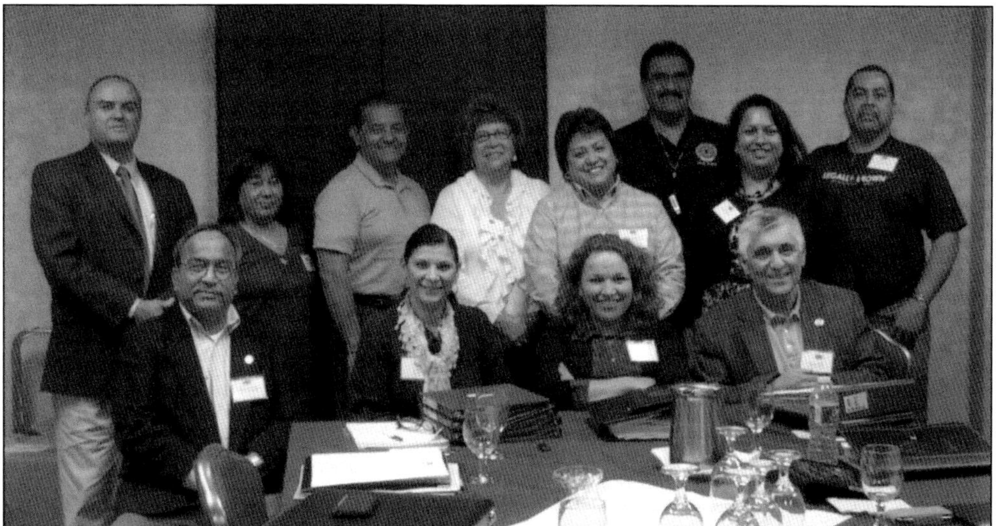

The state board is seen here meeting to discuss possible conference sites in 2011. Through the years, there have been 11 conferences in Austin, 10 in San Antonio, 5 in Dallas, 4 in Corpus Christi, and 1 each in El Paso, Galveston, and McAllen. (Courtesy of Javier Olguín.)

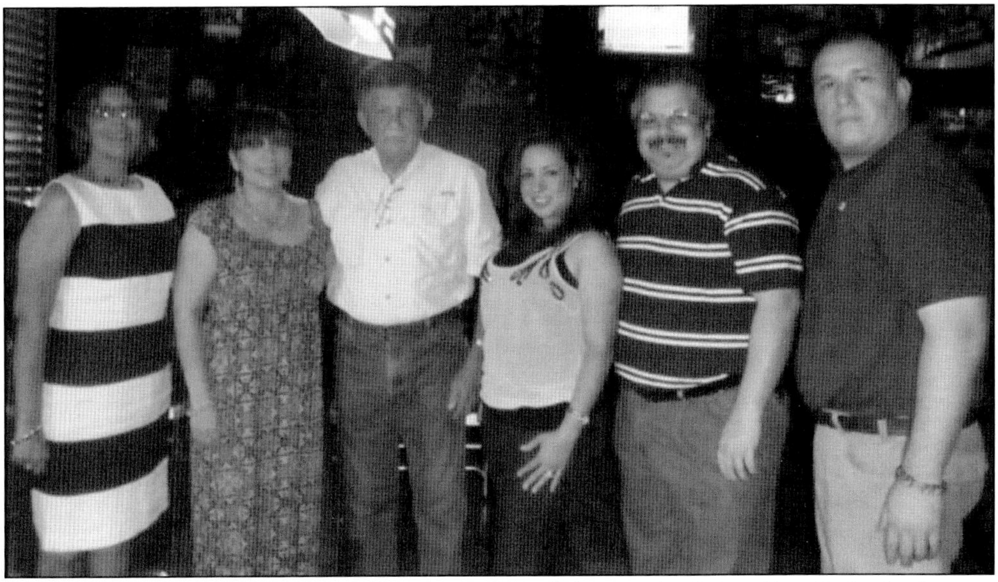

These Laredo TACHE chapter officers are, from left to right, Mary Sue Galindo, Leticia Spillane, Lino Ramírez, Marissa Longoria, René Montemayor, and unidentified. (Courtesy of Marissa Longoria.)

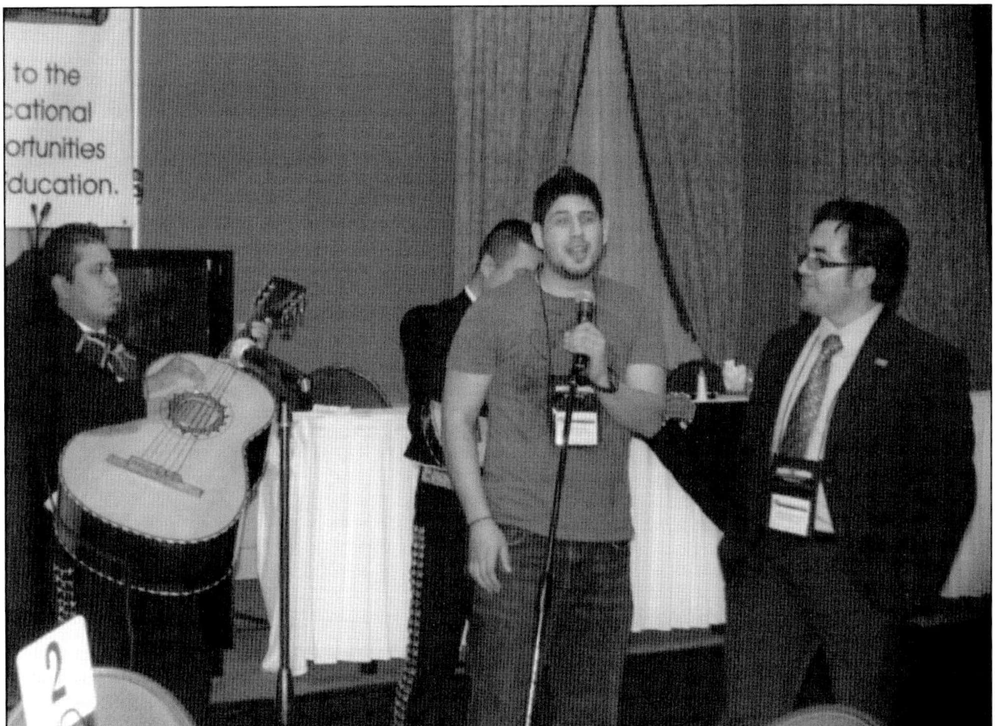

At the 2011 TACHE annual conference, TACHE member Aníbal Ríos of UT-Arlington took to the microphone. Ríos loves to sing and does so at every opportunity. His earlier undergraduate work was done at Tarrant County College–Northeast, where he was a member of OLAS. Gilberto Hernández watches him on the right. (Courtesy of María Aguirre-Acuña.)

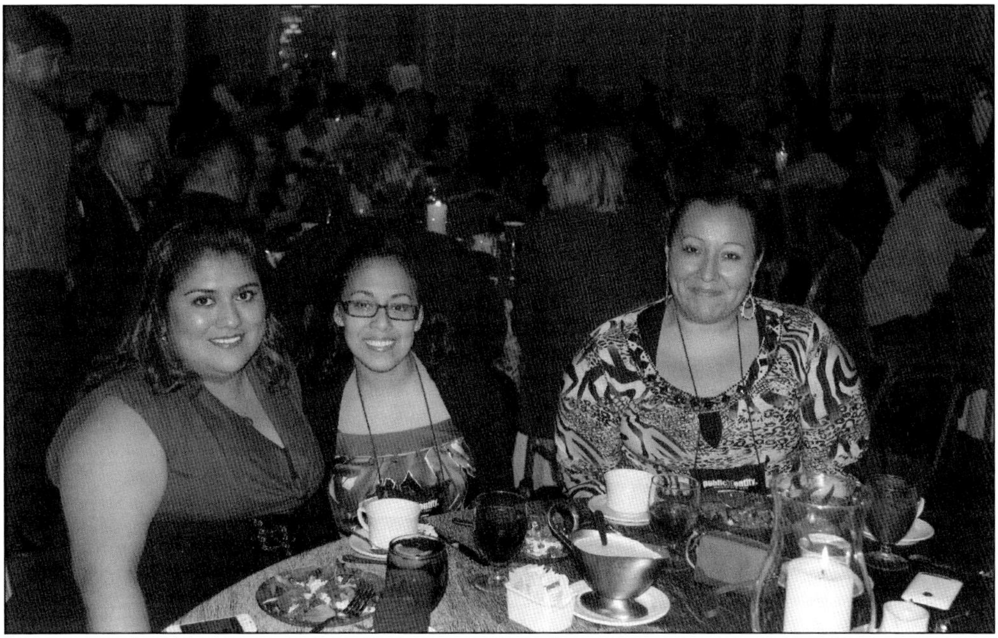

These three students were not yet born when the Mexican American Legal Defense and Education Fund (MALDEF) was founded in 1968. They are, from left to right, Lucy Rojas, Nitza Gómez, and Leticia Villarreal. In 1986, TACHE presented the Meritorious Service Award to MALDEF for its work championing civil rights via litigation. MALDEF has been at the forefront for decades, defending protesting students and litigating complex cases involving affirmative action, testing, school finance, and school segregation, among many others. (Courtesy of Natalia Verjat Gutiérrez.)

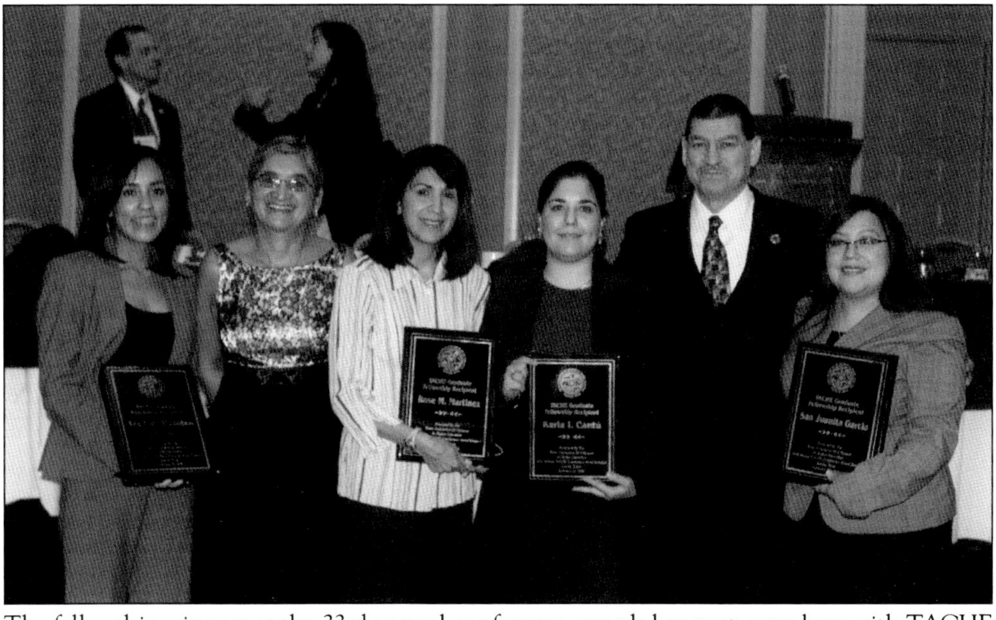

The fellowship winners at the 33rd annual conference awards banquet, seen here with TACHE president Gus Cedillo, are, from left to right, Ana Luz Villalobos (New Mexico State), Rose M. Martínez (UT-Austin), Karla Cantú (UT-San Antonia), and San Juanita García (Texas A&M). (Courtesy of Javier Olguín.)

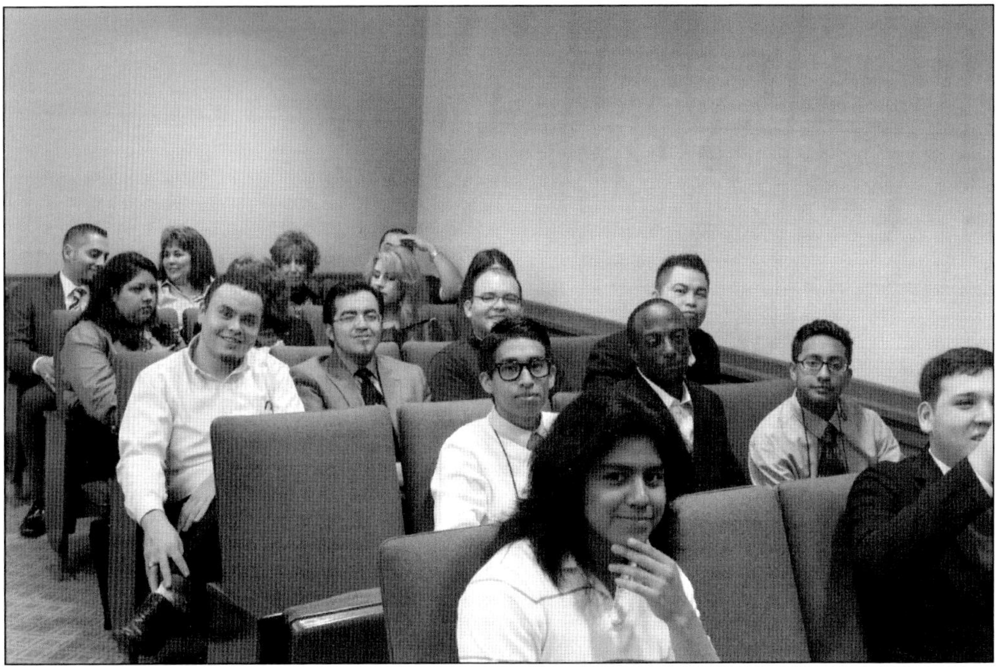

Students from various TACHE chapters listen to training instructions at the capitol before visiting legislators in 2013. They are, from left to right, (first row) Emmanuel Rincón and José Almeda; (second row) Mynor Efraín-Milian, Shamir Iga, and Daniel Sandoval; (third row) unidentified, Gilbert Hernández, Luis Franco, and Fred Fuentes. (Courtesy of Natalia Verjat Gutiérrez.)

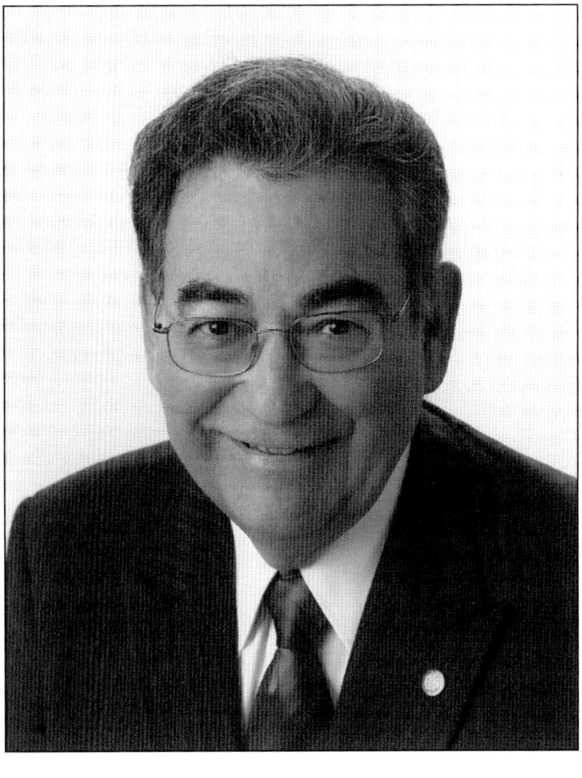

Dr. Rudy Rodríguez, a long-term TACHE member who served as president in 2002, is the only Latino on the Denton Independent School District's board of trustees. He produced the 2009 documentary *The Texas Bilingual Story*. He was also instrumental, along with former TACHE presidents Jude Valdez, Félix Zamora, and Ana "Cha" Guzmán, in establishing the Doctoral Incentive Program in Texas. This TACHE initiative was signed into law in 2003. Unfortunately, the money has currently dried up, but the battle is ongoing to renew funding. (Courtesy of Rudy Rodríguez.)

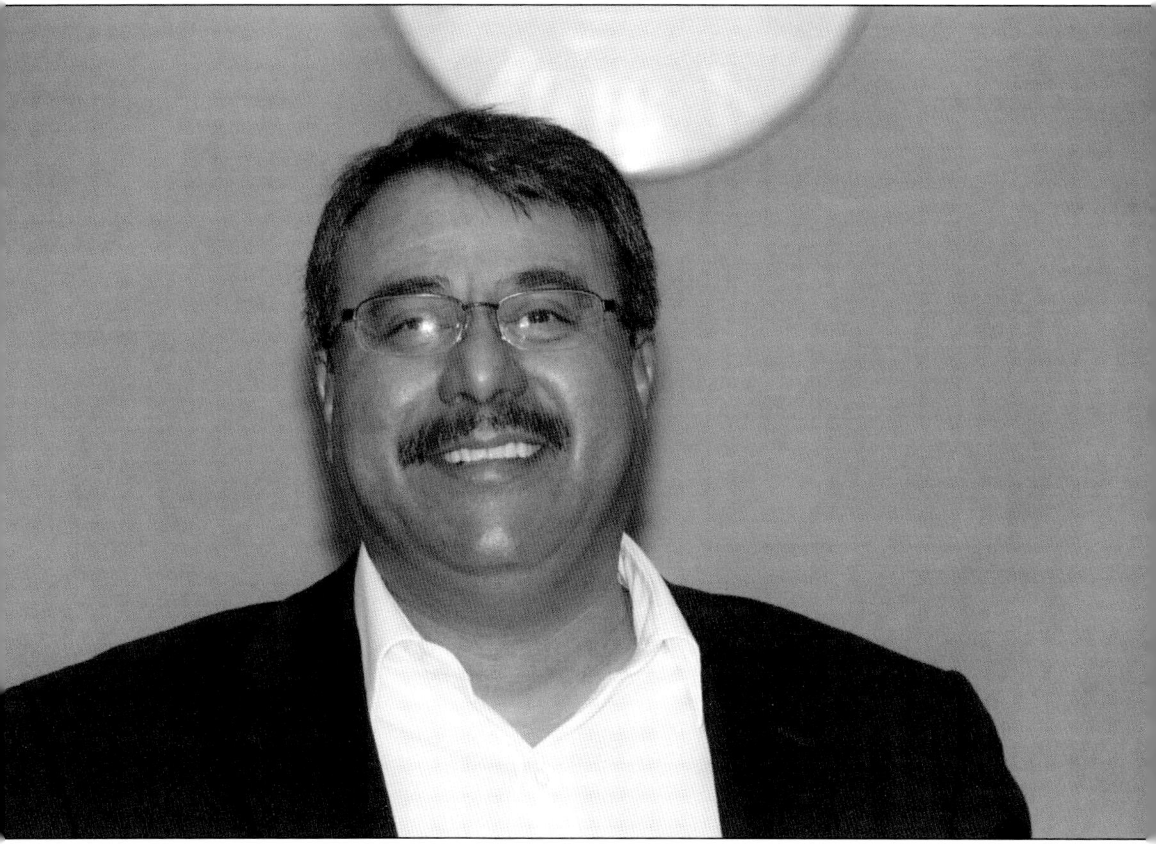

Javier Olguín has a long history of involvement with TACHE. He was a member and then a chapter officer in Austin before moving to Dallas and joining the northeast chapter, where he became a state officer and a board member. He is currently the executive director of the Eastfield-Pleasant Grove campus of the Dallas County Community College District. (Courtesy of Natalia Verjat Gutiérrez.)

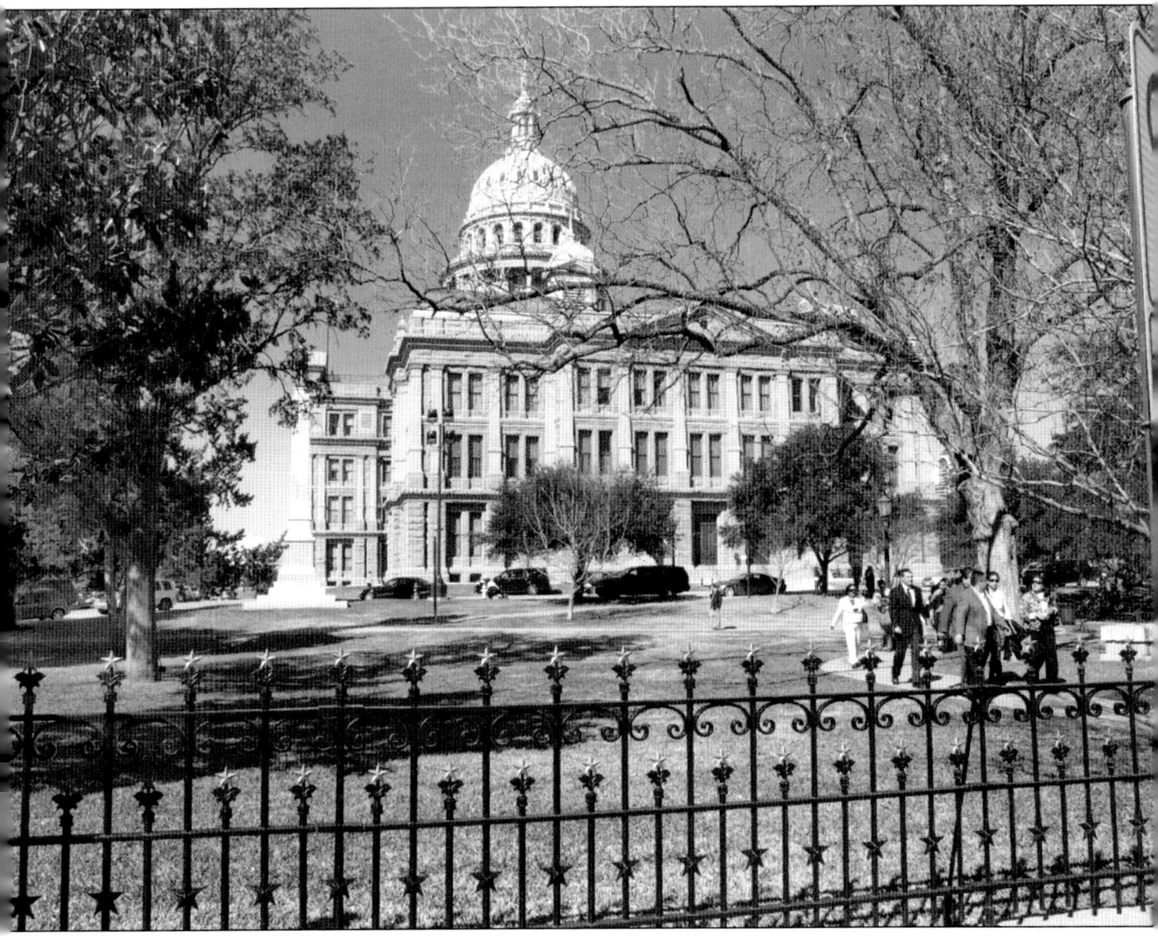

TACHE members are seen here leaving the capitol building after meeting with lawmakers. The Chicano generation is gradually passing away, while the Latino American generation is up and coming. Population forecasts predict that by 2050, one-third of all people in the United States will be Latino. TACHE's original purpose and mission from 1974 must remain front and center for educational reform to continue in the 21st century. (Courtesy of Natalia Verjat Gutiérrez.)

BIBLIOGRPAHY

Acuña, Rodolfo F. *Occupied America: The Chicano Struggle Toward Liberation*. New York: Harper & Row, 1972.

———. *The Making of Chicana/o Studies: In the Trenches of Academe*. New Brunswick, NJ: Rutgers University Press, 2011.

Carter, Thomas P. *Mexican Americans in School: A History of Educational Neglect*. New York: College Entrance Examination Board, 1970.

García, Mario T. and Sal Castro. *Blowout! Sal Castro and the Chicano Struggle for Educational Justice*. Chapel Hill, NC: University of North Carolina Press, 2011.

Grebler, Leo, Joan Moore, and Ralph C. Guzman. *The Mexican American People: The Nation's Second Largest Minority*. New York: Free Press, 1970.

Meier, Matt S. and Feliciano Rivera. *The Chicanos: A History of Mexican Americans*. New York: Hill and Wang, 1972.

Navarro, Armando. *La Raza Unida Party: A Chicano Challenge to the U.S. Two-Party Dictatorship*. Philadelphia: Temple University Press, 2000.

Precious Knowledge: Arizona's Battle over Ethnic Studies. Dos Vatos Productions, Inc., 2011. DVD.

Rodríguez, Rudy. *The Texas Bilingual Story*. 2009. DVD.

Rosales, F. Arturo. *CHICANO! The History of the Mexican American Civil Rights Movement*. Houston: Arte Publico Press, 1996.

Sracic, Paul A. *San Antonio v. Rodríguez and the Pursuit of Equal Education*. Lawrence, KS: University Press of Kansas, 2006.

Strum, Philippa. *Mendez v. Westminster: School Desegregation and Mexican-American Rights*. Lawrence, KS: University Press of Kansas, 2010.

The Origins of the Roberto Hernández Center: The Chapman Hall Takeover and the Creation of the Spanish Speaking Outreach Institute, Milwaukee. University of Wisconsin-Milwaukee Roberto Hernández Center, 2010. DVD.

Treviño, Jesús Salvador. *Eyewitness: A Filmmaker's Memoir of the Chicano Movement*. Houston: Arte Publico Press, 2001.

Valverde, Leonard A., ed. *The Latino Student's Guide to College Success*. Second Edition. Westport, CT: Greenwood Press, 2012.

Walkout. Home Box Office, Inc., 2006. DVD.

Consistent with our mission to preserve history on a local level, this book was printed in South Carolina on American-made paper and manufactured entirely in the United States. Products carrying the accredited Forest Stewardship Council (FSC) label are printed on 100 percent FSC-certified paper.

MADE IN THE USA